# Praise for *The Grain Terminal Elevators of Duluth-Superior*

"The American Midwest's economy—and, indeed, much of the country's—was built through agriculture in the late 19th century. Corn, wheat, and other grains were transformed from mere crops into commodities by the railroads and by the monumental grain elevators that still dot the midwestern landscape. Patrick Lapinski's study of elevators at Duluth—one of the major centers of the grain trade—shows how these structures form a built record of transformations in technology, finance, agriculture, and geography. Unprecedented in its focus and exceptional in the depth of its scholarship, Destined to Lead the World is a vital study of Duluth's museum-like collection of elevator structures and a key addition to the literature on this threatened building type."

**Prof. Thomas Leslie, FAIA. The Illinois School of Architecture**
**University of Illinois at Urbana-Champaign**

# The Grain Terminal Elevators of Duluth-Superior

Minneapolis

First Edition 2024
*The Grain Terminal Elevators of Duluth-Superior.*
Copyright © 2024 by Patrick D. Lapinski.
All rights reserved.

No part of this book may be used or reproduced by any means, graphic, electronic, or mechanical, including photocopying, recording, taping or by any information storage retrieval system, without the written permission of the publisher except in the case of brief quotations embodied in critical articles and reviews.

10 9 8 7 6 5 4 3 2 1

ISBN: 978-1-962834-10-0

Cover and book design by Gary Lindberg

# The Grain Terminal Elevators of Duluth-Superior

Patrick D. Lapinski

Minneapolis

# Table of Contents

Preface . . . . . . . . . . . . . . . . . . . . . . . . . . . . . . . . . . . . . . . . .1
Introduction. . . . . . . . . . . . . . . . . . . . . . . . . . . . . . . . . . . . . .2
1 The Union Improvement and Elevator Company:
   Elevator A. . . . . . . . . . . . . . . . . . . . . . . . . . . . . . . . . . . .8
2 Munger, Markell & Company: Elevator 1. . . . . . . . . . . . . . . 27
3 The 1880s: The Development of Duluth's Elevator Row . . . .39
4 The Rise of Superior as a Grain Port. . . . . . . . . . . . . . . . . . . . .52
5 Expansion of the Union Improvement and
   Lake Superior Elevator Companies . . . . . . . . . . . . . . . . . . 66
6 The 1890s: A Tumultuous Decade . . . . . . . . . . . . . . . . . . . . .75
7 1900 – 1910: The Era of Concrete. . . . . . . . . . . . . . . . . . . . .110
8 The Great Northern Elevator S . . . . . . . . . . . . . . . . . . . . . . .119
9 The Capitol Elevator Company. . . . . . . . . . . . . . . . . . . . . . .133
10 1910 – 1920: A Decade of Growth. . . . . . . . . . . . . . . . . . . .149
11 The 1920s: The Occident Terminal Sets the Standard. . . . .156
12 1925 – 1935: A Time for Expansion. . . . . . . . . . . . . . . . . . 161
13 1940 – 1950: The Farmers Union
    Grain Terminal Association . . . . . . . . . . . . . . . . . . . . . . . .170
14 The 1960s: New Growth with the St. Lawrence Seaway. . .189
15 The 1970s: The Soviet Grain Trade and Embargo . . . . . . . 205
16 The 1980s: Old Faces, New Names . . . . . . . . . . . . . . . . . . 241
17 1990 – 2000: Stability . . . . . . . . . . . . . . . . . . . . . . . . . . . . .260
18 2000 – 2023: Changing Players . . . . . . . . . . . . . . . . . . . . . 268
Conclusion. . . . . . . . . . . . . . . . . . . . . . . . . . . . . . . . . . . . . . 294
Appendix. . . . . . . . . . . . . . . . . . . . . . . . . . . . . . . . . . . . . . . 303
Chronology . . . . . . . . . . . . . . . . . . . . . . . . . . . . . . . . . . . . .311
Acknowledgments . . . . . . . . . . . . . . . . . . . . . . . . . . . . . . . .321
Index. . . . . . . . . . . . . . . . . . . . . . . . . . . . . . . . . . . . . . . . . .323
About the Author. . . . . . . . . . . . . . . . . . . . . . . . . . . . . . . . .336

To my brother Phillip

# Also by Patrick D. Lapinski

*Great Lakes Shipping: Ports and Cargoes*
*Ships of the Great Lakes: An Inside Look at the World's Largest Inland Fleet*
*In The Yard: The History of Fraser Shipyards, 1892-2017*
*In Neptune's Realm: The Maritime Legacy of the Thompson & Norick Hard Hat Diving Family*

# Preface

As a writer and photojournalist, a large part of my life has been dedicated to documenting the Great Lakes maritime industry and the men and women who sail its waters. As a researcher and historian, I have looked closer to my home port of Duluth-Superior to nurture my curiosity. In 2017 I published the highly regarded history of the legendary Fraser Shipyards. This history of the Twin Ports grain industry will add to a body of work that will hopefully inspire further research into this or other areas of interest.

# Introduction

The grain elevators of Duluth-Superior have always been a unique feature of the waterfront. They have dominated the industrial landscape along Rice's Point in Duluth for over a century. In neighboring Superior, they've stood fortress-like, holding the key to the self-proclaimed "City of Destiny" while perhaps symbolically blocking out the view of Duluth across the bay.

Duluth's first export grain elevator was constructed during the winter of 1869–1870. It was easily recognized as the largest building along the undeveloped waterfront. A photograph taken during its construction shows the rectangular structure being erected. Alongside the building are stacks of lumber while workers cover the surface, silhouetted against Lake Superior. It is a very simple image, yet at the same time, very powerful for what it came to represent—the beginning. Elevator *A* was the beginning of not only a new grain elevator and a new grain company, but it marked the nascent point of the region as a world leader in grain handling and export.

The history of the grain trade in the Upper Midwest is vitally linked to the growth and expansion of the American railroad in the region. The railroads were largely responsible for the expansion of the West and the opening of the grain markets. The importance of the railroads in settling this area cannot be understated. Two railroads in particular, the Lake Superior and Mississippi and the Northern Pacific, and later the Great Northern, were the early dominant forces behind the terminal grain elevators in the Twin Ports.

Long before the construction of the first elevator system at Duluth, the need for a cheaper alternative to the existing transportation links between the farm fields of the Upper Midwest and the Eastern and European markets was creating tension. In the early 1860s, Minnesota farm yields of wheat were steady and growing, from just over 5 million bushels in 1860 to just under 10 million bushels in 1865, noted Lester Shippee, Associate Professor of History at the University of Minnesota, in a study of the development of the first railroad connection between St. Paul and Duluth.

> The steadily increasing crops of wheat and other grains, which could find a market in the East and in Europe, were obliged to make use of water transportation in order to reach the railroads to convey them to Milwaukee and Chicago. The northernmost point on the Mississippi touched by a rail-head was La Crosse; here the Milwaukee and St. Paul had reached its most western extension. Throughout the war, then, the only route over which the Minnesota or western Wisconsin farmer could ship his grain, or the merchant import his wares, was made up of the inadequate roads to the Mississippi or one of its navigable branches, and a single railroad connecting river with Lake Michigan.[1]

Between 1862 and 1864, Shippee noted that "the rate on grain from Minnesota points to Chicago and Milwaukee doubled. During the season of 1864, agents of the railroads, acting with representatives of the steamboat lines, met at Chicago and advanced the rate again by from three to eleven cents per bushel, varying with the distance from the railhead; other commodities had their rates raised correspondingly."[2]

---

[1] Lester Burrell Shippee, "The First Railroad between the Mississippi and Lake Superior," *The Mississippi Valley Historical Review* 5, no. 2 (September 1918): 122. Published by: Oxford University Press on behalf of the Organization of American Historians.

[2] Ibid., 123.

The conclusion of the Civil War brought about a renewed effort to link "the navigable waters of the Mississippi River with the head of Lake Superior," wrote Shippee. The rapid growth of the market for food products and lumber in Michigan's Upper Peninsula, along with the growth of crops along the Mississippi valley, "coupled with exorbitant freight charges, impelled to a search for a cheaper route to the Atlantic coast and to Europe."[3]

The battle for a direct rail connection between St. Paul and Lake Superior took many years to resolve. Competing interests on the Wisconsin side of the St. Croix River proposed a line from Hudson to Superior, while interests in St. Cloud, Minnesota, proposed alternatives from their vantage point. After years of legal wrangling, the Lake Superior and Mississippi Railroad (LS&M) was granted the right to build a road from St. Paul to Duluth, essentially connecting the Lake Superior region to the Mississippi River. Between 1861 and 1865, they were awarded money from the Minnesota legislature and federal land grants to aid in the completion of this new line.[4]

The construction of any elevator at Duluth was still years away, and all grain exports via Lake Superior were dependent upon the completion of the rail line to Duluth. The final push was accomplished with the financial backing of Jay Cooke, a Philadelphia financier who was extremely bullish on Duluth. Cooke already owned vast tracts of land in northern Minnesota, and the possibility of mining and its shipment from Duluth played into his long-term plans.

Credit for the rail line is often given to William Nettleton, an Ohio native and resident of Duluth during its formative years, and his brother George. "In 1856, the Nettleton brothers, together with Orin W. Rice, Robert E. Jefferson, and future-Mayor Joshua B. Culver, surveyed the townsite of Duluth, for which service the Nettleton's acquired hundreds of acres of land in the Duluth area. George, who continued residing in Superior, partnered with Culver

---

3    Ibid., 121.

4    Frank King, "Railroads at the Head of the Lakes," *Duluth, Sketches of the Past, A Bicentennial Collection* (Duluth: American Revolution Bicentennial Commission, 1976): 181.

to establish a sawmill, while William became the proprietor of a trading store and established a farmstead on the Minnesota side of Superior Bay."[5]

William Nettleton's obituary in the *St. Paul Globe* noted his enthusiasm for a rail connection between Duluth and St. Paul. "It is said he gave to all railroads land where they now have their terminals and was largely instrumental in the upbuilding of both these cities."[6]

In August 1869, the city of Duluth was buzzing after a visit from officials of the Lake Superior and Mississippi Railroad. The *Duluth Minnesotian* reported that the guests saw all there was to see in the area, and the "conclusions" resulting from the visit that "stand in the nature of a written agreement, signed by the Railroad officials and by our citizens," were detailed within the paper's end of August editions. Among the salient points,

> That the dock and track on Rice's Point is but for a temporary purpose, principally to land the Railroad iron and it is expressly understood that no grain elevator shall be built there.
>
> That a Grain Elevator to hold half a million bushels of wheat shall be immediately commenced on the Bay side of Minnesota Point, near the northern end of the Duluth Bay (sometimes called "Superior" Bay); and that a floating Elevator for temporary purposes, shall likewise be at once built.
>
> That the Railroad track shall be constructed across the head of said Duluth Bay from Rice's Point to Lake Superior at the base of Minnesota Point; and a landing Dock built out into the Lake; and that it is intended to construct also, eventually, branch Railroads on each side of Minnesota Point and down it for about a mile, and a branch Railroad down the North Shore of the Lake for the distance of a mile.
>
> At the end of said mile down the Lake the Breakwater is to be finally constructed, parallel with Minnesota Point, so as to

---

5 "William Nettleton," accessed July 1, 2023, https://en.wikipedia.org/wiki/William_Nettleton.

6 "A Pioneer Stricken: William Nettleton, Founder of Duluth, Killed in Spokane," *St. Paul Globe*, January 21, 1905, p 2.

make a magnificent harbor, a mile square, easy of access and egress, and by its depth of water capable of accommodating the shipping that will go through the St. Mary Canal when it is deepened, as contemplated, to pass grain vessels drawing fifteen or sixteen feet of water.

Led by the Lake Superior and Mississippi Railroad's president William Banning, the party of "railroad excursionists" traveled about the harbor and north shore aboard the steamers *Frost* and *Keyes*, vessels that were "a welcome sight to us weary travelers who had just gone through three day's stage travel over the worst road on this continent" declared a reporter covering the entourage. Members of the Eastern contingent included guests from Philadelphia, Boston, New York City, and London, England, several of them representing the interests of Jay Cooke & Company. During their stay, the guests were lodged with members of Duluth's social elite prior to departing on the steamer *St. Paul* for Marquette and a connecting rail coach back to civilization.

**Duluth, circa 1871. Duluth was incorporated as a city for the first time on March 6, 1870.** Photo: collection of Marie Thompson Norick.

At first, little was mentioned about the expected price tag of the acquisition of a large portion of waterfront property for the railroad at "condemned prices" in return for the Northern Pacific agreeing to build out the harbor at Duluth. The *Minnesotian* reported, "It is expressly understood, and so positively agreed, that the carrying out of these important plans by the Railroad Company depends entirely upon the title to harbor and water frontage being first acquired by the Company in accordance with the agreements and pledges of our citizens..." The demand caused outrage among many residents of Duluth.

Ultimately, Cooke and his Philadelphia associates helped fund the completion of the Lake Superior and Mississippi Railroad by purchasing a half interest in the final section of the line to Duluth. This portion of the railroad made its way from Thomson's Junction east to Fond du Lac, where the constricted path of the St. Louis River emptied into a large estuary before snaking its way along the backwaters to Duluth's shallow bay opposite Minnesota Point. By 1872, the LS&M Railroad was leased to the Northern Pacific, which assumed full operation of the line as part of its expansion to the Pacific Northwest.

In addition to financing the Lake Superior and Mississippi Railroad's completion, Cooke invested heavily in business opportunities throughout the area—land development companies, banks, and hotels, as well as a new Duluth venture, the Union Improvement and Elevator Company, whose principals were ready to commence construction of a grain elevator at the head of the lakes. Cooke had quickly gained entrance into two vital economic areas at the head of the lakes—the railroad and the grain export business.[7]

Time yields tremendous change. The saga of the Duluth terminal grain industry is a story that was broadly told in the book, *Pride of the Inland Seas*, a history of the Port of Duluth. This book will take a more detailed examination of this critical industry. It takes a long step back to examine the origins of the first terminal elevator built in Duluth. At the time, Duluth was just taking shape as a united group of communities ringing the lakeshore. In March 1871, the first Duluth city charter was completed.[8] Development along the rugged hillside would be based as much upon vision as upon hard work. The ability to look to the future was as important an asset as the ability to swing a hammer.

---

[7] Glenn N. Sandvik, *Duluth: An Illustrated History of the Zenith City* (Woodland Hills: Windsor Publications, Inc., 1983), 30.

[8] Ibid., 31.

# 1
# The Union Improvement and Elevator Company – Elevator *A*

The vision of the future was strong in the eyes of several of Duluth's founders. The end of the American Civil War and the subsequent expansion of the Plains Territory marked the beginning of a new era in the growth of the war-torn nation. The Lake Superior region, despite its isolation, was still a place where you could write your own ticket. With a bit of ambition and creativity, the possibilities were limitless. This potential was borne out by the seemingly unusual pairing of two men to form Duluth's first grain elevator company.

Colonel Charles Hinman Graves moved to Duluth in 1869 to begin a new life away from the army. He had just retired from military duty after faithfully serving his country during the War of the Rebellion. Earning respect and honor as a soldier during his involvement in major battles at Bull Run, Williamsburg and Chancellorsville, Graves was severely wounded at Gettysburg but recovered to finish his career.[9]

In the remote wilderness of Lake Superior, Graves decided upon a business focused on selling fire insurance, forming the firm of C. H. Graves and Company in 1869. He also began trading in bulk

---

9   Judge Charles E. Flandrau, ed., *Encyclopedia of Biography of Minnesota* (Chicago: Century Publishing & Engraving Company, 1900), 1:274.

commodities at the head of the lakes, mainly salt and lime.[10]

At about the same time, Roger S. Munger began thinking about his possibilities away from the public and social life he and his brothers enjoyed in St. Paul. The Mungers were professional musicians, but each separately yearned to do more with their lives. Talk of the opportunities awaiting those at the tip of Lake Superior came with the arrival of each train now that the railroad operated a regular schedule north from the capital city.[11]

Munger moved to Duluth, where he became associated with the retired colonel. The unusual combination of a military hero and a reluctant musician saw great potential for the grain trade via the waters of Lake Superior. With his salt trade contacts, Col. Graves believed his success in trading salt could just as easily be duplicated with grain. All Graves needed was an elevator and some financial backing, so he formed a partnership with Munger and Clinton Markell to create the Union Improvement and Elevator Company.

Clinton Markell was one of Duluth's most influential pioneers. He was born in Geneva, Ohio, in 1832, where he operated a successful dry goods business before moving to Superior, Wisconsin. According to a brief biography of Markell, in a project to document historical east-side residences, he became convinced that Duluth was "the coming city at the Head of the Lakes." As a result, Markell joined with James D. Ray, John I. Post, Dr. A. B. Robbins and Sidney Luce to purchase a tract of land they platted in 1856 as the town of Portland (now the Portland Division of Duluth). Duluth had a population of only 200 when Markell first resided there. His efforts to build a city were recognized by being elected the city's second mayor in 1870.[12]

---

10   Ibid., 274.
11   Ibid., 269.
12   Intensive Survey of Duluth's East End Neighborhood, Larson Fisher Associates, p. 18.

**Union Improvement and Elevator Company Elevator A, Duluth's first grain elevator, built by Joseph T. Moulton in 1869.**
Photo: University of Minnesota Duluth, Kathryn A. Martin Library, Northeast Minnesota Historical Collections, on loan from the St. Louis County Historical Society.

Substantial financial backing came from business tycoon Jay Cooke. The Union Improvement and Elevator Company was incorporated in Minnesota in 1868 with a $500,000 capital investment. Long-term plans called for the construction of a second elevator at Stillwater, Minnesota, to facilitate the movement of grain arriving by riverboat or barge along the St. Croix and Mississippi northward by rail to Duluth for export.[13]

There was great excitement when plans were announced for Duluth's first export grain elevator in November of 1869 in *The Duluth Minnesotian*. It was reported that the Union Improvement and Elevator Company planned to erect a structure "capable of unloading twenty cars in an hour, and containing *five* Receiving Elevators and *three* Shipping Elevators. As 1,000 bushels are computed as the loading proper to every *three* cars, this Elevator will handle about 70,000 bushels of wheat per day."

---

13 John L. Harnsberger, "Land, Lobbies, Railroads and the Origins of Duluth," *Minnesota History* 37, no. 3 (September 1960): 89–100.

The influence of Jay Cooke on the Union Improvement Elevator Company can be seen in the firm's first operational structure. George C. Thomas of Jay Cooke & Co., Philadelphia, was appointed president of the elevator company, with Charles B. Newcombe, Esq., of Boston, vice-president, and Charles S. Hinchman, also of Philadelphia, secretary and treasurer. The board of directors, including Thomas and Newcombe, reflected the financial interests of the East Coast. J. Hinckley Clarke and J. H. Seaver (Clarke & Co. bankers, Philadelphia) and Robert Henry Lamborn of Philadelphia (secretary and treasurer of the Lake Superior and Mississippi Railroad Company) were paired with local representation on the board consisting of Gen. George B. Sargent, who was an early settler and land surveyor, and Col. Graves.[14] Whether of their own accord or not is unclear, but Munger and Markell were not a part of the governing board when the company was incorporated.

The arrival of Newcombe in Duluth by stagecoach in November 1869 was all the assurance needed that the great elevator project would soon be underway. The board appointed Newcombe as the managing director of the Union Improvement and Elevator Company.

As a representative of Jay Cooke's interests in Duluth, Newcombe was quick to remind Duluth officials that the work was contingent upon the railroad's acquisition of large tracts of waterfront property in return for their participation. At the time of Newcombe's arrival, the exact site of the proposed elevator had not been determined. "If the condemnation of the property necessary to the business of the Railroad, and hereafter also of the Northern Pacific Railroad, are made cordially and promptly, we shall see this great building arise in its magnificent proportions in just the spot we all desire it to stand, assuring the prosperity of us all..." wrote the editors of *The Duluth Minnesotian*. They also admonished those who might oppose the wholesale exchange of valuable waterfront property, stating, "We hope and trust our resident citizens will pursue no short-sighted policy—nor countenance non-resident property holders in an embarrassing course."

---

14 "Looks Like Business," *Duluth Minnesotian*, November 6, 1869.

It was no surprise to insiders that the first month of the decade found Duluth on the precipice of a new beginning. On Saturday, February 5, 1870, Newcombe placed an advertisement for carpenters "to work on the CRIBS, DOCKS and ELEVATORS of the Union Improvement and Elevator Company, Duluth, Minn."[15] A week later, on February 15, Jay Cooke's Northern Pacific Railroad commenced construction at Thomson's Junction near Carlton, Minnesota, on its transcontinental route west of the Great Lakes. Within a couple of years, Cooke was leasing the Lake Superior and Mississippi track section he helped build, which terminated at Duluth. This seemingly insignificant section was crucial to the development of the Northern Pacific because it provided direct rail access to the port at Duluth. The Northern Pacific now had a clear line to the water outlet at Lake Superior.[16]

The Chicago-based elevator architect Joseph T. Moulton designed and built the elevator. Construction of Elevator *A* began in the spring of 1870.[17] Moulton was much sought after as an elevator architect when the wheat fields of the Upper Midwest were opening and the Twin Ports had no export facility. Leaving behind much of what he recognized as the civilized world, Moulton knew when he arrived in Duluth that, as an architect, he could play an important part in its growth. He could see the potential for many more elevators. History shows that he was right.

Moulton was hired on commission to build a grain elevator for the Union Improvement Elevator Company. Already waiting in Duluth to meet with Moulton was Charles B. Newcomb, superintendent and managing director of the "Great Grain Elevator of Duluth," by which the project was referred to in the local press.

Joseph Tilton Moulton was born on August 27, 1826, in Gilford, New Hampshire, beneath the shadow of the White Mountains. The young boy was the great-grandson of General Jonathan Moulton,

---

15  "Wanted Immediately, Carpenters," *Duluth Minnesotian*, February 12, 1870.

16  Ibid., 182–183.

17  Walter Van Brunt, ed., *History of Duluth and St. Louis County* (Chicago: American Historical Society, 1921), 3:192–193.

who earned his distinction during the Revolutionary War. Moulton's father was a farmer with a practical instinct. His sons worked in the fields during the summer. In the winter, Moulton attended school, hungry to learn and find a way out of his situation. A posthumous biography of Moulton said, "He acquired a good education, which business experience and the practical duties of his life largely supplemented." He was said to have excelled when working with mechanical devices.

Moulton would not be tethered to the horse and harness. At the age of nineteen, he left the farm, moving to Waltham, Massachusetts. There, he found work at Waltham Bleachery. Proving to be an intelligent worker, he soon advanced above his entry-level peers, but Moulton had interests that would lead him in another direction. While working at Waltham, he found time to learn the carpenter's trade, at which he excelled.

The ten-year span that accounted for his twenties began with the nineteen-year-old Moulton marrying Maria Babcock in April 1846 in Lowell, Massachusetts. The couple soon had three small children—Charles, William, and George. Once again, Moulton was restless. This time, eying the rapidly growing "west," Moulton moved his family to Chicago, a metropolis being built lock, stock and barrel out of lumber. There was plenty of work for a man with his newly honed skills. By the age of twenty-eight, Moulton had found a trade that sustained his family for the next three decades. "He mastered the business in every detail and made such continued progress that he became one of the most prominent contractors throughout the entire west," lauded his Freemason colleagues in their *Compendium of Freemasonry in Illinois*.

Historian, Professor Thomas Leslie captures Moulton in his early years in Chicago. Leslie writes that Moulton "emigrated to Chicago in 1853, gaining experience in elevator operation and construction by taking work as a laborer in one of the city's riverfront structures. After opening a contracting business with engineer Alexander Miller—who had assisted Van Osdel with the Newberry and Dole elevator—Moulton revolutionized grain elevator construction and design by standardizing construction and incorporating new conveying innovations to provide more efficient operation."

As Moulton prepared for his trip to Duluth, he reflected on the break that had jump-started his career. The year was 1855, and his son, George, who would one day inherit and build upon the business, was three years old. As an architect, Joseph Moulton's first elevator was the 700,000-bushel Sturges-Buckingham Elevator *A* on the mouth of the Chicago River.

Going forward, Moulton's design would become the standard for elevators.

> With a key location adjacent to the Illinois Central railyards and the river's mouth, Moulton's structure nearly doubled the city's storage capacity. Within two years, Moulton built a second structure, 50 percent larger on an adjacent site. At 130 feet tall, Sturges and Buckingham's so-called *A* and *B* elevators represented the state of the art in elevator construction.[18]
>
> Grain was shoveled from Illinois Central cars into hoppers next to and below the tracks. From there, conveyer belts fitted with metal scoops carried it to a narrow cupola at the structure's peak where they discharged grain into two stacked boxes. The first, a "garner," held a thousand bushels. When full, it discharged into a hopper below that weighed the batch and allowed a grader to take a sample for inspection. Depending on the quality, graders could then direct the incoming shipment to a specific bin below by a rotating chute, ensuring that each bin would contain grain of equal quality. The elevators could then discharge weighed and graded grain into ships through chutes on the wharf side.

---

18 Thomas Leslie, "Chicago's Other Skyscrapers: Grain Elevators and the City, 1838–1957," *Journal of Urban History*, May 28, 2020, https://doi.org/10.1177/0096144220925446.

The grain firm was founded by banker Solomon Sturges and brother's-in-law C. P. and Alvah Buckingham, merchants from Ohio, according to the *Encyclopedia: Chicago History*. Moulton's pioneering innovations for Sturges and Buckingham set elevator standards for the next fifty years.

> Steam power ran shafts, pulleys and belts that filled elevator's cupolas with motion and sound. Belt conveyors were shaped into vees that prevented spillage or into slopes that discharged into bins. Self-contained mechanical legs limited spillage while belt tightening systems assured constant speed and operation. Grain could be switched into circuits that cleaned, dried or sifted it if a grader determined that it was inferior in quality while powered shovels attached to chain drives reduced the time it took to empty a rail car. Systems that accepted grain from hoppers underneath these cars, or that tilted full cars to discharge their contents to one side, sped up this process. These advances largely automated receiving, handling and storing grain, which was critical given Chicago's perpetual labor shortage and the trade's seasonal nature. Loading a 40,000-bushel lake boat took a dozen laborers an entire day in the 1840s. In Moulton's elevators, one worker could move this much grain out of rail cars in an hour, and by the 1880s a typical elevator with more powerful steam engines and more sophisticated handling equipment would quadruple this capacity.

Moulton's next known work came in 1863 when he built a large elevator in Toledo for the Michigan Southern Railroad. The *Chicago Tribune* lauded his work, saying it "combines strength, durability, and accuracy." Moulton was praised as having built a structure "which will not only be a credit to that city but will stand as a monument to the enterprising skill of its architect." During the 1860s, Moulton also constructed a large elevator on the Mississippi River at Dunleith, Illinois (now East Dubuque).

Flywheel for drive belt on machinery floor of Peavey Globe Elevator, 1992.
Photo: author.

After the Sturges-Buckingham elevator, Moulton perfected his design, letting gravity do the work by releasing the grain from the top of the elevator in a series of stages that included weighing, cleaning and grading before distribution to bins.

> Bins were at the heart of Moulton's system. They formed the bulk of an elevator's structure and bore the tremendous weight of thousands of bushels. Bins had to be designed for the grain's dead weight and the bursting stresses caused by its fluid pressure. Experiments established that bin walls carried most of a tall grain column's weight through friction, while a bin's floor carried only a shallow pyramid of grain above it. Brick or stone walls could not develop the strength in tension necessary to contain tall columns of grain.

Instead, Moulton relied on "crib construction," which became the standard in Chicago. Two-inch thick timber planks, ranging in width from four to eight inches, were nailed and spiked together horizontally, with wider planks at the bin's base and narrower ones at its top. These planks provided increasing strength toward the base of the bins where the outward pressure of grain was greatest and were aided by iron tie rods running across or around each bin. Crib construction was resource-intensive. Such "somber piles of joining" were only economical while lumber flowed through Chicago in vast quantities.

The Duluth elevator introduced George Mayhew Moulton into the family business. George was born in Readsboro, Vermont, on March 15, 1851, prior to the move to Chicago. "He was educated in the public schools of Chicago, to which city his parents had moved in 1853. On his graduation in 1868 from Central High School, he entered his father's business, that of designing and building grain elevators. In January 1870, he went with his father to Duluth and aided in the construction of the first grain elevator built in that section of the country. He was secretary to the vice-president and general manager of the Elevator Company at that time."[19]

When construction in Duluth began in earnest in the spring of 1870, the young superintendent, Charles Newcombe, thought it would be a great idea to begin each workday by assembling the men for a morning prayer. The novelty soon wore off on the recalcitrant laborers, as noted by Duluth historian Walter Van Brunt. "By the end of the first week, the prayers were being replaced with catcalls and objects hurled in the direction of Mr. Newcombe. In lieu of the successful completion of the elevator, as well as his own safety, Newcombe decided to drop the prayer service from the morning activity roster."[20]

Over the summer of 1870, the shell of the elevator, 150 feet in length and sixty-five feet in depth, quickly rose along the lakefront. Details of the construction were reported in the *Duluth Minnesotian*.[21]

---

19   Leslie.
20   Van Brunt, 192.
21   "The Great Elevator of Duluth," *Duluth Minnesotian*, September 24,

> It is built, in its exterior walls, of plank 2 by 8 inches, laid flatwise and log house fashion, and these walls are interlocked and spiked together with the interior walls, which are made of planks 2 by 6 inches, and which form the Grain Bins - the whole constituting a very solidly laid and strong structure, requiring 150,000 feet of two-inch planking for the outside walls, and 50,000 feet of two-inch plank for the inside or "bin" walls. The exterior walls are carried up on the front and back sides for 51 feet 2 inches, when the roof slope commences and rises at about an angle of 30 degrees until, at 15 feet from the main side walls, it strikes the walls of what is termed the "Cupola."

An outlook platform ringed the cupola. From 102 feet above the dock, the view "is one of the handsomest panoramas, landscape and water scenery, that the world presents." Thirty feet above the roof rippled a twenty-four-foot American flag representing thirty-seven undivided states.

Elevator *A* was powered by a steam plant housed in a brick structure located on the south end of the elevator with a "brick chimney stack 102½ feet high, 9 feet 8 inches square at the base, tapering most beautifully to 4 feet 4 inches at the top..." Steam was generated by two great boilers located in the brick building. During its first year of operation, Newcombe placed advertisements for bids on 500 cords of wood to feed the system.

> These boilers are 16 feet long and four and a half feet in diameter and filled with 64 three and a half inch tubes with full fire fronts and all modern improvements. The engine that gives motion to it is a very fine one of 100-horse capacity by the Northwestern Manufacturing Company of Chicago with a steam cylinder 24 inches diameter and 30 inches stroke. The flywheel

1870.

> is 14 feet in diameter and weighs five tons. The power is communicated from the engine by means of a large 12-foot pulley on the flywheel shaft and upon a pulley three feet diameter on the line shaft to the top of the building and immense belt revolves giving motion to the solid line shaft above and this shaft drives all the machinery this main belt is a monster of its kind, being made of one continuous piece of rubber and five ply three feet wide and 200 feet long and weighing 1800 pounds.

Prior to providing the details of the interior construction, the newspaper described in detail the laying of the foundation to support the structure and to it from the perils of Lake Superior. It may seem trivial in modern times, but this was challenging construction in 1870 and would set the standard for future building within the harbor.

> To secure depth of water enough for vessels loading with grain to lay alongside of the elevator, it was of course necessary to make a foundation in the lake itself. To do this a strong crib work of heavy timbers hewn on the underwater sides and interlocked with timber "grillage" and bolted together with 10,000 Iron bolts each an inch square and 30 inches long, was constructed on the ice last winter and then sunk by loading the entire crib with stone. To constitute these foundation cribs, there were used 800,000 feet of 12 by 12 pine timbers and 1,500 cords of stone, the heaviest kind of trap rock, having a specific gravity of 160 pounds to the cubic foot. When the cribs were sunk and filled, walls of stone laid in hydraulic cement, were built upon them - first a wall 4 feet thick and 5 feet high as a foundation for the outside walls of the building to rest upon, and then of 3 feet 6 inches thick and 5 feet high for cross walls every ten feet across the foundation to support the "bin" partitions.

**Interior of House *1* at Globe Elevator where box cars either unloaded into a graded pit beneath or were loaded by chutes from above. (Modern steel hopper rail cars were too wide to fit between the support posts).** Photo: author.

At track level, the large beams formed a cathedral-like canopy beneath which rail cars could be brought in, unloaded, and removed. Working upward, located above the bins, the upper stories of the elevator were housed within the cupola, where the grain was received, weighed, cleaned if necessary, and distributed via chutes to the bins through hatches located on the bin floor. On these floors, unlike the main support and bin walls, the structural timbers stretched vertically and diagonally in support of the walls and floors. Even with the machinery in place, the floors were often airy and breathtaking work spaces.

The description of the conveying method to "elevate" grain from track level to the top of the cupola gives us insight into a system that Moulton designed to perfection, leading the path forward for further development in the following decades. [See the Appendix for more details.]

A novel feature in the Duluth elevator was the use of an arresting or "friction" pulley to stop any of the belts individually without shutting down the entire hoisting system. Moulton first used this new device in the Sturges-Buckingham elevator and carried over to the Union Improvement facility. Prior to this, when the weigher at the top desired to arrest the hoisting capacity of any one belt, he had to signal to the person feeding the grain into the elevator foot multiple stories below, bringing the entirety of the operations of the entire building to a standstill.

On September 24, the first receipt for a carload of grain was recorded. Elevator *A* was open for business. A small ceremony took place at the Union Improvement Elevator site, a comingling of principals Clinton Markell, Col. C. H. Graves and Roger Munger, along with laborers and men of commerce. Joseph T. Moulton was presented with an ebony cane and a jar containing a grain sample from the first shipment. The family of Mr. Moulton would later donate that sample to the St. Louis County Historical Society for its archives.[22]

**Drive belt pulley for marine leg on water side of Globe Elevator House 1.** Photo: author.

---

22 "Hardy Workers Flocked Here In 1870 When Building Began," *Duluth News Tribune*, October 14, 1931.

Within a few weeks of the opening of the Union Improvement Elevator Company, a fire broke out on Sunday, October 8, 1871, in Chicago. News of the conflagration reached Duluth soon after, giving everyone pause to speculate on the possibility of a similar event occurring along Minnesota Point or Superior Street, let alone their new grain elevator. In Chicago's great fire, a quarter of the grain storage space, receiving and shipping facilities were burned.[23] The lost capacity resulting from the fire was over 1.5 million bushels, an amount nearly four times the capacity of Duluth's 350,000-bushel Elevator A.[24]

Although the Chicago Board of Trade was closed for a week, grain continued moving through Chicago in great quantities, supported by monies from New York and Milwaukee. "The grain received during that week aggregated not less than 1635 car loads, or 649,000 bushels, and the shipments amounted to 220,460 bushels, to move which required the outlay of fully $165,000. Most of these funds were brought direct from New York, but a portion of the money was obtained from Milwaukee." Despite the losses, statistics show the movement of Midwestern grain was vitally important to the nation's food supply chain and the economy.

In comparison to Duluth, Chicago was the wheat capital of the Midwest. To accommodate the large grain business of the city, there were seventeen public warehouses (elevators) with a united storage capacity of 11,580,000 bushels. In addition, there were quite a few small storehouses with an average capacity of about fifty thousand bushels. These were independent of the storehouses for the keeping of flour, pork products and other articles of produce.[25]

With the Duluth elevator up and running, the Union Improvement and Elevator Company soon requested bids for the construction of an elevator at Stillwater, Minnesota, which it wanted ready by the spring season.[26] At the start of 1871, the stockholders of

---

23 Elias Colbert and Everett Chamberlain, *Chicago and the Great Conflagration Chicago* (Northern Illinois University: 1872), 331.
24 *Chicago: Tales of the Great Lakes* (Secaucus, NJ: Castle Publishing), 19.
25 Ibid., 130.
26 "Attention Contractors," *Stillwater Messenger*, December 16, 1870.

the Union Improvement concern met in Philadelphia on January 11 at which Charles Newcombe, noted as a resident of St. Paul, was elected president and Jay Cooke vice president. Duluth was represented by George Spencer, retained as secretary and treasurer, and Charles Graves as a member of the Board.[27]

The first yearly grain totals for the Union Improvement elevators, published at the end of 1871, provides the following statistics: the receipt of 1,402,142 bushels of wheat at Duluth's Elevator *A* and the shipment of 1,387,680 bushels. Elevator *B* at Stillwater listed receipts of wheat at 1,112,720 bushels, and similar numbers in shipments (1,111,224 bu.) were recorded between its opening on June 8 and the close of navigation on the Mississippi and St. Croix Rivers on November 22. An additional facility, Elevator *C*, under lease in Hastings, Minnesota, reported receipts of 59,344 bushels of wheat, with shipments of 51,626 bushels. The statistics, reported by Charles Newcombe, were notated as "showing a remarkable development of the grain business for the new route via Duluth and Lake Superior."[28]

In November, a reporter for the *Boston Weekly Advertiser* tagged along with an inspection party of commissioners appointed by President Grant to inspect the progress of the Northern Pacific Railroad between St. Paul and Duluth, "to spy the land, its offerings and opportunities in the interest of the public and the profession, and to report plainly and truthfully what he might see, hear and observe." His report was reproduced by the *Duluth Minnesotian* several months later, in February 1873.[29]

From the perspective of an outsider not tied to Duluth, the report provided an interesting insight into the Union Improvement and Elevator Company's operation.

---

27 "The Union Improvement and Elevator Company," *Duluth Minnesotian*, January 21, 1870.

28 "Statement of the Receipts and Shipments of Grain by the Union Improvement and Elevator Company," *Duluth Minnesotian*, December 21, 1871.

29 "A Northern Pacific Trip," *Duluth Minnesotian*, reproduced from the *Boston Weekly Advertiser*, February 8, 1983.

> This was the second year of the practical operation of the elevator, and this the month of the most constant and favorable business... Last year its rates for handling were so high as to amount practically to a prohibition, but better counsels have prevailed this fall and the charges now are but one cent to one cent and a half per bushel – no more than other elevators of the West – and as a consequence the receipts of grain have been large and constant. Last night fifty thousand bushels of wheat left Stillwater and will be here today, while as many more are ready to leave to-night. The Improvement Company have their elevator "B" at Stillwater, and there transfer to the cars wheat brought in boats from as far down the Mississippi as Winona, while cars of the Northern Pacific are freighted at St. Paul, Minneapolis, Carver and all intermediate points along the line with grain for transshipment at Duluth.

The reporter noted that the wheat shipped from Duluth was destined for Buffalo, with "the millers of that city preferring the Minnesota spring wheat to that from any other section of the country." As a quick aside, hard spring wheat was high in protein, but I the 1870s was difficult to process. Soft winter wheat, grown in southwest Minnesota in great quantity, was easier to process, so millers traded higher quality for efficiency. Innovation in the milling process, pioneered in Minneapolis, led to the ability to use the protein rich hard spring wheat in the flour milling industry. Hard spring wheat grown in the Red River Valley, destined for mills in Buffalo, was shipped through the port of Duluth.

It was noted that the shipment of grain from Duluth via the canal at Sault Ste. Marie contributed to abolishing the rate tariff imposed on wheat by steamboat shippers the previous season out of Milwaukee and Chicago.

> Last year Duluth wheat was steadily quoted two or three cents a bushel higher in Buffalo than the "Milwaukee club," and the same preference is apparent in the prices this fall. One reason among others by which this state of facts is explained here is, that the softer grain of Iowa and Illinois is mixed in the Milwaukee elevators with the better wheat of the farther north, while the Minnesota flint and fife wheat finds its way through Duluth direct and unadulterated to the consumer. The shipments to Buffalo and the New York ports have been increased this year by the abolition of the discriminating freight tariff which the steamboat companies last year imposed, in consequence of the reduced cargo which can be taken through the Sault Ste. Marie, compared with that through the Mackinaw straits amounting in large vessels to ten thousand bushels. Last year three cents more per bushel were charged for carrying wheat from Duluth to eastern lake ports, than from Chicago and Milwaukee, - this year the rates are equal, and Duluth prospers and rejoices. The single elevator which is now sufficient for the transshipment of the wheat at Duluth is likely to demonstrate two things by this season's work, the advantage of Duluth as a shipping port, and its own insufficiency for the business of another year.

Direct competition was fierce for the Duluth elevator against the already well-established Great Lakes grain ports of Milwaukee and Chicago. The cost of doing business was high, and the rhetoric was constant. Perseverance and business savvy were often needed to see beyond the year's grain receipts. The projected development of the Red River Valley wheat fields helped keep the future dreams of the Duluth elevator firm intact. On September 12, 1879, *The Northwestern Miller* reported, "The Union Improvement and Elevator company are building an addition to their elevator *A*, at Duluth,

Minn., which will make it the largest elevator in the state. It will be 260x60 feet and 114 feet high."[30]

A final note in the accomplishment of Elevator *A* as a historic first was the installation of the first telephone in Duluth at Elevator *A*, as documented by Walter Van Brunt in his history of Duluth and St. Louis County.[31]

> In 1876, Philadelphia Exposition, Mr. Walter Van Brunt, who promoted and operated the first telephone exchange in Duluth, read of the invention of the telephone and sent for two instruments, which he connected on a private line between C. H. Graves & Co. office, with which he was associated, and a nearby elevator "A."

---

30 "Milling News Items," *The Northwestern Miller* 8, no. 11 (September 12, 1879): 174.

31 Walter Van Brunt, *Duluth and St. Louis County, Minnesota: Their Story and People* (Chicago: The American Historical Society, 1921), 1:257.

# 2
# Munger, Markell & Company – Elevator *1*

It was inevitable that more elevators would follow. The collaborative effect of the success of Elevator *A*, combined with Duluth's exploding growth, led to the need for increased elevator capacity. The year following the start of Elevator *A* saw the incorporation of Duluth's second grain export elevator company.

The firm of Munger, Markell & Company was incorporated in 1872 at Duluth. Along with Roger S. Munger and Clinton Markell were two of Roger Munger's brothers from St. Paul—Russel and Gilbert.[32] Roger Munger and Markell were already involved as principals of the Union Improvement and Elevator Company. They would build their new elevator in what was known as the inner harbor parallel to the Lake Superior and Mississippi Railroad tracks, near Dock Street and 5th Avenue West.

Construction on Elevator *1* began in 1873 and completed in 1874 for $60,000. It was smaller in dimensions than Elevator *A*, with a storage capacity of 200,000 bushels. The main building stretched 120 feet, and its height reached a maximum of 54 feet. The front portion of the elevator containing the "elevators, cleaners, scales and weigh hoppers" was fifty-four feet high, and the rear portion, "which contained the grain bins on the ground floor," was thirty-six feet

---

32  *Encyclopedia of Biography of Minnesota* (Chicago: Century Publishing and Engraving Company, 1900), 1:269.

high. The elevator foundation was built on wooden pilings sunk into the clay bottom of the bay. A brick boiler house stood twelve feet to the east of the main elevator.[33]

A second dock ran along the east side of the elevator and was generally used to store barrels of salt belonging to Col. C. H. Graves's export business. Immediately to the west were the docks and warehouses of the Northern Pacific, separated by a small bridge.[34]

A brief notation in *The Duluth Minnesotian* contributed by "Seacher" describes some of the elevator's details provided during a tour of the facility led by Clinton Markell in the fall of 1874.

> **It has six set of Fairbanks scales, and two of Barnard & Lea's separators, with a capacity of 600 bushels each per hour. To do the work of the elevator they have placed one double engine of 40 horse and one single engine of 32 horsepower. The building is iron-clad, and has a wharfage of 500 feet, and being within the inner harbor can load boats at any time.**[35]

The design of the elevator was based on the Chase plan developed in 1873 by the Chase Elevator Company of Chicago. Chase was a milling firm that developed a studded-wall design as an inexpensive alternative to the cribbed elevator design employed by J. T. Moulton and Sons. In the US Department of Interior's documentation of Minnesota grain elevators compiled in 1990, the patented Chase system was first used in Peoria, Illinois. While this study is not intended to be a detailed account of elevator construction, it is useful to note some of the details of this system as it would be the only time this method would be deployed in Duluth-Superior.

> **The Chase design is interesting for at least two reasons. The first involved the plan of the bins and the**

---

33 "The Duluth Elevator Fire," *St. Paul Globe*, March 8, 1880.
34 "Destruction of Elevator," *Duluth Tribune Weekly*, March 6, 1880.
35 *Duluth Minnesotian*, October 10, 1874.

> transport system. The Chase employed a double row of grain bins extending behind what was called the "transfer house," now known as the workhouse. Grain was received in the transfer house, elevated to the top, and then delivered to the bins with a belt conveyor. This was a new development over the previous design of allowing the grain to gravity-flow from the elevator head into nearby bins.

> The second interesting feature of the Chase elevator appears in one of two views of a Chase structure published in the 1880s. Clearly visible in the engraving are three horizontal bands extending around the entire building at equal intervals between the foundation and the eaves, a distance of perhaps 30 feet. The bands are punctuated by small circles at intervals of some 3 to 4 feet... The "bands" are sections of wooden plank, and the "circles" along their length are the ends of tie rods that extend across the elevator interior to cross-brace the bins... The Chase elevator is an example of an innovative plan that pointed to terminal-elevator design, but structurally it was a simple, traditional studded country-elevator.[36]

Buoyed by the success of the grain export business and the overall growth of the city, the young community of Duluth was dealt a serious setback with the financial collapse of Jay Cooke's enterprises. The diversity of businesses Cooke had invested in, particularly the Northern Pacific, surpassed his ability to support them. On September 18, 1873, Cooke's financial empire came crashing down in what became known as the Panic of 1873, beginning a four-year economic depression. The collapse devastated the Duluth area, which relied on Cooke-backed enterprises.

---

36   Ian R. Stewart, "Grain Elevators in Minnesota to 1945," *Minnesota Historical Society*, 1990.

Duluth's population, which had exploded from several hundred in 1869 to over 3,500 by 1873, quickly withered. As a public entity, the city of Duluth could not overcome its debts and was forced to dissolve its charter. It would be another five excruciating years before the town of Duluth again regained its status as a city.

The crash of 1873 also caused the eventual loss of the Lake Superior and Mississippi Railroad. The line could not fully recover and was reorganized in 1877 as the St. Paul and Duluth Railroad. It took over operations along the Duluth waterfront previously run by the LS&M before being absorbed into the Northern Pacific.

The Northern Pacific, under the direct leadership of Jay Cooke, eventually proved more resilient. It took several years, but Cooke persisted, re-establishing himself in the railroad industry. His stock interests in the grain business, namely one hundred shares of stock in the Union Improvement and Elevator Company, were auctioned off at a par value of fifty dollars each at the end of December 1873.[37]

By January 1874, Elevator *1* reported over ten thousand bushels on hand for the upcoming shipping season. Munger and Markell were pushing deep into western Minnesota and the Dakotas for their grain, soliciting business from growers along the St. Paul and Sioux City Railroad and the Northern Pacific.[38] By early April, the amount on hand at the elevator was just under fifty-four thousand bushels.

Munger, Markell & Company, with fingers in both elevator enterprises at Duluth, aggressively scoured the wheat fields of western Minnesota, particularly the Red River Valley and the farms of the Dakota Territory. The rapid onset of Duluth as a grain port continued reaping benefits for western farmers. In late 1875, Munger & Markell were building a country line elevator at Goose River, North Dakota, and were expecting to have in excess of twenty thousand bushels on hand before spring.[39] A line elevator is one of multiple elevators usually owned either by a railroad, such as the

---

37 "Stock Incorporated Companies and Interest in Joint Stock Companies," *Philadelphia Enquirer*, December 27, 1873.

38 *Duluth Minnesotian,* January 24, 1874.

39 *Brainerd Tribune*, November 23, 1875.

Great Northern or Northern Pacific, or by a company, in this case Munger & Markell. The grain harvested locally would be sent first to the line elevator and later loaded into boxcars and sent to the larger terminal elevator at Duluth.

The burgeoning wheat market led to large-scale farming in the Red River Valley. One of Munger & Markell's early customers was Oliver Dalrymple, manager and operator of a "bonanza farm" in the Dakota Territory located on 13,440 acres of Northern Pacific land. The land was principally owned by George Cass, president of the Northern Pacific.[40]

Dalrymple started in Minnesota with a farming operation near Cottage Grove, Minnesota, circa 1874, where he became known as the "Minnesota wheat king." He lost his farm speculating on the grain market but reacquired his fortune in the Dakota Territory in the mid to late 1870s.[41] Dalrymple, Munger and Markell forged a solid business relationship. In late August 1877, according to the *Duluth Minnesotian*, Dalrymple arrived in Duluth. "He came to see the shipping of his wheat, which is arriving this week, and is of a first-class quality. He has arranged with Munger, Markell & Co. to handle 180,000 bushels of it..."[42]

In time, the relationship between Dalrymple and the Duluth elevators soured, leading Dalrymple to look at building his own elevator facilities in Bayfield, Wisconsin, editorialized the *Northwestern Miller* in July 1885 in its "The Elevators" section. "He has never been satisfied with his treatment at Duluth, and has been compelled to demand special bins there, so that Duluth elevator employees call his grain 'sacred wheat.' By and by it is expected that Mr. Dalrymple will put up mills, somewhere, and grind his own wheat."[43]

---

40  Cathy A. Langemo, "Oliver Dalrymple," *Prairie Public NewsRoom*, published May 18, 2022, https://bit.ly/3UQvU5d.

41  "Dalrymple Farm," Fargo, North Dakota: Its History and Images, accessed June 13, 2023, https://bit.ly/3TaWQey.

42  *Duluth Minnesotian-Herald*, August 25, 1877.

43  "The Elevators: Facts About Old and New Ones Throughout the Country," *The Northwestern Miller* 20, no. 1 (July 3, 1885): 14.

Fortunes were being made on the wheat fields of the Upper Midwest as crops went from subsistence to export commodities, feeding a growing demand on the East Coast. The elevator operators at Duluth were another piece of the supply chain they were in the process of building. The coming decade would see the explosive growth of the wheat market and the development of Rice's Point as the place to do business in Duluth.

The decade of the 1880s brought a new player into the elevator business in Duluth. The Lake Superior Elevator Company incorporated in 1880 with an operating capital of $20,000. The incorporators were C. H. Graves, Roger S. Munger, Clinton Markell, and John Q. Adams of St. Paul. The new company became almost a sister company to the Union Improvement & Elevator Company with its roster of officers, including the familiar faces of Graves and Munger, each listed as vice presidents. Luke Arthur Marvin, a St. Paul merchant who moved to the region in 1861 and most recently served as Duluth postmaster between 1875–1880, was appointed secretary and George Rupley treasurer and elevator superintendent.[44] Gilbert Munger of London, England, was also a co-owner of the elevator.

The Lake Superior Elevator Company entered into an agreement with the Northern Pacific Railroad to construct an elevator with a one-million-bushel capacity. Lake Superior's Elevator B became the first elevator built on Rice's Point on property owned by the Northern Pacific. For their part, the railroad added new track sections to service the elevator.

In addition to the contract for Elevator B, the Lake Superior Elevator Company agreed to build at least three additional structures on the Northern Pacific site.[45] Railroads such as the Northern Pacific were finding the amount of wheat on their lines exceeded their capacity. More terminal elevators at Duluth would help free up storage space.

---

44 Lake Superior Elevator Company, Articles of Incorporation. Minnesota Secretary of State. Minnesota archives 112.F.14.4F, vol. E, 134–137.

45 "Tally One More for Duluth," *Duluth Tribune Weekly*, November 16, 1883.

**Lake Superior Elevator Company Elevator *B* was the first elevator built on Rice's Point in 1880.**
Photo: Lake Superior Maritime Collections, UW-Superior.

To maintain the competitive edge in their business, the railroads sought deals that could give them the advantage of a complete cycle of transportation from the country line elevators to the eastern mills via the Duluth elevators.

The construction of Elevator *B* was typical of the day. The main structure was timber framed with an iron-clad exterior that provided a layer of fireproofing. Once again, the architect was J. T. Moulton and Sons of Chicago, "the builder of the Vanderbilt elevators in New York, and of other large elevators throughout the country. He considers it the best one he's ever built. The superintendent is John M. Rich, Esq., formerly engineer of Munger, Markell & Co.'s elevator and overseer of the new house from the day the first pile was driven."[46]

Unique to its contemporaries, Elevator *B* was equipped with shipping legs on both sides of the elevator, allowing for loading vessels from either side. June 1, 1881, marked the first time that two

---

46 "Monster Elevator," *Duluth Weekly Tribune*, October 1, 1880.

boats were loaded simultaneously at a Duluth elevator.[47] The details of Elevator *B* and Annex *C* were detailed by the *Northwestern Miller*.[48]

> Elevator *B*, built in 1880, is situated in the inner harbor and has a receiving capacity of 350 cars in ten hours. The power in this elevator is furnished by an upright 640-horsepower condensing engine with a 42x42 cylinder with steam supplied from two steel boilers six feet in diameter and sixteen feet long. The power from the engine is carried to the main shaft by a six-ply rubber belt forty-six inches wide and 290 feet long. The main shaft runs the entire length of the house on the upper floor and has ten paper friction pulleys that run the receiving elevators for conveying the grain from cars to the scales. Cross-belts from the main shaft run the shipping elevators, six in number, which are used for elevating grain for shipment. Each elevator belt has a carrying capacity of 5,000 bushels per hour, making the total elevating capacity 80,000 bushels per hour. On the floor below the machinery are the scales, 16 in number, into which the elevators discharge. Ten of these are used for weighing cars and have a capacity of 50,000 lbs. each. The other six are used for shipping and have a capacity of 30,000 lbs. each. These scales are all Fairbank's Standard, recently strengthened to meet the increasing size of cars. Test weights are kept with them, and they are constantly tested, and their accuracy has become proverbial.
>
> Next below is the spout floor, where one sees only a confusing wilderness of spouts leading to bins in all parts of the house. Next below is the ground floor, on

---

47 *Duluth Daily Tribune*, June 1, 1881.
48 "Duluth Elevators," *Northwestern Miller* 15, no. 13 (March 30, 1883): 311.

which are the railroad tracks, steam shovels, cleaning machines, etc. The tracks in this house will accommodate twenty cars, and ten can be unloaded at once, so that while one track is being cleared another can be filled with cars. The cars are unloaded by the steam shovel, a very interesting automatic machine, which, by means of weights, throws itself in and out of gear, and then winds and unwinds the rope attached to a large shovel. By means of this, one man can unload a car in seven minutes, while it would require four men to do the same work by hand. The rapidity with which work can be done in this elevator is something wonderful. The barge *Hiawatha* has received a cargo of 44,500 bushels in one hour and forty minutes, the schooner *Adams* 62,000 bushels in two hours and forty minutes, with cars unloading at the same time.

Two hundred and fifty feet west of elevator $B$, stands elevator $C$, a mammoth structure equal to elevator $B$ in size, and surpassing it in storage capacity, as none of the room is taken up by machinery. This building is used simply as a store-house, and all grain is carried into it from elevator $B$ by means of a horizontal belt, 1480 feet in length, the longest conveying belt in the world. This belt is run from the main shaft in elevator $B$, and carries grain at the rate of 10,000 bushels per hour, and by means of a tripping machine can be made to discharge into any bin in the house.

The grain is drawn from elevator $C$ to elevator $B$ by means of another horizontal belt in the lower floor and from elevator $B$ is delivered to boats.

Prior to the advent of self-unloading vessel technology, grain arriving at elevators from ships was unloaded using a marine leg, a vertical conveyor system with metal buckets attached to a moving rubber belt. The leg, once lowered into the cargo hold of a vessel, scoops the grain into the buckets and raises the grain to the top of the elevator. The invention of the marine leg is largely credited to Joseph Dart, who first employed his device in Buffalo. Many, but not all, of the elevators in the port had at least one marine leg. Elevator *E* for example, had two legs capable of unloading 20,000 bushels per hour,[49] but most were in the range of 10,000 to 15,000 bushels per hour.

When it comes to loading a vessel, a similar set of legs, located on the water side of the elevator, are used to transfer grain from the storage bins to shipping bins where the grain is blended and weighed just prior to being loaded. The equipment is still called a leg, but more specifically a shipping leg. The origin of the term is consistent with other nomenclature that is already used to describe other areas, such as the spout floor, or the scale floor. Leg is simply another word to describe a part or function of the elevator that is easily understood by everyone.

* * *

The good fortune accorded to all at the start of the new decade was not favored on the firm of Munger, Markell & Co. Fire broke out in Elevator *1* on Saturday, March 6, 1880.[50] The fire was first reported late in the afternoon and quickly engulfed the structure. "The fire engine was immediately gotten out, but by reason of its great weight and the depth of snow, something near half an hour elapsed before it reached the burning structure…"[51]

Little could be done to save the elevator despite the valiant efforts of the elevator crew, the fire department and local citizens. By midnight, the framework had dissolved under the flames leaving burning mountains of grain that were only recently stored for shipment.

---

49 Note: Data from Norris Grain Company, circa 1945.
50 "Destruction of an Elevator," *Duluth Tribune Weekly*, March 6, 1880.
51 "Burning Bread," *St. Paul Globe*, March 8, 1880.

Duluth's first major grain elevator fire was a spectacle as well as a terror for the young community. The memory of the devastating fire in Chicago did little to lessen the fear. Flames, fanned by a slight wind, spread out across the surrounding hillside while the intense heat caused several nearby buildings to catch fire.

All the grain in the elevator was insured, forty thousand bushels of wheat and one hundred twenty-five thousand bushels of corn, except for four rail cars of corn that had recently arrived. C. H. Graves & Co. faced losses of upwards of ten thousand dollars for damage to seven thousand barrels of fully insured salt stored on a nearby wharf. Unfortunately for the Munger and Markell concern, the structure itself was vastly underinsured for such a tragedy. The machinery inside the elevator, which had been recently upgraded to better facilitate the handling of grain, contributed greatly to the value of the loss. The value of Elevator 1, its contents and the dock were estimated to be one hundred fifty thousand dollars at the time of the fire, with a total of one hundred seventeen thousand dollars of insurance spread out over at least seven different insurance firms.[52]

Duluth pioneer Jerome E. Cooley recalled the fire in his memoir of the early days of Duluth, writing,[53]

> Another fire was the Munger and Markell elevator which stood on the bay front about a hundred feet east of Fifth Avenue west, where the Clow line of boats now land. About 500,000 bushels of wheat were in the elevator at the time. It was built on pile, the bins running down to the water level. The bins, which were full, made excellent flues and gave the fire a good draft.
>
> The wheat ran into the bay and furnished food for the wild ducks and gulls until spring. Wheat-fed ducks certainly offered a welcome diversion from an all-fish diet.

---

52 Ibid.
53 Jerome Eugene Cooley, *Recollections of Early Days in Duluth* (Duluth: self-published, 1925), 51.

The fire dealt a devastating blow to the young company. "From the time of the completion of the elevator up to the year 1878 it was a losing investment," reported the *St. Paul Globe* several days after the fire. "In 1878 the firm realized a small profit and last year the profit was greater. The prospects for 1880 were exceedingly flattering, but the fire deprives the firm of all chance of profit from handling this year's crop."[54] Disheartened, Russell and Gilbert Munger retired from the grain business after the fire. The company regrouped and continued under the abbreviated name of Munger and Markell.[55]

Munger and Markell never rebuilt their grain elevator. After the fire, the firm concentrated more on the real estate development side of their business. The musical past was evidently still strong in the heart of Roger Munger when they built the Grand Opera House of Duluth in 1883. Munger maintained a strong interest in the grain business. His dream of opening a flour mill at Duluth was realized years later in 1888 with the organization of the Imperial Mill.[56]

The loss of Elevator *1* cut the grain capacity of Duluth almost in half. The nearly completed Elevator *B* for the Lake Superior Elevator Company coupled with the expansion of the Union Improvement and Elevator Company overcame any anxiety felt as a result of the devastating fire.

---

54 "The Duluth Elevator Fire," *St. Paul Globe*, March 11, 1880.
55 *Encyclopedia of Biography in Minnesota* 1:269.
56 *Annual Report for the Year Ending December 31, 1888*, Duluth Board of Trade, 36–37.

# 3
# The 1880s: The Development of Duluth's Elevator Row

The decade of the 1880s brought tremendous commercial growth to Duluth and its grain business. In *The Wheat Market and the Farmer in Minnesota, 1858–1900,* business historian Henrietta Larson noted this period as the one that put Duluth on the map. "The change which more than any other affected Minnesota's wheat trade in the late seventies and the eighties was the rise to a position of importance of the local primary markets, Minneapolis, and Duluth.... The phenomenal rise of Duluth as a wheat market began at that time."[57]

In a summary of the year 1882, *The Northwestern Miller* stated, "Taken altogether the year just closed has shown Duluth to be steady and surely advancing to the position of the market of the granary of the continent, and in the hands of the men who are at present engaged in the grain business here, we are confident that ere long it will be the great northwestern wheat market." The reporter noted that improvements in the total of ten thousand dollars had been made to Elevator A.[58]

The grain trade is a numbers game defined by an array of tables and statistics—bushels received versus bushels shipped. For the

---

57 Henrietta Larson, *The Wheat Market and the Farmer in Minnesota, 1858–1900* (New York: Columbia University, 1926), 126–127.
58 *The Northwestern Miller* 15, no. 3 (January 19, 1883): 70.

Duluth wheat trade, there was a definite change in these numbers, a coming of age as a force in the national marketplace. It was a time when the development of the farm regions in the Northwest pushed the rapid expansion of elevators at Duluth. It was the time when everything came together.

Duluth and the western farmlands experienced a grain explosion. Elevator capacity at Duluth jumped from just over three million bushels in 1883 to over nine million the following year. Just three years later, by 1887, the storage, handling, and shipping capacity doubled to just under twenty million bushels. Larson noted, "The amount of wheat received increased from an annual average of 1,692,503 from 1876 to 1880 to an average of 9,159,162 from 1881 to 1885." Wheat receipts and shipments went from just over nine million in 1883 to over twenty-five million in 1884.[59]

In response to this rapid growth, the Duluth Board of Trade was established in 1881. The Board's purpose was to help regulate and control the commerce emanating from the city of Duluth, including the rising sale of grain.[60]

The following statement was given in the overview of the archives of the Board of Trade.

> **The Duluth Board of Trade was organized in 1881 to improve the methods of trading in, and dealing with, an increasing volume of wheat being sent to Duluth, Minnesota, for market or shipping. The original incorporators were George Spencer, Clinton Markell, Andrew J. Sawyer, Owen Farguson, William T. Hooker, Wilmer W. Davis, Roger S. Munger, Charles H. Graves, and Walter Van Brunt.**

---

59 Ibid., 127.

60 *Report of the Federal Trade Commission on the Grain Trade*, Terminal Grain Markets and Exchanges, (Washington, DC: Government Printing Office, 1920), 2:155.

In 1883 the Board of Trade moved into offices in the Metropolitan Block, on the north side of Superior Street between First and Second Avenues West. In 1886 the Board moved to its own newly constructed building at the southwestern corner of Superior Street and Third Avenue West. The building was destroyed by fire in February of 1894. In March of 1895 the organization moved into another new building, for which plans had already been made before the 1894 fire, at the northwest corner of First Street and Third Avenue West.

The Duluth Board of Trade building at 301 West First Street was designed by noted Duluth architects Oliver Traphagen and Francis Fitzpatrick. It was the last large commission received by this architectural partnership, which dissolved in January, 1896. In 1905, Chicago architect Daniel Burnham designed the addition to the north side of the building and redesigned the Trading Room.

The First Street building had a fire in 1948, but was repaired and continued to be used by the Board of Trade. The Duluth Board of Trade was dissolved in 1972.[61]

In the first report from the secretary to the Duluth Board of Trade dated January 16, 1883, the receipts of wheat for 1882 were 4,198,833 bushels.[62] (It should be noted that in 1882, wheat was the only crop handled at the port.) This was an increase from the previous year's total of 1,283,266 bushels. Duluth was well on its way to becoming a major player in the nation's grain trade.

The annual report published by the Board of Trade listed the overall capacity of Duluth's elevators at 2,660,000 bushels. It noted that

---

61 Duluth Board of Trade records, https://bit.ly/3OYHffU.
62 Duluth Board of Trade, *1882 Annual Report*, January 16, 1883, p. 4.

an additional capacity of 1,100,000 bushels was gained with the recent completion of the Lake Superior Elevator Company's Elevator C.[63]

The decade of the eighties would see the return of J. T. Moulton and Son, led now by George Mayhew Moulton, to construct a new series of elevators in Duluth for the Union Improvement and Elevator Company and the Lake Superior Elevator Company. The Lake Superior Elevator Company erected Elevator's C, D, G, and Store House No. *1* between 1882 and 1887. The Union Improvement and Elevator Company added Elevator's E, F, and H in the same period. In addition to the new construction, the pioneering Elevator A was enlarged to a capacity of 560,000 bushels.

"The houses are arranged to operate in pairs, C being an annex to B, G an annex to D, and F an annex to E. The grain is received and shipped in the operating houses and transferred to and from the annexes by means of belt conveyors. The entire storage capacity of this system is over 11,000,000 bushels..."[64] In an overview of their elevator business, George Moulton contributed the following statement retrospectively in 1902 about the use of the "annex" in grain handling.[65]

> **The nature of grain handling business is often such as to require the storage of large bulk of grain for extended periods of time without the necessity of excessive elevating facilities. For this condition the "Annex" system is admirably adapted to secure large storage capacity at comparative low cost per bushel. This system was introduced by us in Duluth, being the pioneer in that line of construction. Elevator C, F, G, and I of the Consolidated Elevator Co., and Elevators 2 and 3 of the Globe Elevator Co. are prominent examples of this plan of construction...**

---

63   Ibid.

64   Geo. M. Moulton & Co., *Builders, Architects and Engineers* (Philadelphia: G. M. S. Armstrong, 1902), 28.

65   Ibid., 14.

> The bins or tanks may be built of wooden plank in the usual form of elevator bin construction, or of steel in square or circular form, or of hard-burned clay tile and cement strengthened with steel members. In the case of circular steel or tile bins, they may be either connected or detached.

The Union Improvement and Elevator Company's Elevator *F* was a wood-framed, iron-clad storehouse located at the head of the slip. It was a scant 60 feet in length but held 1.5 million bushels. It had no loading machinery and was connected to Elevator *E* via a ground-level brick-covered conveyor. To the east of *F* stood Elevator *E* at 92 feet in length with a storage capacity of 1.2 million bushels. At the end of the slip was Elevator *H*, with a slightly larger capacity of 1.5 million bushels.

\*\*\*\*

The exponential growth of the nation and the grain trade lent the opportunity for other companies to join in at the head of the lakes. The St. Paul and Duluth Railroad, which had taken over the operations of the bankrupt Lake Superior and Mississippi Railroad after the Panic of 1873, followed the lead of the other railroads in vying for the lucrative Duluth grain trade.

The railroad organized a new division, The Duluth and Western Elevator Company, announcing the construction of an elevator to begin in late 1883. Initially, the elevator operated from January 1884 until August 1887 under a lease to Minneapolis milling pioneer George H. Christian. The Board of Directors for the Duluth and Western Elevator Company consisted of grain commission merchant Wilmer W. Davis, Craig Cofield (grain buyer for the Northwestern Grain Dealers Association and former superintendent of Elevator *A*), Dwight G. Cutler (Cutler-Magner Co.) and C. A. Gilbert, all of Duluth. Edward Locke and Frank R. Bunker of Minneapolis rounded out the board.[66] Incorporation took place on November 22

---

66  *Duluth and Western Elevator Company: Articles of Incorporation.* Index to Incorporations, 1858–1906. Minnesota Historical Society Archives, 112.H.11.6F

with a capital stock of $200,000 with a right to increase to $1,000,000. "The number of shares shall be 4,000 of $50 each, all stock to be paid on call of assessment by the directors of the corporation, the highest amount of indebtedness at one time not to exceed $50,000," reported the *Minneapolis Journal*. Out of the lot, Craig Cofield assumed the role of general manager.

The plant consisted of two structures. The smaller of the two, Elevator D, a 50,000-bushel grain dryer, was built first. The main building, Elevator E, was situated about 250 feet west of the dryer building. Elevator E had a capacity of a half-million bushels. The first trainload of wheat was unloaded at the elevator in September 1884.[67] The elevator was initially misidentified as Elevator F in *The Northwestern Miller*.[68]

Elevator E was also commonly known as Elevator Q. In most newspaper grain receipt references, the elevator was listed as Q, although the Sanborn Map Company fire insurance maps used by the city list the structures as Elevator D and E, respectively.[69] Confusion over the name of the elevator was met with some comic derision within the industry at large. "Trouble has been experienced in deciding on a title for the large elevator at Duluth, recently leased by Geo. H. Christian. Sometimes it is dubbed *Northwestern*, then *St. Paul & Duluth*, and often Elevator Q, but the best hit of all was made by an old sailor who looked it all over and decided it should be called the "Dolly Varden.""[70] The reference to a character from a Charles Dickens novel, later used for fashionable women's clothing, is unclear but possibly destroys the myth that sailors of the era were illiterate.

---

67 "Duluth's Great Fire," *Lake Superior News*, December 4, 1886.

68 *The Northwestern Miller* 17, no. 20.0 (May 16, 1884).

69 *St. Paul and Duluth Elevators: Insurance Maps of Duluth, Minnesota* (New York: Sanborn Map Co., May 1885).

70 "The Elevators: Facts About Old and New Ones Throughout the Country," *Northwestern Miller* 20, no. 1 (July 3, 1885): 14.

**Elevator *E* and grain dryer Elevator *D* of Duluth and Western Elevator Co., with conveyor gallery built in August 1884. Elevator *A* is on the right with new addition.** Photo: University of Minnesota Duluth, Kathryn A. Martin Library, Northeast Minnesota Historical Collections, on loan from the St. Louis County Historical Society.

The Duluth and Western elevators were located behind the Union Improvement's Elevator *A*. Several sections of track divided the two work sites. To facilitate the loading of lake vessels, the Duluth and Western constructed an enclosed overhead conveyor gallery extending out from the elevator over the tracks to the dock.

A unique quality of Elevator *Q* was its popularity with the citizens of Duluth. The window-paned cupola that housed the receiving legs along the north face of the elevator was an eye-pleasing addition. Elevator *A*'s box-shaped utilitarianism was easily outdone by the rather stylish newcomer.

During the construction of Elevator *Q*, some doubt was raised about the structural integrity of the elevator's foundation. A report issued by the Bradstreet Commercial Agency's St. Paul office stated: "Their building has been condemned as unsafe, and the Chamber of Commerce has decided to do business with their wheat checks. The facts of the case seem to be that Lock (sic) has misled the other investors and put up a building which is unsafe for business and stands idle. The investors seem to regard themselves as victimized (thereby meaning and intending to charge the plaintiff with the crime of having deceived, defrauded and victimized his associates in said company). The company cannot be considered as having a basis of any credit."[71]

Edwin Locke, one of the Duluth and Western incorporators as well as president of the Northwestern Grain Dealers' Association, filed a twenty-five thousand-dollar libel suit on August 25 in the Hennepin County district court in opposition to Bradstreet's "defamatory" statements. By September, the suit had reached the United States Circuit Court. Outside of the courtroom, Locke went on the offensive with a letter to the editor of the Minneapolis *Star Tribune* published in the newspaper on September 9.

> **No business man can allow such an attack to pass unnoticed, and in refutation thereof, I would ask that you publish the following letters, viz.:**
>
> **Duluth and Western Elevator Company Elevators D and E, Duluth, Minn. Aug. 15, 1884.**
>
> **We the undersigned associates of Mr. Edwin Locke of Minneapolis, in the Duluth and Western Elevator Company, pronounce as false and malicious the information now being circulated by the commercial agencies to the effect that Mr. Locke has swindled or victimized his associates in that enterprise. The report has been started by parties hostile to the interests of the elevator company, and the for the purpose both of injuring the credit of the company and also the country houses with which Mr. Locke is concerned. There is no foundation of truth whatever in the report.**

---

71 "A $24,000 Libel Suit," *Star Tribune*, August 26, 1884.

D. G. Cutler,
W. W. Davis,
C. Cofield.

Minneapolis, Minn., Aug. 20, 1884. – I pronounce as wholly false and untrue the report issued by the Bradstreet Commercial Agency on or about August 13, 1884, in reference to the Duluth and Western Elevator Company to the effect that its elevator has been condemned as unsafe, its wheat checks declined, and the other investors misled and victimized by Mr. Locke. I am fully conversant with all the facts in the case, and am heavily interested in the company. I am satisfied that our investment has been honestly and wisely managed under the direction of Mr. Locke, and will prove highly profitable. Frank R. Bunker.[72]

Company officials hired contractors to place an extra set of timbers throughout the lower story of the elevator to strengthen the structure. They pointed out the security of the foundation and even invited reporters to the site to survey the construction. In fact, most of the building rested on solid bedrock. To answer critics, the balance of the foundation was reinforced with heavy timbers.[73] The application by the Duluth and Western Elevator Company to be made regular with the Board of Trade was withdrawn until the construction was completed.

While Locke prepared for his day in court, the first grain was unloaded at Elevator *E* on October 6 with company officials stating they expected to make their first shipment later that week. It is uncertain whether any grain was loaded onto a vessel at Duluth. By the end of the month, a second attempt to be made regular with the Duluth Board of Trade was again rejected. A "Special Dispatch to the *Tribune*" from Duluth detailed the cause and effect of the action.

---

72   "A Complaint and Correction," *Star Tribune*, September 6, 1884.
73   "The Duluth and Western Elevator," *Duluth Weekly Tribune*, September 26, 1884.

The wheat men in this city are considerably worked up over the action of the Board of Trade this morning refusing to make the new elevator of the Duluth and Western Company regular, so that receipts for grain stored therein might be used at the banks as collateral. When the house was first completed application was made by the committee to have it endorsed by the Board of Trade. A committee of that body was appointed to inspect the structure. The company learned that a report after receiving was made that it would be disfavorable and withdrew the application. The house was then strengthened and after receiving considerable wheat and making two shipments the company again made application to be recognized by the Board of Trade. A committee was again appointed and inspected the house. The committee also employed an attorney to look into the financial condition of the company. This morning the committee reported that as far as could be ascertained, the house was perfectly safe and in good condition for the storage of grain. The report was accompanied by a certificate from several prominent architects and also from the Chief Engineer of the Manitoba Railroad to the effect that the structure was perfectly safe. Twenty members of the board were present this morning when the matter came to a vote, and the report was rejected by a vote of 10 to 10. The elevator company feel rather discouraged, as they have about one hundred thousand dollars invested, and for the present the house will undoubtedly be idle. The company thinks in substance that the action of the board in this matter conclusively clinches that fact that no individual unwilling to enter into the pool with the two elevator companies now doing business here need attempt to come in and engage in that sort of an enterprise, and that is will have a tendency to give the wheat trade here a severe setback.

On January 16, 1885, the jury ruled in favor of the defendant. Locke failed in his attempt to disprove the financial condition of the elevator company. A week later, the operation was sold to Minneapolis miller George H. Christian for approximately eighty-five thousand dollars.[74]

The ownership under George Christian provided stability to the company, leading to an expansion of the Duluth and Western operations. Thanksgiving 1886 saw *E* (still locally referred to as Elevator *Q*) increase the elevator's capacity by another half-million bushels within two weeks of completing an annex on its west side. In only their second year of operation, the owners had much to be thankful for.

Their jubilation soon ebbed, however, following the destruction of the elevator in a spectacular fire on the night of November 27. Along with the Duluth and Western elevator, Duluth's pioneering Elevator *A* was also destroyed.[75] The fire claimed three lives. Of the three, one was reported to have jumped nearly eighty feet from the upper story of Elevator *A* to escape the flames. The body of one of the workers was never recovered.

According to eyewitness accounts, the fire began on the east side of Elevator *E* and quickly spread. Reporters for *The Weekly Northwestern Miller* wrote,

> **From the place of starting the flames spread all over the top of Elevator *Q*, lighting up the whole eastern part of the city. They gradually ate downward along the bins and sides, and soon extended to its annex on the west, which was nearing completion. While the fire progressed on these two buildings, every effort was made to save elevator *A*, across the tracks from *Q*."**

---

74  Note: After the sale, Locke faced a series of suits filed against him and his organization, The Northwestern Grain Dealers' Association, which occupied the courts for several years.

75  "Duluth's Great Fire," *Lake Superior News*, December 4, 1886; and "Duluth's First Great Fire," *Duluth News Tribune/Cosmopolitan*, November 18, 1951.

> Half a dozen streams were turned on the fire while the elevator company worked on the inside of the building. There were two dozen men scattered over the building working with hose and buckets, and they staid [sic] at their post, some in top stories, 80 ft above ground, until after the fire had caught in many places and the owners had ordered them out. As the flames grew hotter the men were compelled to fall back and leave the elevator to its fate. The fire first caught at the windows, which were broken by the heat, the iron sides preventing the flames from getting a footing at any other place. The fire was kept out of $A$ for nearly an hour, the heavy iron sheathing on it and $Q$ keeping the former from igniting sooner. Elevator $A$ could have been saved but for the new annex to $Q$, which was not yet sheathed and which made a terrific heat.[76]

Speculation leaned toward the theory that workers installing a conveyor belt earlier in the day may have left a lamp burning, although no lamp was ever found. An hour after the fire in Q was reported, the nearby Elevator A was ablaze. Workers at A already had their pumps running at maximum capacity, pouring water over the roof and down the sides of the elevator. The heat from the fire in the Duluth and Western Elevator was so great that the water evaporated into steam long before reaching the bottom of the building.

The monetary value of Elevator Q was placed at eighty thousand dollars, with an additional fifty thousand invested in the new annex, which was two weeks from completion and empty. At the time of the fire, Elevator Q had 401,580 bushels of wheat in storage, nearly all of it destroyed or damaged. Elevator Q and its annex were valued at one hundred thirty thousand dollars but only insured for one hundred thousand. Its grain contents were insured for $212,000 before the fire.

---

76 "Big Elevator Fire at Duluth," *Northwestern Miller* 22, no. 24 (December 3, 1886): 576.

With its two-year-old addition, Elevator *A* was valued at one hundred twenty-five thousand dollars. Inside the elevator bins were 340,445 bushels of wheat, 122,000 bushels of corn, 14,000 bushels of flax seed, 6,000 bushels of oats and 2,000 bushels of barley. Insurance on the elevator prior to the fire was reported as $87,750, and the contents were insured for $301,950.

Within several hours, the fire had destroyed the first and last elevators built along the outer harbor of Duluth. Nearly one dozen neighboring structures were destroyed as well. Despite the loss of the elevators, Duluth surpassed Chicago in 1886 as the leading shipper of grain on the Great Lakes. A Duluth newspaper declared, "We can now justly claim Duluth as the greatest wheat receiving and shipping center in the country…"[77]

---

77 "Duluth and Other Points," *Duluth Tribune*, January 3, 1886.

# 4
# The Rise of Superior as a Grain Port

By the late 1880s, the race by the railroads for supremacy at the head of the lakes began taking shape on the Wisconsin side of the harbor, and the coming decade of the 1890s would be dominated by elevator construction in Superior.

The Manitoba line of James J. Hill's St. Paul, Minneapolis & Manitoba Railway was in fierce competition with the Northern Pacific. They sought a similar Lake Superior outlet for their grain traffic. Aside from the Northern Pacific, the main competition for Hill's railroad was the grain interests in Milwaukee and Chicago. The Lake Michigan interests lobbied hard against diverting any grain moved east of the Mississippi toward Superior because the elevators at Duluth had already cut deeply into their volume and profits.[78]

The Manitoba line secured the property and desired location to begin its operation at West Superior. The Great Northern road from Hinckley to Duluth was completed and operational early in 1887.[79] At West Superior, the railroad wasted little time moving in an army of workers. [See the Appendix for more details.]

Those who received stock in the Great Northern Elevator Company were some of the industry's powerful leaders—Frank H.

---

78  Martin Albro, *James J. Hill and the Opening of the Northwest* (St. Paul: Minnesota Historical Society Press, 1976), 361.

79  "Duluth-Superior Harbor Handles Grain Quickly," *Duluth News Tribune*, July 19, 1925.

Peavey, George Van Dusen, William H. Dunwoody, John Crosby, Charles Martin, Charles A. Pillsbury, H. P. Upshaw and David C. Shepard. In a summation of the funds expended, the construction of the Elevator *A* in Superior was again noted,

> The funds for constructing the grain elevator at Superior by the Lake Superior & Southwestern Railway Company and leased to the Great Northern Elevator Company under agreement of November 17, 1886, were advanced by the LS&SW Ry Co., the later company is acquiring the 1748 shares above referred to carried them as an investment in its accounts to June 30, 1887...

Among many things, R. C. Burdick, a pioneer of Stearns County, Minnesota, was a grain inspector in Minnesota for the Northern Pacific prior to his assignment as president. Shortly after the incorporation of the elevator company, Burdick resigned his position as chief grain inspector for the state to accept the job as manager of the Great Northern Elevator *A* in Superior.[80] Vice-president William Cullen Farrington was a St. Paul native who began as a clerk with the railroad, rose to prominence and eventually became president of the Northern Steamship Company among other roles with the Great Northern.

In 1886, Hill's vision of a grain trafficking empire began with the formation of the Great Northern Elevator Company of Minnesota and the erection of Elevator *A*. Hill wrote,

> I have felt quite clear for some time that the large and rapidly growing lake business of Duluth could not be done with any degree of expedition or for reasonable cost without largely increased terminal facilities and I have so far as the Manitoba Co. is concerned taken time by the forelock and our new elevator at West

---

80 "The Grain Inspector Resigns," *St. Paul Daily Globe*, November 26, 1886.

> Superior can handle as many cars daily as all the elevators combined on the Duluth side...[81]

Residents of Superior were at first skeptical of the elevator. Many believed the construction would most likely never occur. By the beginning of March, however, Fagin & Co. of Duluth commenced excavation work in preparation for the pile driving. The skeptics soon vanished as the construction rapidly advanced.

"The foundation of this mammoth structure well deserves notice and description," wrote *The Superior Times*.[82]

> In its construction, piles were driven as far as they would go, a few feet apart, placing thereon heavy planking, upon which mammoth stone piers were erected, covering the entire area of the foundation, which was filled in with dirt, the top of the foundation being on a level with the bank and a little above the water's edge. Engineer Thomas, who has the work in charge for the Manitoba Company, and whose opinion should be authority on this matter, informs us that no better foundation could have been put in anywhere else.

**The Great Northern Railway's Elevator *A* was the first elevator built in Superior.** Photo: Lake Superior Maritime Collections, UW-Superior.

---

81   Ibid, 285 and 360.
82   "The Great Northern Elevator," *Superior Times*, November 27, 1886.

The Grain Terminal Elevators of Duluth-Superior

The contractor hired for what would be called Great Northern Elevator *A* was John A. McLennan of Chicago, "who bears a worldwide reputation in this line, as being at the head."[83] The Great Northern's use of McLennan broke the exclusive hold on elevator construction in Duluth held by the Chicago firm of J. T. Moulton and Son. A Canadian by birth, McLennan settled in Chicago in 1863 at the age of fifteen, where he became a very successful builder and architect. He constructed his first grain elevator in 1879. Throughout his career, McLennan built elevators in Chicago, Detroit, Toledo, Cincinnati, Joliet, New York City, Council Bluffs and Burlington in Iowa, and the Great Northern in West Superior.

> He is a painstaking architect, employing competent assistants and skilled labor and can be relied upon to combine elegance and beauty with economy of space. He will cheerfully furnish estimates to all who intend building grain elevators and give entire satisfaction. As a talented member of the profession his ambition is to excel, and his record is one of permanent enterprise and prosperity.[84]

McLennan believed he had developed a more efficient method for moving grain within the elevator, which the *Times* described as the elevator neared its completion in late 1886.[85]

> The machinery throughout the entire length of the building is of the latest pattern, some parts of which are late inventions of the contractor, and can be found in no other elevator in the world. One of the principal features of the entire work is its simplicity in all departments, and the ease with which grain can be handled,

---

83  Ibid.
84  *Half-century's Progress of the City of Chicago*, The Leading Manufacturers and Merchants (Chicago: International Publishing Co., 1887), 99.
85  "The Great Northern Elevator," *Superior Times*, November 27, 1886.

> with less human aid than is usually required in other structures of this kind.

> A row of huge tanks are placed beneath the first floor in the basement, ten in all, for receiving the grain from the cars, on each side of which tracks are laid the entire length of the building, receiving grain from both sides enabling them to unload twenty cars at one time. Each of these tanks is provided with a double set of elevators one for unloading and the other for transferring and shipping purposes. There are ten shipping bins on the side next to the slip, into which grain is elevated when prepared to ship. On receiving grain from the cars, it is elevated directly to the scale floor, which is very near the top, where there are ten of Fairbanks' scales capable of weighing 6,000 bushels, and after being weighed is transferred by means of spouts to the several bins. The elevator belts are of 4 ply rubber and represent over one mile in length.

After the construction of the elevator for the Great Northern, McLennan submitted a patent request in September 1886 for his own elevator design. It was granted in October 1887.[86]

> My invention relates to certain improvements in the construction and general arrangement of store-houses or elevators for storing, cleaning, or transferring grain and other agricultural products.

> Heretofore it has been the practice in constructing large elevator-buildings to place all the receiving-elevators in line, leaving a distance between each elevator nearly the

---

86   Grain Elevator: John A. McLennan, of Chicago, Illinois: U. S. Patent Office, Letters Patent No. 371,343.

> length of a railway-car, and to locate the shipping or transferring elevators in one or more lines parallel to the line of receiving-elevators, but in different tiers of bents of the building. This arrangement necessitates separate lines of shafting on machinery-floor for running the different sets of elevators, causes complications in spouting, and necessitates the employment of different gangs of men if shipping and transferring are done at the same time, and causes much delay and loss of time in the general management of the elevators.
>
> **The object of my invention is to overcome these difficulties, to reduce the cost of erecting and equipping such establishments, and to so arrange the elevators that the work of the house may be systematized and facilitated, thus reducing the running expenses.**

When completed at a cost estimated to be $1.5 million, Elevator *A* had a bin capacity of 1,750,000 bushels, making it the largest elevator in the Twin Ports. The Eastern Minnesota Railway supplied rail service. The outside dimensions were 395 x 50 with a height of 150 feet. The smokestack for the steam power plant registered five feet higher than the workhouse at 155 feet high.[87] The internal engines and boilers were manufactured by the Southwark Foundry & Machine Company of Philadelphia, the details of which the company provided to *The Superior Times*.[88]

> They have placed in the building one Porter & Allen high speed, automatic engine, with a cylinder 26 inches in diameter and a 42-inch stroke, making 120 revolutions per minute, capable of 750-horse power, about three times the power needed to drive this one

---

87 *Great Northern Elevators: The Eye of the Northwest* (Superior: City of Superior, 1890), 172.

88 "The Great Northern Elevator," *Superior Times*, November 27, 1886.

elevator. There are four steel boilers, 16 feet long and six feet in diameter, of the horizontal tubular pattern, the best manufactured. It is possible to get more power out of these engines, with less fuel, than any others manufactured. The main shaft is 18 inches in diameter and 24 feet long. The engine room is supplied with a feed pump for the boilers and fire pump, also an engine for the driving a dynamo of 150 32-candle power incandescent electric lights, placed in the building by the United States Electric Light Co., of Chicago. The engine room is an addition to the main building and built of white brick, with a smoke-stack 155 feet high, five feet higher than the elevator, out of the same quality of brick used for the engine room.

The first railcar of wheat arrived at the elevator on December 9, 1886, marking the entrance of Superior, the self-proclaimed "City of Destiny," into the grain handling business. Two days later, by a vote of ten to one, the Duluth Board of Trade made regular the new Great Northern elevator in West Superior, where five hundred cars of wheat were now on the tracks as elevator officials awaited the decision. Difficulties in getting the new machinery to work properly caused some initial delays in filling the elevator, but the problems were resolved. The propeller vessel *Cuba* is the first known vessel to load at the elevator, carrying fifty-four thousand bushels of wheat bound for Buffalo on May 20, 1887.

In reference to the term 'made regular,' the regulation of all Twin Ports elevators was done through the Duluth Board of Trade. Company offices were required to be established at Duluth. The terms governing the inspection and weighing of grain at Wisconsin elevators by inspectors from Minnesota became a thorn in the side to Wisconsin legislators and Superior citizens. In the early days of the Twin Ports grain trade the presence of a strong Board of Trade in Superior was virtually non-existent and all elevators operated through the Duluth Board of Trade.

## The Grain Terminal Elevators of Duluth-Superior

\* \* \*

Within one year of the initial Great Northern Elevator Company development at West Superior, a new system of elevators was completed to the east of the Great Northern property. Located on land owned by the Chicago, Minneapolis, St. Paul and Omaha Railroad, the new elevator was built by A. J. Sawyer, noted for his Duluth grain commission business.

> The West Duluth Elevator Co. has contracted with J. T. Moulton & Sons for the building of an 800,000-bus elevator and a 2,000,000 bus consort on the grounds of the Omaha railroad at West Superior, Wis., both to be completed before Oct. 1, and also to build before that date, if notified to do so, a 2,000,000 receiving elevator, making a total capacity of 4,800,000 bush. The location of the elevators is about 300 ft east of the West Superior side of the Northern Pacific bridge. The elevators will be 227 x 84 ft, with bins 60 ft deep, while the boiler house will add 90 ft to the length. The annex will be 540x88 ft, with bins 55 ft high at the eaves and 67 ft at the center. The machinery will be driven by an engine of 700 hp, and the two houses will cost $350,000. Moulton & Sons are the contractors on the new Lake Superior and Union Improvement elevators, now building, which have a capacity of 3,000,000 bus.[89]

---

89 "The Elevators," *The Weekly Northwestern Miller* 23, no. 7 (February 18, 1887): 149.

**Timber framing at roof of cupola along west wall of Globe Elevator House 1.** Photo: author.

Andrew Sawyer was born in Gasport, New York, in rural Niagara County. Like many of the city's early pioneers, he arrived in Duluth in 1869.[90] Sawyer initially operated a grocery business, a small log building a block or so up from Superior Street, called A. J. Sawyer & Co. He was soon heavily involved as a grain commission agent in Duluth.

On August 13, 1870, the *Duluth Minnesotian* reported,

> **A. J. Sawyer received the first carload of grain (oats) from St. Paul to Duluth over the L.S.& M.R.R. It was forwarded by Grain-Buyer Eames.**

Then, on October 31, 1872, the *Minneapolis Star Tribune* reported,

> **A. J. Sawyer received the first cargo of wheat over the L.S.& M. railroad two years ago, and a day or two since, Messrs. Sawyer & Davis received the first carload of**

---

90  *Superior Times*, March 5, 1892.

> wheat ever shipped over the main line of the Northern Pacific to Duluth. This wheat came from Messrs. Kemper & Draham of Perham, a little village seventy miles west of Brainerd; and we have been astonished to learn that there are about ten thousand bushels of wheat to be shipped from that single station to Duluth... If the *first year's crop*, at one single little station—where, probably not *one* acre in *twenty thousand* is under cultivation produces a surplus of ten thousand bushels—what limit shall we place to the surplus wheat crop of that region, a few years hence, when every acre of the broad and fertile valley of the Red River shall be under a high state of cultivation?

Sawyer expanded his interests to include the construction of numerous elevators along the Northern Pacific line in North Dakota. One of his earliest attempts was in Eldridge, where he built a forty-thousand-bushel facility.[91] The next year, he commenced construction of a larger elevator in Valley City, which added to his growing grain commission business.

Sawyer was a founder and principal stockholder of the North Dakota Elevator Company based in Jamestown, North Dakota. "This is one of the most extensive and wealthy companies in the northwest, which is as prolific of great enterprises as it is of wheat production," lauded the *Jamestown Weekly Alert* on August 27, 1885.

> This company operates a system of elevators extending from Blum station, east of Jamestown, west to Bismarck and all along the line of the Jamestown and Northern from Jamestown to Minnewaukan, including the Moose River branch so far as completed.

Within a year of constructing the new elevators in Superior, Sawyer consolidated the management of his North Dakota

---

91  *Jamestown Weekly Alert*, August 1, 1884.

"Sawyer" elevators with those of the North Dakota Elevator Company. They were expecting to add a dozen more country line elevators in the coming year of 1886 along the rural portions of the Manitoba line.

Sawyer was building a large grain enterprise along the western rail lines. The significance of the construction of the elevators meant that more North Dakota wheat would now be going through the port of Duluth rather than to Minneapolis, according to a report in the Duluth newspapers.

> The amount of wheat estimated to come out by this new line is put at a million and a half bushels, nearly all of which is to come to Duluth. This Duluth & Manitoba is to open a country hitherto without adequate railroad facilities, and the wheat formerly raised along that section has gone in great part to Minneapolis.[92]

The new Sawyer elevators were a unique departure from the norm in elevator construction at the head of the lakes. This would be the first time a real "system" was constructed at one time. Reports prior to the construction noted the ownership group as the P. B. Weare-Sawyer-Dunwoody-Peavey-Crosby syndicate. "They will be distinctively Duluth elevators, but will be on the other side of the river to avoid bridge charges."[93] Up to this point, the companies operating in Duluth, the Union Improvement, and the Lake Superior, had each built their elevators individually. Annexes were added at later dates to expand their operations.

Out of the new ownership group, Portus B. Weare is an interesting story. In brief, he was born in a log cabin in rural Otsego, Michigan, in 1842. As a young man, he became a fur trader in Montana. As the

---

92 "A New Elevator System," *Jamestown Weekly Alert*, September 2, 1886.

93 "Duluth Doings," *The Weekly Northwestern Miller*, January 21, 1887. Note: The local Duluth tug companies added a $10 surcharge for assisting vessels across the harbor to West Superior, which led to the elevator maintaining its own tug at the dock during the early years of operation.

riches of the fur trade waned, Weare moved to Chicago in the mid-1880s, where he became involved in the grain trade.[94] Weare served as a member of the board of directors of the elevator company. The others in the ownership group were all men linked to the milling and grain industry in Minneapolis.

The Sawyer site contained three major structures—a workhouse and two annexes. All three structures were laid out in a linear manner, running north to south. The capacity of workhouse House No. *1* was one million bushels, while Houses *2* and *3* were storage annexes of two million bushels each.[95] All the structures were wood frame construction with iron-clad exteriors. The contractor for the Sawyer System was J. T. Moulton and Son, the firm responsible for the construction of all the elevators in Duluth at the time.

The spout, or circle floor, where grain is distributed. Globe Elevator House **1**. Photo: author.

---

94 "Portus B. Weare," Wikipedia, https://en.wikipedia.org/wiki/Portus_B._Weare.

95 "The New Elevator Systems," *Inter Ocean*, Superior Regional Center, WPA Project #10117, October 15, 1887, 14–15.

A sawmill was set up at the site. The Sawyer system, as the local paper, the *Superior Leader*, called the new elevator complex, looked to the forests southwest of Superior for its lumber supply. Trees were felled along the Pokegema River and hauled by horse teams to the rail lines, where they were loaded onto flatbed cars to be relocated to the elevator site. The materials for the elevators were then cut to specification on an as-needed basis.[96] To complete the three buildings, over twelve million feet of lumber were anticipated, as well as ten thousand kegs of nails to hold it all together.

Like most structures of its size, Elevator *1* and annexes *2* and *3* presented an amazing amalgam of dimensions and statistics—a cost of $700,000, a total capacity of five million bushels, fifteen-thousand-bushel scales, over thirteen feet of conveyor belts, a 520-horsepower engine operated at sixty-five revolutions per minute, with 16,000- and 26,000-pound flywheels driving the machinery. A sixty-five-foot chimney capped off the boiler at the north side of the No. *1* house.[97]

As with all major projects, the construction of an elevator generated many jobs in the young community. The size and scope of the Sawyer system were certainly no exception. Upwards of three thousand men were employed throughout construction at the elevator site. The labor force at the lakehead was made up largely of immigrants. They were a rugged group, often separated by language and culture yet brought together by a passion to succeed in this new land. Many remained in the Duluth-Superior area, adding to the growing diversity stirred into the Twin Ports cultural melting pot.

In February 1887, the Sawyer System was officially incorporated under the name of The Duluth Elevator Company. Among the officers of the company along with Sawyer were Frank H. Peavey, corporate treasurer; John Crosby; William H. Dunwoody, vice president; and Lester R. Brooks (all of Minneapolis,) plus George G.

---

96   Jay Van Horn, interview with author, Superior, WI, February 12, 1994.
97   *Inter Ocean*, Superior Regional Center, WPA Project #10117.

Barnum.[98] Peavey eventually played a much bigger role in the grain business at the head of the lakes.

Citizens of Superior took offense at seeing the word "Duluth" so brazenly fashioned upon the elevator system's exterior walls. Rather than accord them their due respect, it was preferable for the Superior newspapers to refer to the elevators as the Sawyer System. To better handle the operations of his grain business, Sawyer moved to Minneapolis in the summer of 1887 and relocated the offices of the North Dakota Elevator Company to Duluth. As for the name of the elevator company, that would be resolved later.

---

98 "Sawyer Elevator System," *Superior Leader*, March 12, 1893; and *The Weekly Northwestern Miller* 23, no. 7 (February 18, 1887): 149.

# 5
# Expansion of the Union Improvement and Lake Superior Elevator Companies

"Elevator *H*, the new 1,500,000 bushel house which the Union Improvement & Elevator Co. is about to build will be located out in the bay in front of *E*," reported *The Weekly Northwestern Miller* at the beginning of December 1886.

> Work on the foundation cribs was finished Tuesday, and they will be filled at once. As soon as the ice forms in sufficient thickness, piles will be driven, and by next fall the house will be complete. It will ship from both sides and will cost about $350,000. The burned elevators will be rebuilt at once, though perhaps in another location.[99]

The Union Improvement and Elevator Company added Elevator *H* to their holdings in 1887. Elevator *H* became the last elevator built for the Union Improvement and Elevator Company.

> The finishing work is being put on Elevator *H*, at Duluth, owned by the Union Improvement & Elevator Co. Its size is 333½ x 84 feet, 228 bins, 18 Fairbanks scales and 9 cleaners. The engine is the largest in Duluth,

---

99   *The Weekly Northwestern Miller* 22, no. 23 (December 3, 1886): 571.

> having a capacity of 900 horse power. J. T. Moulton & Sons are the builders. The capacity is 1,500,000 bus. And the cost, with dock, about $300,000.[100]

The growth continued with the completion of a storehouse located at the head of the slip.[101] The previous year, the Lake Superior Elevator Company purchased four hundred feet of waterfront property between Elevator *E* and the adjacent Ohio Central Barge and Coal Dock Co's coal dock, at a cost of forty thousand dollars for the expansion. Elevator *2*, alternately Store House No. *2*, officially opened its doors on April 27 of that year, owned and operated by the Lake Superior Elevator Company.[102]

The location of the storehouse was unique in respect to the company's other structures. By the time the Lake Superior Elevator Company built Store House *1* in 1883, the company had literally run out of room along the slip where its other buildings were located. As a result, *1* was built at the head of the slip between the existing Lake Superior and Union Improvement elevators. The elevator is listed as a storehouse on the Sanborn Map Company's fire insurance drawing. The rail car unloading capability of the 1.75-million-bushel storehouse was rated at one hundred twenty thousand bushels every twenty-four hours.

The Union Improvement and Elevator Company also built two wheat warehouses. Warehouse No. *2* was located next to the Northern Pacific tracks at Third Street off the water. The last built was Warehouse No. *3*, built in late 1886 and considered a winter storage building at 80 x 500 feet with a capacity of seven hundred

---

100   *The Weekly Northwestern Miller* 24, no. 22 (November 25, 1887): 574.

101   Note: Sanborn Fire Insurance map of 1888, p. 33, shows two warehouses labeled Warehouse No. 2 (200') and Warehouse No. 3 (272' x 112') along 3rd Street, on the west side of the C. St. P. M & O tracks. These two structures were connected to Elevator *F* via a bridge and trestle tramway. Both of these structures are gone from the 1908 Sanborn edition of Duluth.

102   Duluth Board of Trade, *Annual Report*, December 31, 1887. Note: The Lake Superior Elevator Company Warehouse *1* would later be designated as Storehouse No. *1* by the Consolidated Elevator Company in the 1890s.

thousand bushels. The two previously built storage sheds had been removed earlier in the year after the spring grain rush was over. Warehouse No. 3 would meet with a similar fate once its temporary purpose was concluded.[103]

The classification of grain storage structures as annexes/storehouses/warehouses was important for the elevator companies because these structures received a lower insurance rate. The state Railroad and Warehouse Commission, meeting in Duluth with city officials, reviewed the policy, concluding,

> These buildings are constructed for insurance reasons, as by putting a portion of the bins at a distance from the others, better rates are secured. Practically they are separate bins of one elevator, and the commission decided to treat elevator and annex as one.[104]

In all instances, the Duluth elevators were built with timber, following a method known as crib construction. In his book *The Design of Walls, Bins and Grain Elevators*, Milo Ketchum described the process.

> In this construction, pieces of 2" x 4", 2" x 6" or 2" x 8" are laid flatwise, so as to break joints and bind the structure together, and are spiked firmly. This makes a strong form of construction, and one very cheap with the former low price of lumber.

The outside walls of the elevators generally consisted of an exterior sheeting of galvanized corrugated iron.

\* \* \*

The Duluth Board of Trade's 1887 annual report listed the increased capacity of the Twin Port's elevators at 8,050,000 bushels following

---

103 "New What Warehouse, Rice's Point," *Duluth Daily Tribune*, December 21, 1884.

104 *The Weekly Northwestern Miller* 22, no. 27 (December 31, 1886): 670.

the completion of the new Duluth-Superior complexes. Total wheat receipts for the year were only 17,136,275 bushels, against 22,424,950 for 1886. Shipments aggregated 19,761,586 bushels of wheat and a quarter-million bushels of corn and coarse grains. Of the wheat shipped, 16,080,000 was No. 1 hard wheat, all going by vessel except for sixty thousand bushels.[105]

The combined capacity of the elevators in Duluth-Superior eventually grew to a tremendous 19,450,000 bushels. Newspaper and trade advertisements pictured the Duluth elevators in a combined panorama across the harbor skyline. This striking image would come to depict the famous "Elevator Row" of Duluth.

**Postcard view of Rice's Point and Duluth's Elevator Row, circa 1910.** Postcard: author's collection.

The Board of Trade, for its part, counted the Superior elevators as part of the Duluth system. The fact that the Superior elevators operated under the laws of the State of Minnesota gave the Duluth Board of Trade jurisdiction over grain inspection at the Superior elevators.

The annual reports published by the board spelled out their claim regarding the Superior elevators.

---

105 Duluth Board of Trade, *Annual Report*, December 31, 1887, p. 36.

> Their warehouse receipts are made 'regular' on the Duluth Board of Trade, and they are under heavy bonds to this Board of Trade, guaranteeing that the offices shall be established and maintained in Duluth, and that their business shall be conducted strictly according to the laws of the state of Minnesota and the rules and usages of the Duluth Board of Trade. They are in all respects Duluth elevators except the ground they stand upon.[106]

The abilities of the Duluth elevators were extolled as "unsurpassed anywhere in the world." The report went on to detail the speed at which the grain was handled.

> The propeller *"Onoko"* carries 90,000 bushels of wheat—equivalent to 180 car loads. She has often arrived at the elevators after 7 o'clock in the morning, and been outside of the harbor with her cargo in place before noon of the same day. On one occasion this work was all done in 135 minutes, and the vast cargo of No. 1 Hard Wheat was weighed out of the elevator in eighty minutes. On one occasion two vessels, a steamer and consort, carry 130,000 bushels, arrived in the harbor at 4 p.m. By 6, two hours later, both were on their way to Buffalo, loaded. This rapid handling of freight is of great advantage to vessels trading at Duluth, saving them hours and days of valuable time.[107]

\* \* \*

In early 1888, an expansion began in West Superior with the construction of a second elevator on the property of the Great Northern Elevator Company. The new building, Elevator *X*, became

---

106 Duluth Board of Trade, *Annual Report*, December 31, 1887, p. 37.
107 Ibid.

a storage annex to the already existing Elevator *A*. The capacity of the new elevator was 1.5 million bushels.[108]

Elevator *X* was located south of *A*, off the waterfront. Movement of grain to the ship loading elevator was done via a conveyor system connecting the two structures. The combined capacity of the two Great Northern elevators was 3.5 million bushels.

**The southeast side of the original Elevator *X*, built in 1888 at West Superior.** Photo: Lake Superior Maritime Collections, UW-Superior.

The elevator building was 514 feet long and consisted of two rows of bins that ran through the center of the structure. On either side of these bins ran the conveyor galleries sandwiched between the inside bins and a set of bins along the outside walls. The architect for this elevator was John McLennan of Chicago.

The *Superior Times* noted in July 1888 that the project was progressing well but had some issues.

> The work of putting in the foundation has been necessarily slow for several reasons. The weather which has been bad for building enterprises, has played a prominent part, while the difficulty of procuring stone and the cramped facilities of handling material and the

---

108 "The New Elevator," *Superior Times*, July 28, 1888.

working of men which is occasioned by the numerous railroad tracks, has rendered progress difficult.[109]

At the south end of the elevator was a headhouse for the receiving leg for incoming grain from railcars. The headhouse held the cleaner, shipping bins and the machinery to operate the elevator.

> **These elevators are one of the signs of the times, and speak more eloquently than words of the importance of West Superior as a distributing point. The completion of the Eastern railway of Minnesota now puts us in direct intercourse with all of that great territory traversed by the Manitoba railway, and the rich products of its harvests must pass through the elevators at the head of the lakes on its way to Eastern and European points.[110]**

As construction on the new elevator at West Superior continued into the fall, the Manitoba Railway transferred the ownership of Elevator A, "the largest single elevator in the world," along with the new elevator, to the Eastern Minnesota Railroad Company.[111] Superintendent Albert Cross continued in his role with the new company. A circular issued by Henry Minot, president of the Eastern Railway[112], stated,

> **This company this day assumed the control and operation of Great Northern Elevator A at West Superior, Wis., with storage capacity for 1,800,000 bushels, and will soon have completed an additional house to be known as Great Northern Elevator X, with capacity for 1,500,000 bushels. Wheat for these elevators should be consigned, care of the Eastern Railway Company of Minnesota, either at Hinckley, Minn., or at West Superior, Wis.**

---

109 Ibid.
110 Ibid.
111 *Record and Union*, Rochester, Minnesota, October 12, 1888.
112 "The Eastern Minnesota," *Duluth Evening Herald*, October 4, 1888.

With the control of the Great Northern Elevator now in the hands of the Eastern Railway Company, petitions were put forth to dissolve the Great Northern Elevator Company of Minnesota. The petition was scheduled to be heard at a special hearing scheduled by Judge Orlando Simons of the State of Minnesota District Court, Second Judicial District, for December 15, 1888.[113]

* * *

On the Duluth side of the harbor, the talk of the day was the completion of the city's first flour mill. The Imperial Mill was largely due to the ambition of Roger S. Munger, who was previously involved in the Munger, Markell elevator. Munger believed that someday Duluth could possibly be the greatest flour manufacturing city in the country.

In starting the mill, the Imperial Mill enlisted the aid of Bradford Clifford "B. C." Church, Jr., a successful miller from Sterling, Illinois.[114] The construction of an elevator with a capacity of 350,000 bushels to service the mill is of interest to this history of the Twin Ports grain trade.

Timothy Allen "T. A." Olmsted, grain inspector at Duluth and one of the founders of the mill, was appointed vice president of the Imperial Mill. Olmsted is credited with performing the first grain inspection in Duluth and for being the "originator of the No. 1 hard grade, being the first to give it that name."[115] He was born in Vermont prior to moving to Iowa where, during the Civil War, he was the commander of Company E, 27th Regiment Iowa Volunteer Infantry. By the time he mustered out of the service in 1865, he had been promoted to the rank of captain.

* * *

The decade concluded with an overall elevator capacity of the Twin Ports reaching 20,800,000 bushels. The short-lived *Duluth*

---

113 *St. Paul Daily Globe*, November 20, 1888.
114 Duluth Board of Trade, *Annual Report*, December 31, 1888, pp. 36–37.
115 "T. A. Olmsted Dead." *Duluth News-Tribune*, December 9, 1899.

*Daily News* looked optimistically ahead in their annual year-ending compendium for 1889.

> The Great Northern company have just completed Elevator *X*, the only addition to the elevator capacity of Duluth for 1888. Yet, with this extraordinary capacity, the growing demands of the rapidly developing Northwest promise to make a large increase necessary at an early day. New farms, covering vast areas of the most productive wheat lands in the world, are being opened up each season, and the railroad systems building to Duluth bring to our doors the product of those sections heretofore remote. The elevator system of Duluth is destined to lead the world in its perfection of construction, facility in handling grain and vast storage capacity.[116]

---

116 "Duluth's Elevators," *Third Illustrated Annual Edition of the Duluth Daily News* (Duluth: Duluth News Co., 1889), 28.

# 6
# The 1890s: A Tumultuous Decade

The 1890s were a tumultuous decade for the Duluth-Superior grain industry. The decade saw the maturation and consolidation of two Duluth elevator companies—one rocked with scandal— the introduction of new players, the battle for control of grain inspection between Duluth and Superior, and a bitter dispute over trading on the "futures" markets between the Chicago Board of Trade and Minneapolis-Duluth-Superior grain interests, which ultimately led to the loss of one of the industry's leading grain merchants.

As the grain market expanded westward, the direct costs of shipping from Duluth began to produce greater profits than shipments via Milwaukee and Chicago. The increased geographical distances from the farm fields of Minnesota, especially the Dakotas, increased shipping costs via rail to Milwaukee and Chicago, decreasing the economic value of the Lake Michigan ports in the Upper Midwest grain trade. It was cheaper to go directly to Duluth-Superior, where elevator capacities were being pushed to their limits.

Wheat receipts that had tripled in the 1880s continued expanding at an astounding rate. The ten-year span from 1883 to 1894 saw a growth in receipts and shipments from just over nine million to twenty-three million bushels.[117] The start of the decade saw the reincorporation of the Union Improvement and Elevator

---

117 Duluth Board of Trade, Annual Reports 1884–1894.

Company as a Minnesota business in a move away from the Jay Cooke connections that led to its initial incorporation in the state of Pennsylvania. C. H. Graves, Melvin J. Forbes, George Rupley, Theodore B. Casey of the Duluth and Winnipeg Railroad, and Reese M. Newport, land agent with the Northern Pacific, were listed as incorporating members. The Lake Superior Elevator Company filed amended articles with increased operating capital intended for reinvestment in the elevators so they could continue having a strong share of the Duluth market.[118]

The Lake Superior Elevator Company used a portion of the new capital raised with the reincorporation to purchase controlling interests in the Northern Pacific Elevator Company and the Red River Valley Elevator Company, both of Minneapolis, to be used as "feeders" for its Duluth elevators.[119] The Northern Pacific company operated 120 line elevators along the Northern Pacific road, while the Red River Valley Elevator Company had a roster of approximately forty line elevators. The two purchases were part of a strategy to bolster the supply of grain entering the harbor for export.

At a meeting of its board of directors, C. H. Graves was elected president of the Lake Superior Elevator Company, with Roger Munger as vice president. Graves was also elected president of the Union Improvement Elevator Company and the Northern Pacific Elevator Company. The boards of all three companies included the familiar names of Melvin Forbes, George Rupley and A. D. Thomson.

Coming on the heels of a burst of elevator construction along Rice's Point in the 1880s, the announcement of a small elevator for the Imperial flour mill appeared almost as an afterthought in the local papers.[120] Duluth's Imperial Mill was grabbing headlines

---

[118] "Duluth," *The Weekly Northwestern Miller* 29, no. 21 (May 23, 1890): 538.

[119] *The Weekly Northwestern Miller* 30, no. 2 (July 11, 1890): 31.

[120] Note: It should be noted that the inclusion of the Twin Ports flour milling industry is out of the scope of this study of the port's terminal grain elevators, but is included here because this elevator eventually became designated as Capitol 5, a part of the Capitol Elevator Company system in the early 1900s.

for its high-quality flour and the splashy advertising of its products. To increase its output, the stockholders voted to authorize the construction of a wood-frame storage elevator on the west side of its main milling building. Following the call for bids in the spring, the contract was let to the St. Louis firm of James Stewart & Co. to construct the elevator by August. By mid-July, the foundation was well underway, and advertisements were placed in the local papers seeking one hundred carpenters and laborers. Delays in the project at mid-summer eventually pushed the completion back into late fall before the 350,000-bushel elevator received its first shipment of fifty thousand bushels of wheat on November 24.

As noted, Duluth's elevators were now built within the safe confines of the harbor and away from the fury of Lake Superior. That didn't account for much on March 9, 1892, when the biggest storm in memory rocked the Upper Midwest, causing widespread damage at the head of the lakes. "The storm was the worst Duluth has had since records have been kept," stated the local weather observer.[121] The Duluth elevators of the Lake Superior and Union Improvement companies took a beating during the storm.

> The conveyor gallery leading to elevator $B$ was blown down, and, in falling, it crashed through the dock. At $C$ the metal on the roof and side walls was torn away in great sections, The conveyor gallery between $D$ and $G$ was also torn away, and in falling it crashed through a corner of the dock. The only damage to $I$ was the stripping of the metal, almost entirely, from the roof. The gallery between $E$ and $F$ was blown down. The costly belting in these galleries was ruined and considerable of the machinery badly damaged. At $H$ the brick oil room was destroyed. A peculiar feature here is that from the way the walls fell it would seem that great pressure had been brought to bear against them from the inside, as they all bulged outward. The roof

---

121 *Duluth Evening Herald*, March 10, 1892.

and about two-thirds of the brick work of the boiler room, and the roof and about half the brick work of the engine room at *H* were destroyed. The breeching and flue of the boiler were damaged and two safety values and two steam pipes were broken, the steam thus being able to escape. The wind was from the northwest, and at 8:30 in the evening it reached a maximum velocity of 60 miles an hour. Manager George Rupley estimated the damage to be in the range of $15,000.[122]

Two months later, in mid-May, the collapse of the temporary conveyor trestle between Elevators *B* and *C* caused substantial damage to the wooden steamer *David W. Rust* when part of the trestle fell onto its after cabins, taking away the smokestack. The vessel owner sued the elevator for damages to the vessel. The temporary trestle was put up because the elevator was receiving a large amount of grain at the time and needed to be able to move it efficiently from the annex to the elevator. Plans were in the works to install a ground-level reversible belt as a permanent replacement.[123]

A district court judge concluded,

> The trestlework owned and built by this defendant company, and erected near the side of the dock where the *Rust* was moored, was structurally in an unsafe condition, and known to be so by the owners. The defendant company was legally in fault in permitting boats to moor at the place where the *Rust* was dropped down..."

However, the court concluded the vessel captain, even though the ship's engine was under repair, did not direct his crew to move the vessel further down the dock away from the conveyor by means of its mooring lines. The captain chose instead to walk over a mile

---

[122] *The Weekly Northwestern Miller* 33, no. 12 (March 18, 1892): 437.
[123] "Wind, Rain and Storm," *Duluth Weekly Tribune*, May 20, 1892.

distance to seek help from a local tug company, during which time the overhead conveyor collapsed onto the deck of the vessel.

> The wind was fresh, but not blowing a gale. The vessel was provided with ample appliances for moving her by hand…There was nothing in the existing conditions, shown by the evidence, to prevent successful action on the part of those in charge of the vessel. They were in fault, and contributed to the injury sustained.[124]

The damages were ordered to be split between the vessel owner and the elevator company. The year continued with more bad headlines the following month when a House committee was created to investigate an alleged breach of rules and regulations regarding the shipment of uninspected grain from the Lake Superior Elevator Company's Elevator *D*. Dubbed the "Wheat Steal" by the *Minneapolis Daily Times*, the scandal reverberated through the Minnesota grain industry. A special committee was appointed based on a resolution adopted by the House of Representatives in the State of Minnesota "to investigate charges that a certain Duluth elevator had stolen 60,000 bushels of wheat belonging to farmers and to ascertain whether or not such was not the general practice among bonded elevators or warehouses…" The committee was composed of farmers plus two Democrats representing the majority and two Republicans representing the minority. On April 17, 1891, each side presented their reports to the full house with the conclusion that further investigation was needed.

A condensed version of the majority report presented by R. J. Hall appeared in the *Minneapolis Daily Times*.[125]

> John Loftus, now night foreman of Elevator *H*, Lake Superior and Union Improvement elevator companies,

---

124 "Sullivan et al. v. Lake Superior Elevator Co.," *The Federal Reporter* 56, (St. Paul: West Publishing Co., 1893).

125 "That Wheat Steal," *Minneapolis Daily Times*, April 18, 1891.

in 1889 temporary foreman of Elevator $E$, said he worked at night in January, February and March, 1889, with a crew of eight or nine men. He received an order from Mr. Rupley, superintendent, to load the cars at night, and it was understood that the cars were to be loaded without the state inspector and state weigher being there. He received from Mr. Rupley double compensation for his night work, and it was understood that this matter was to be kept secret by himself and crew.

Leopold Arlo, watchman, knew cars were loaded from elevator $E$ in February, 1889, at night without state inspection or state weighing. The cargoes were loaded with wheat and marked "screenings." Chief Deputy Grain Inspector Fulton, of Duluth, testified to the non-inspection of this cargo.

Mr. Arlo, recalled, said in 1888 the elevator company shipped from elevator "H" 20 cars in the night on the Northern Pacific cars, without the knowledge of the state weighmaster, and that the cars were marked "screenings." Mr. Rupley, superintendent, and Mr. Marvin, assistant superintendent, were present at the time of shipment. Foreman Sharvey told the men that if anyone asked what they were doing down there at night to tell him "They were loading out screenings." Mr. Arlo further testified that in 1886 he knew of boats which carried from elevators $E$ and $F$ 200,000 bushels of wheat, and further, that were almost all Transit line boats.

The books of the Transit company and the state inspectors were compared for the years 1886 to 1891. From such comparison it appears that on Jan. 24 1896, the inspector's books showed inspection on propeller $B.\ W.$

> *Blanchard* 31,033 bushels of wheat, but the books of the Transit company give 38,023 bushels, the propeller carrying 7,000 bushels of wheat on which there is no record of inspection.
>
> The report continued detailing the shipment of grain and screenings from elevator to vessel with discrepancies, as well as grain "being taken into the elevators and then loaded out, reinspected and loaded out at a higher grade than it went in at..."
>
> In 1890 there were 392 cars loaded with wheat and shipped out of Duluth, of which the record fails to show any inspection, and the list shows that there were willed from Duluth 140 cars billed as screenings."
>
> In the years 1888, 1889 and 1890 the list shows there were 651 cars loaded and shipped from Duluth, which the record of inspection fails to show. These cars, estimated at 600 bushels per car, would reach the amount of 390,000 bushels.[126]

A Chicago publication called *The Western Rural and American Stockman*, in its Alliance and Grange column, carried a portion of the report and, in these words, lambasted George Rupley for refusing to testify to aspects of the report.

> Those elevator companies, it seems, constitute themselves courts of law as well as dens of robbers; pass

---

126 Note: The primary delivery method for grain sent to the elevators at the head of the lakes was by rail in boxcars. The grain was loaded into the cars at one of the line elevators and sealed shut across the openings with grain doors, heavy wooden planks fastened together and strong enough to hold back the weight of the grain. The grain had to be hand shoveled to remove it from the boxcar. In the 1880s it was a labor intensive and time-consuming process.

> upon the constitutionality of laws with the same facility they show in appropriating to their own use whole cargoes of wheat and make the most private of all private business the doings of the public elevators of Duluth. Surely the time has arrived when it must be determined which is supreme in the land; law and the people or capitalistic combines.[127]

In May, the committee investigating the alleged theft of grain visited Elevator *E* in Duluth to inspect the elevator and view the procedures for taking grain into the elevator, weighing it, storing it and shipping it from the facility.

> From the top of the vast caverns with capacity for thousands of bushels of grain, a lantern was lowered fifty or sixty feet so that the committee might see the interior. The bottom lining of sheet iron worn bright by the action of grain in loading vessels, was clearly visible, and even the aperture fifteen inches or so in diameter, which is the exit to the boat, was distinctly seen. At the bottom of each of these great bins, where pipes leave the side of the elevator to connect with the boat, is a pocket holding perhaps a carload. Much has been said by witnesses regarding these pockets, and so one of them was very scrutinized by the committee. It could be reached only by climbing from the ground floor up a ladder made of cleats on big beams… The committee appear to be satisfied that the elevators are so constructed that wheat stealing is hardly possible, and pockets under shipping bins are not used for concealing grain.[128]

---

127 "Investigating Wheat Buyers," *The Western Rural and American Stockman*, May 9, 1891.

128 "Can't Pick Pockets, The Investigating Committee Finds Duluth Elevators in Proper Shape," *St. Paul Globe*, May 19, 1891.

Hearings continued into the summer with more witnesses testifying before the committee. Emphasis was placed on the inspection of the grain at Duluth elevators. In July, the committee adjourned until the following year when the minority presented its findings. By this time, the furor had faded as the issue fell from the headlines, and the daily activity of the elevators continued without further scrutiny.

Rupley remained as the general manager of the Lake Superior Elevator Company and survived an attempt on his life in late August from a disgruntled former employee, William Anderson. After pulling a revolver on Rupley, the two men struggled and the hammer of the gun came down on Rupley's finger as Anderson screamed, "You don't know who I am. I am God Almighty."

Anderson was discharged from his job at one of the elevators prior to transforming into a religious zealot. The *St. Paul Globe* reported, "Early yesterday morning he was found selling church entertainment tickets, claiming he was Jesus Christ and had return tickets to heaven for 50 cents apiece."[129] Anderson was upset about the practice of buying wheat on speculation, which led him to Rupley.

Rupley was considered a large man. Several years before the incident, the same St. Paul newspaper compared his appearance to President Grover Cleveland.

> If Mr. Rupley had stood beside President Cleveland on the grandstand Monday night it would have been hard to tell them apart, except that one has a sallow complexion and the other's is a delicate pink. In avoirdupois I should judge that their weight was about the same, for it is a standing joke in Duluth that when George Rupley stands at the harbor entrance of the Zenith City the opposite shore tips up.[130]

\* \* \*

---

129 "Claims To Be Jesus," *St. Paul Globe*, August 25, 1891.
130 *St. Paul Globe*, August 16, 1887.

The W. W. (William Wallace) Cargill Company of La Crosse, Wisconsin, operated two terminals along Lake Michigan—one at Green Bay and the other at Milwaukee. The decreased activity at these ports forced Cargill to find an alternative location to maintain the amount of trade for which he competed at the Lake Michigan ports. Historically, Cargill entered the grain business in Conover, Iowa, having moved his family from Janesville, Wisconsin, following the end of the Civil War.

> **W. W. became the proprietor of a single grain warehouse at the end of the McGregor & Western Railroad, where he collected and stored grain for trade. Two years later, his brothers (Samuel and Sylvester) joined him, constructing a second warehouse and lumberyard in nearby Lime Springs, Iowa.**[131]

The railroad did not spur the large growth in the area that Cargill had probably anticipated, so he was faced with a decision to remain or leave and grow. In 1875, Cargill moved to La Crosse, Wisconsin, to establish a stronger regional presence for his grain business.

The Cargill's actively entered the grain trade at Duluth in 1892 with the establishment of the Cargill Commission Company, a branch of the Cargill Elevator Company. Fred Lindahl managed the office.[132] According to the first published history of Cargill, Inc., in 1945, Lindahl was described as "an experienced grain man, and an excellent administrator. The office was a great money maker practically from the beginning, and at a later period in this history was the main standby of the business."[133]

Fred Lindahl "was becoming a legend at Cargill," having begun his career as a country elevator manager at Hope, North Dakota,

---

[131] "The Warehouse that Started it All," January 1, 2015, https://www.cargill.com/history-story/en/FIRST-GRAIN-WAREHOUSE.jsp.

[132] *The History of Cargill, 1865–1945* (Minneapolis: Cargill, Inc., 1945), 25–26.

[133] Ibid., 25–26.

for James F. Cargill in 1884, according to W. Duncan MacMillan in his memoir of the MacMillan family. "Lindahl opened the firm's Duluth office, which operated largely as a separate organization." He took young John McMillan, Jr., under his wing, showing him how to work as a cash grain buyer and pit trader. Lindahl stayed on the job for fifty-five years, retiring at age eighty in 1940. MacMillan wrote,

> Fred E. Lindahl always held a special place in John Jr's affections. He helped shape the destiny of the Cargill Company and my father's career as well. In 1940 John Jr. held an eightieth birthday and retirement party for Lindahl at our home in Orono. Amazingly enough, Lindahl did not learn to drive a car after he was eighty. He died in 1945 in St. Petersburg, Florida.[134]

Cargill's entry into the Duluth-Superior grain industry came at a contentious time as the dispute between regulation of the elevators by the Duluth Board of Trade, hence, Minnesota, came into direct conflict with the state of Wisconsin, which was in the process of taking control of grain inspection in that state, particularly in Superior. Concurrently, it was also a time when the practice of options trading was being contested by Senator William D. Washburn, Republican of Minnesota, and Representative William H. Hatch of Missouri, chairman of the House Committee on Agriculture.

The idea of futures trading was not new in 1892. It was practiced in a number of industries. By way of a simple introduction, a futures contract is a standardized agreement between a buyer and a seller to exchange an amount and grade of an item at a specific price and future date."[135] The item or underlying asset in this case is an agricultural commodity, wheat.

---

134 W. Duncan MacMillan, *MacMillan, The American Grain Family* (Afton, MN: Afton Historical Society Press, 1998), 197.

135 Joseph, Santos, "A History of Futures Trading in the United States," EH.Net Encyclopedia, edited by Robert Whaples. March 16, 2008. URL https://eh.net/encyclopedia/a-history-of-futures-trading-in-the-united-states/.

Commodity traders buy and sell futures contracts on an exchange that is operated by a voluntary association of members. In Duluth, the Duluth Board of Trade provided buyers and sellers the infrastructure (trading pit), legal framework (trading rules, arbitration mechanisms), contract specifications (grades, standards, time and method of delivery, terms of payment). Only exchange members were allowed to trade on the exchange. Nonmembers could trade through commission merchants – exchange members who service nonmember trades and accounts for a fee.[136]

The bill, which defines options and futures, has come to be popularly known as the Anti-Option Bill. It was introduced by Mr. Hatch of Missouri in the House and by Senator Washburn of Minnesota in the Senate. The Hatch Anti-Option Bill is very sweeping and practically puts an entire stop to the Board of Trade dealings in options and futures. It provides that each speculator shall pay a license fee of a thousand dollars annually for conducting his business plus the sum of twenty cents per bushel for grain sold on futures or options and five cents per pound for all cotton, hops, pork, lard or bacon sold in this way.

The tax was purposely designed to be so high that dealers could not continue their business of futures and options. Mr. Hatch succeeded, after months of effort in the House, in securing the passage of his bill by a large majority. However, Mr. Washburn did not have as much success in the Senate. His bill was not so radical, as it permitted futures and options so long as the dealers handled the actual commodity instead of an imaginary commodity. The Senate discussed Mr. Washburn's measure for three weeks until it was evident that the opponents of the bill intended to talk it to death. This is a senatorial tactic occasionally used to kill an unpopular measure.[137]

The Hatch Anti-Option Bill was akin to swatting the hornet nest. Opposition was vocal and vigorous within the terminal grain

---

136 Ibid.
137 Alfred S. Johnson, ed., "Miscellaneous Acts: The Fifty-Second Congress," *The Quarterly Register of Current History: History of the Year 1892* 2 (Detroit: Current History Publishing Co., 1892), 182.

elevator industry from Duluth to Minneapolis. A meeting held by the Minneapolis Chamber of Commerce put Washburn in the same room with about thirty grain and elevator representatives, including C. H. Graves, A. J. Sawyer, Frank H. Peavey and George W. Van Dusen. When given the floor, Washburn laid out his views. "'It is a well-known fact," he said, "that wheat speculation or short selling of grain is detrimental to the grain business. The need of some law to prevent it is necessary. I realize that this bill is as yet a crude affair and would like you all to express your opinion on it." In response, the elevator men argued that,

> ...the illegitimate speculators that Senator Washburn claims to be after do not number over ten percent of the grain interest, and that to drive them out of business on the basis proposed in the bill would be to ruin 90 per cent of the grain traders who are legitimate buyers of wheat, for the bill practically prohibits any but the manufacturer and consumer from buying wheat.[138]

Speaking in opposition to the bill as proposed, Graves spelled out the objections of the Duluth Board of Trade.

> The Bill as it stands... would allow a man who has 100,000 bushels of grain to sell for delivery at a future time, but that purchaser could not re-sell it to anyone except a miller until the time when the grain was actually delivered to him. If he became financially embarrassed or wanted to close up his business he could not divest himself of that contract, and heretofore it would make it quite dangerous for a man to buy grain for future delivery and would tend to reduce the number of customers for grain.[139]

---

138 "They Don't Like It: Grain Men Pitch into the Washburn Bill," *Minneapolis Star Tribune*, January 3, 1892.

139 Ibid.

Washburn conceded that he would need to make some adjustments to his anti-options bill but hung tough on his line of thinking in response to the criticism.

> What I want to see is a time when the supply and demand will fix the value of property. I want to interfere just as little as possible with legitimate business. There is a legitimate buying for future delivery—as in the case when there is something on hand to deliver. The elevator men buy for future delivery, and do it legitimately. It is perfectly legitimate to sell an article for future delivery, if you have the article to deliver. It isn't legitimate or right to gamble. What I want to do is to stop gambling in wheat.

Later that month, after some modifications, the battle over the anti-options bill continued. In favor of the anti-option bill was Minneapolis miller Charles Pillsbury. In opposition was Andrew Sawyer, a member of three grain exchanges. In an interview with the *St. Paul Globe,* Sawyer was said to have "worked himself up to a fever of excitement over the Washburn option bill" and was vociferous in his language regarding Pillsbury and flour milling interests.[140]

> They don't propose to prohibit the selling of flour for future delivery. Why don't they put that under the same heading as gambling? Seventy-five per cent of all the flour is sold for future delivery, from one to three months. These schemers propose to wipe out the elevator men and prevent them from selling wheat in advance. At the same time they take advantage of selling futures in flour, making the gambling in that staple instead of in wheat. It is the most complete scheme of robbery I ever saw, and then they have the assurance of asking congress to endorse it.

---

140 "The Pot Boiling," *St. Paul Globe,* January 22, 1892.

That same day, a cartoon featured caricatures of Pillsbury and Sawyer leaning out of their respective elevators with rifles in hand, clearly on opposite sides of the bill.[141] Sawyer spent the next few weeks traversing the country to testify before Congress in opposition to the anti-option bill. For his efforts, he was rewarded with a victory when the Senate failed to pass the legislation. In the aftermath of the anti-option bill, both Representative Hatch and Senator Washburn lost their bids for re-election and never held office again.

The anti-option bill had a far more detrimental long-term impact on A. J. Sawyer. His travels and the stresses he endured over the bill led to failing health. During the first week of March 1892, Sawyer died at his Minneapolis home "from complication of diseases brought on from overwork and nervous strains." He was fifty-seven years old and was buried at Lakewood Cemetery.

* * *

The arrival of Cargill in the Twin Ports was favorably looked upon. They had, in fact, been courted by local business interests to build in Superior, particularly flour miller Almeron A. Freeman.[142] A. A. Freeman was a La Crosse miller who established the three thousand barrel per day Freeman Mill along Superior's Hughitt Avenue slip in 1891. It was undoubtedly through this La Crosse connection that Freeman became acquainted with William and Sam Cargill. Freeman was anxious to have the Cargills build an elevator on or near Connors Point.

In late December 1892, the Cargill Elevator Company announced its plans to build an elevator in Superior's East End, an area known as "Old" Superior. "In that year the Superior Terminal Elevator Company was formed with W. W. Cargill taking a two-thirds interest and S. D. Cargill one-third."[143] This location was somewhat of a surprise to the community. Instead of building near the existing sites along the West Superior harbor, the Cargill's chose to build in

---

141 *Minneapolis Star Tribune*, January 22, 1892.
142 "Successful Grain Men," *Superior Daily Leader*, December 22, 1892.
143 *The History of Cargill, 1865–1945* (Minneapolis: Cargill, Inc., 1945), 25.

the area generally considered the domain of Superior's flour milling industry. The Consolidated Land Company of Superior was offering the property at reasonable prices to encourage development in that part of Superior.[144]

The Superior Terminal Elevator Company, *K* and *L* were owned by the Cargill brothers. Photo: Copyright Cargill, Incorporated. Used with permission.

The Cargill's chose the Toledo Pier as the construction site for their new elevator. A day later, they generated some confusion by moving the site to the opposite pier. On December 23, 1892, the contract was let to the Barnett & Record Company to drive a minimum of four thousand pilings for a foundation on the Montreal Pier opposite the Toledo.[145]

The Superior Terminal Elevator Company was incorporated on February 20, 1893, with an operating capital of five hundred thousand dollars. William W. Cargill of La Crosse was appointed president, with his brother Samuel D. Cargill of Minneapolis vice president. William S. Cargill and Emory J. Tull of La Crosse and William Thompson of Superior rounded out the roster of incorporators.[146]

---

144 "Another Large Elevator," *Inland Ocean*, January 1, 1893.
145 "The Mill Is An Elevator," *Superior Leader*, December 22, 1892.
146 "Superior Terminal Elevator Company, Articles of Incorporation," *Superior Daily Call*, February 21, 1893.

Completion of the elevators was scheduled for the start of the 1893 shipping season. By early spring, work was well underway to meet the deadline and the two new grain houses were taking shape. Elevators *K* and Annex *L* were rated with a 2.5-million-bushel capacity. Licensing applications were made by the Cargill's to the Duluth Board of Trade to conduct business under the rules and regulations of the laws of the State of Minnesota.

All Twin Ports elevators were regulated through the Duluth Board of Trade. Company offices were required to be established at Duluth. The terms governing the inspection and weighing of grain at Wisconsin elevators by inspectors from Minnesota had become a thorn in the side of Wisconsin legislators and Superior citizens. The Superior Terminal Elevator Company inevitably became embroiled in this controversy, along with other Superior elevators.[147]

In addition to constructing Elevators *K* and *L*, the Cargill's announced plans to build another pair of elevators opposite the Cargill concern for the Belt Line Elevator Company. This was great news for the city of Superior. These elevators would add an additional 2.5 million bushels.

January 14, 1893, marked the date of incorporation of the Belt Line Elevator Company. A capital stock of six hundred thousand dollars was raised and divided into six thousand shares. The incorporators of the Belt Line were attorney Ralph C. Pope,[148] Duluth bank teller Ghent R. Smith, and William B. Perry.[149] Prior to the formation of the Belt Line, the true owners of the proposed new elevators were revealed to be Edmund Joseph Phelps and Albert J. Harrington. Mr. Phelps was appointed treasurer of the Belt Line, and Harrington was named president at the time of incorporation.

---

147 Ibid.

148 "Ralph C. Pope was married at Superior's Fairlawn mansion to the niece of Superior mayor Pattison's spouse," *Mineral Point Weekly Tribune*, June 11, 1896.

149 Corporation Record, Book A, p. 471, Douglas County Court House, Register of Deeds; "Belt Line Elevator Company," *Superior Times*, January 1, 1893; WPA Project #10157, 212.); Peavey Company, Belt Line Elevator Minute Books, 7 (Minnesota Historical Society Archives 145.K.20.3) listed as January 25, 1893.

Phelps was born in Ohio, where he was a farmer early in life, leaving that life for a short stint as a teacher and then a banker before founding a furniture business in 1870. He moved to Minneapolis, where he continued in the "artistic" furniture trade. In 1883, Phelps, along with Eugene A. Merrill, organized the Minnesota Loan & Trust Company. Not one for standing still, he left that venture to become associated with Frank Peavey in the grain business.[150] Phelps eventually became president of the Belt Line Elevator Company.

**The Belt Line Elevator Company, Elevators *M* & *N*, circa 1900.** Photo: author's collection.

Albert Harrington was a respected man in the grain and flour business. His professional association with the Van Dusen-Harrington flour interests was well known in milling circles. Harrington was born in New York and attended West Point after his family moved to Minnesota. After leaving the military academy due to poor eyesight, Harrington went to work for his cousin, Charles Harrington, at the G. W. Van Dusen Company. In 1888, the stock of the G. W. Van Dusen and Co. and the Star Elevator Company was sold to investors in London. The Van Dusen business merged with

---

150 *History of Minneapolis: Gateway to the Northwest* (Chicago-Minneapolis, The S. J. Clarke Publishing Co., 1923).

Charles Harrington's Minneapolis grain business, becoming the Van Dusen-Harrington Company on December 23, 1889. Following the merger, Albert moved from Rochester to Minneapolis, where he became a grain dealer of his own accord.

Interestingly, the Superior Terminal Elevator was directly influenced by the Belt Line elevators. Historian Wayne Broehl, Jr., wrote that Sam Cargill,

> ...went to Barnett & Record [who] had recently completed an elevator for Mr. Harrington [of the Van Dusen-Harrington Co.] on the site adjoining Cargill... when they asked what kind of an elevator he wanted, he told them that what was good enough for Albert Harrington was good enough for him, and to go ahead and build it... exactly like the one they just completed.[151]

The Superior Terminal elevators and the Belt Line elevators were designed and planned by the Edward P. Allis Company of Milwaukee. Details for the elevators, including the machinery used inside, were provided under the supervision of their milling engineer, William D. Gray, a native of Lauder, Scotland. He moved to Milwaukee in 1876 to work in the flour mill construction division of the Edward P. Allis Company.

His biography *The Northwestern Miller* noted Gray "was the designer, inventor, and caused to be introduced the roller now known as Gray's patent noiseless roller, containing solid cast-iron frame, belt drive and more and finer adjustments than any other roller that ever was built up to that time,"[152] with vast experience in the Washburn-Crosby Mill in Minneapolis.[153] In addition to

---

151 *The History of Cargill, 1865–1945* (Minneapolis: Cargill, Inc., 1945), 25; Wayne Broehl, Jr., *Trading the World's Grain* (Hanover, MA: University of New England Press, 1992), 79–81.

152 William D. Gray, The *Northwestern Miller* (May 16, 1900), 952.

153 Ron Cookson, "William Dixon Gray (1843–1920)," Mills Archive, May

the elevators, the Edward P. Allis Company was responsible for a number of the flour mills adjacent to the elevator sites. Among them were the Lake Superior Mill, the Listman Mill and the Anchor Mill, comprising the heart of Superior's flour industry.[154]

The Belt Line Elevator Company's Elevator *M* and Annex *N* were built by the Barnett & Record Company along the Toledo Pier. Barnett & Record began driving piles the second week of January 1893 for the "Phelps-Harrington" elevators, reported the *Superior Times* in an article derived from information in *The Northwestern Miller*.

> The Harrington plant will have room for 2.5 million bushels—1.75 million bushels in the warehouse and .75 million bushels in the shipping house. The contract calls for the completion of the Harrington plant April 1. Mr. Harrington says there will be 1,000 men at work on both plants by February 1. It will require 500 carloads of lumber for each elevator and about 5,000 kegs of nails.[155]

Elevators *M* and *N* were completed during the 1893 shipping season. Completion came on the heels of an accident described as "one of the worst accidents that has occurred in this city for a long time." The fate of the workers was the talk of the day following the collapse of a section of scaffolding.

> The scaffold on which the men, all carpenters, were working had been adjusted that morning and was thought to be perfectly secure, but in some way the

---

5, 2020, https://new.millsarchive.org/2020/05/05/william-dixon-gray-1843-1920/. Note: "First installed his machines at the Schoellkopf & Matthews mill at Niagara Falls, in 1878, but more prominently installed them in the Washburn 'Experimental C Mill' the following year with many other mill installations credited to him in the following years."

154 *At the Head of the Lakes* (Milwaukee: Edward P. Allis Co., 1893), Superior Regional Center, LS 917.7512 Atl, Vault.

155 "One Thousand Men on the Elevators," *Superior Times*, January 14, 1893.

> rope at one end became detached and all of them, five in number, fell to the floor fifty feet or more below and inside the crib walls.

The injured workers were lifted out of the crib via a rope pulley system before being taken to St. Francis Hospital in Superior.[156] All of the men survived, some with serious injuries. The fiancée of one of the injured workers married him at the hospital so she could remain by his side during his recovery. It was the first reported marriage at St. Francis Hospital in Superior.

Aside from the lettering painted on the side walls in billboard-size letters identifying the elevators, in appearance, they were hard to tell apart. The combined capacity of the two outfits was seven million bushels.

\* \* \*

The 1895 session of the Wisconsin state legislature brought about a new law establishing public warehouses and providing for grain inspection at Superior. Efforts to make the Superior elevators operate under Wisconsin regulation soon snared the Belt Line company in controversy. The Belt Line was regulated, as were all the elevators in Superior, by the rules of the Duluth Board of Trade. The establishment of a Board of Trade at Superior, which forced local elevators to open offices in Superior, follow Wisconsin regulations, resulted in a legal battle that would not be fully resolved for another ten years.

An article in the *St. Paul Globe* declared "War at Superior" to describe the battle brewing between elevator operations in the port and the attempt to enforce new grain inspection rules. District Attorney Henry Sloan lodged "a complaint against the Belt Line Elevator company and demanding judgment for $1,000, the maximum penalty for failure to keep offices open in this city, where their plant is situated, and for neglecting to comply with section 8 providing for a report of the week's business to be posted in their offices. The

---

156 "Five Fell Fifty Feet," *Superior Times*, April 8, 1893.

law was enacted and this prosecution is made at the instance of the Superior Board of Trade. The measure is very obnoxious to the Minnesota grain men who fought bitterly against its passage."[157]

Refusing to budge, the elevator operators would not comply with the new law, forcing the state of Wisconsin to compromise on its enforcement. In mid-January of 1896, in a meeting between the Minnesota Railroad and Warehouse Commission, representatives of the Superior Board of Trade and parties from the three Superior elevators—the Belt Line, The Globe Elevator Company, and the Superior Terminal Elevator Company—reached an agreement to resume grain inspection under of Minnesota laws.[158] The temporary solution did not fully satisfy officials in Wisconsin. Throughout the following summer, talks continued until a more permanent agreement was reached that fall.

In an editorial opinion offered in the *Superior Times* following a "spirited" mid-summer meeting at the Board of Trade in Superior, the paper wrote,[159]

> ...While the *Times* would be glad to see Wisconsin inspection adopted, if it can be done without injustice to any interests here, we are clearly of the opinion that its enforcement at this time would result in great inconvenience and loss to the city and to the fine array of mills and elevators that have located here within the past five years, plants costing in the whole not less than $10,000,000 and to which we always point with the greatest of pride. We say, as some of our citizens said at the meeting, let these industries determine for themselves which inspection is for their interest: let us not meddle with their business plans; their capital and not ours is interested; if they suffer we suffer; their prosperity is ours... certainly to say the least the

---

157 "War At Superior," *St. Paul Globe*, October 8, 1895.
158 "Commission Acts On It," *Minneapolis Daily Times*, January 14, 1896.
159 "Grain Inspection," *Superior Times*, July 25, 1896.

> rankest kind of presumption for any citizen, however well meaning he may be, to intermeddle in this great business industry of Superior, supporting, Mr. Hurd of the Daisy Mill estimates, not less than 3,000 persons, especially citizens who have not a dollar invested in these enterprises. Such socialism should be frowned upon by all sensible people. Under the guise of aiding Superior these agitators are able to irreparably injure the good name and fame of our fair city.

A new agreement, reached by mid-summer, called for the continuation of wheat inspection under the rules and regulations of Minnesota. The Superior Board would be allowed to inspect coarse grains and "as much wheat as the elevators will buy under the new system, the elevator and mill men agreeing to co-operate in making the Superior board a success."[160]

Even with a compromise in place, tensions continued that fall when James J. Hill refused to accept a consignment of wheat from the Terminal Storage Company at the Great Northern elevator in Superior because it had been weighed in Wisconsin. The railroad commissioner for Wisconsin heatedly demanded the Great Northern either open its doors as a public warehouse or he would file papers to "compel them to do so or become private houses." The Terminal Storage Company filed suit against the Great Northern, claiming that the refusal of the car of barley "greatly damaged their business."[161] They demanded thirty thousand dollars in damages. By November, Duncan McKenzie, Commissioner of Railroads for Wisconsin, was asked to drop the suit against the Great Northern by attorneys for the Terminal Storage Company, who were taking the railroad to court for damages,[162] bringing a close to another chapter in the drama over grain inspection at Superior.

---

160 "Superior Compromises," *Chippewa Herald-Telegram*, August 8, 1896.
161 "Must Accept Grain," *Lake Geneva Herald*, September 26, 1896.
162 "Dropped The Proceedings," *Eagle River Review*, November 26, 1896.

\* \* \*

Despite the favorable rulings, the Belt Line Elevator Company entered its third year of operation on shaky financial ground. Rumors persisted throughout the shipping season that the company would either fold or be reorganized to alleviate its financial obligations. A special meeting of the stockholders was called in August 1896 "…for the purpose of considering and determining the advisability of the sale and disposition of the property belonging to the Company and the terms upon which said sale shall be made…"

Belt Line secretary Edmund Phelps detailed the state of the company finances, including several large losses reported the previous year. "The largest loss of all, namely, about $30,000 was made by the President himself, (Albert Harrington) speculating upon his own account and taking the funds of the Company to pay his losses with, which sum he stated he was unable to make good…"[163]

The following two weeks saw the conclusion of business by the Belt Line Elevator Company and the sale of the elevator to a new company retaining the Belt Line name.

\* \* \*

As Superior grew in prominence as a grain port, ripples occurred on the Duluth side as the Union Improvement Elevator Company and the Lake Superior Elevator Company became financially distressed. Plans for the "settlement of the affairs" of the two elevator companies had been underway since that spring when stockholders and secured and unsecured creditors appointed committees to look into the dissolution of the two firms. Tangentially, the fate of the Northern Pacific Elevator Company was placed into the hands of Judge Walter Sanborn in St. Paul.[164]

In January 1885, Judge Sanborn "issued an order directing Assignee Forbes (Melvin Forbes) to sell at the court house in Moorhead, Minn., on October 29, the terminal houses of the Lake

---

163 Belt Line Elevator Company, minute books: August 19, 1896, meeting of stockholders at Superior, Wisconsin (MHS Archives, 145.K.20.3).

164 *Weekly Northwestern Miller* 37, no. 14 (April 6, 1894): 504.

Superior Elevator Co. and the Union Improvement Elevator Co. All bidders are required to deposit $5,000 earnest money. In each case, provision is made for paying first liens and bringing the rest of the proceeds into court for distribution."[165]

The Union Improvement and Elevator Company, assessed at $597,000, and the Lake Superior Elevator Company ($810,000) were purchased by Emerson Peet of St. Paul for an unnamed syndicate, merging the two firms into one operating entity.[166] Melvin Forbes was announced as the president of the new Consolidated Elevator Company, effective November 15, 1894.[167]

Emerson William Peet was by no means a grain merchant, but he held stock in several of the Duluth elevators. In practice, he was involved in the insurance business during his lengthy career. He moved from Texas to St. Paul in 1885, soon becoming a vital part of the business community. His obituary lauded Peet as a "pioneer actuary" and the dean of the insurance profession.

> His wide acquaintance with men and institutions elsewhere induced him to add to his insurance business the handling of investment securities of one kind and another. During the first six or seven years of his residence in St. Paul he carried on a very active business in mortgage loans, and municipal and corporation bonds. In this way he became familiar with the resources and possibilities of the city and state and very much interested in their development.[168]

---

165 *Weekly Northwestern Miller* 19, no. 3 (January 16, 189): 530.
166 "Peet Buys Elevators," *St. Paul Globe*, November 4, 1984.
167 "The World's Greatest Grain Mart," *Duluth Evening Herald*, June 28, 1900.
168 "Death Ends Illness," *St. Paul Globe*, April 18, 1902.

Vessel loading at Consolidated Elevator *E*. In background is Elevator *H* and *I*. Photo: Lake Superior Maritime Collections, UW-Superior.

Melvin J. Forbes, the president of the Consolidated Elevator Company, first arrived in Duluth in 1870. He came from Boston where he was engaged in the stationery business. In Duluth, Forbes started his own book and stationery company, which he ran until 1874.[169] He then became a bookkeeper with the grain commission firm of George W. Spencer & Co., eventually becoming a partner in the business.

Forbes, a charter member of the board (Duluth Board of Trade), served as the board's president from 1885 to 1886. Together, he and Spencer commissioned renowned St. Paul architect George Wirth to design the board's first headquarters, the Metropolitan Building, at 113–119 West Superior Street. During the same time, he served as the Board of Trade's president.

Before he married, Forbes—like so many other single men of means in 1880s Duluth—lived at the St. Louis Hotel on Superior

---

169 *Geyer's Stationer* 43, no. 1078 (July 3, 1907): 22.

Street and was a charter member of the Kitchi Gammi Club. Forbes also belonged to Northland Country Club, the Duluth Curling Club and the Duluth Boat Club.[170]

The Consolidated Elevator Company was incorporated with a capital of half a million dollars. "By terms of the reorganization, the old stockholders will lose all their old stock," explained Forbes, "which will be wiped out. Each stockholder will be allowed to subscribe for the stock of the new company, one share for each four formerly held."

> The reorganization committee arrived at Duluth Thursday. With the assistance of Attorneys F. B. Kellogg and C. A. Severance of St. Paul, the committee arranged all the details and made the transfer. The reorganization committee comprise the of following gentlemen, who are interested in the new company: F. H. Parker, Morton S. Paton, George B. Cooksey, of New York; George Ripley, Boston; C. H. Clark, Philadelphia; B. E. Walker, Toronto; C. A. Mair, Chicago; E. W. Peet, St. Paul. At the meeting here on Friday the following board of directors was elected: Messrs. Clark, King, Ripley, Mair, Parker, Cooksey, Peet, Spencer and Forbes. These directors elected the following officers: M. J. Forbes, Duluth, president and general manager; George B. Cooksey, New York, vice president; A. F. Hepworth, Duluth, secretary. An executive committee was also elected, comprising the following gentlemen: Messrs. Spencer, Forbes, Cooksey, Parker and Peet, Mr. Spencer being chairman. This action closed a difficulty which began a year previously when the Lake Superior and Union Improvement companies went into receivership. The new company has an abundance of capital with which to operate the reorganized system. C. A. Marshall, Superior and Duluth, Nov. 19.[171]

---

170 "Melvin Jackson Forbes," https://www.ancestry.com/family-tree/person/tree/164195610/person/322282281469/story

171 *Weekly Northwestern Miller* 38, no. 21 (November 23, 1894): 818.

The reorganization had little impact on the daily operation of the system of elevators and warehouses. Consolidated at first relied upon the capacity and age of its elevators to help them reign as the major grain handling power in Duluth. By the end of the decade, Duluth's Consolidated Elevator Company became one of the largest systems in the Great Lakes grain trade.

\* \* \*

On an individual level, this was a time of growth for Frank Peavey as a grain merchant. The F. H. Peavey Company expanded into a powerhouse. Peavey started out in Sioux City, Iowa, selling farm implements.

> In 1874, he solved the problem of why the farm implements were not selling. There was no ready market for the farmers to sell their grain. With their capital they built a 6,000 bushel capacity blind horse elevator at Sioux City, Iowa, and built other elevators all along the old Dakota Southern Railway to Minneapolis, MN.[172] [173]

Peavey moved his base of operations out of Iowa to Minneapolis, where he grew his business with the expansion of the railroads by continually adding to his series of line elevators. His initial involvement in the Twin Ports with the Duluth Elevator Company gave Peavey the opportunity to operate in the port without a heavy capital investment.

By 1895, Frank Peavey was appointed president of the Duluth Elevator Company following the death of A. J. Sawyer.[174] In August 1894, the dissolution and reincorporation of the Duluth Elevator Company was announced and the elevators at West Superior came

---

172 "The Peavey Story, Iowa and Minnesota," RootsWeb, https://bit.ly/3TwxbNI.

173 The reference to a blind horse is not common and not further defined within the Peavey history. It could be taken at its literal meaning; they used a blind horse to walk in circles to elevate the grain.

174 Peavey Company: Globe Elevator Minute Books, p. 22 (MHS Archives, 145.K.20.11 (b)).

under the operation of the new Globe Elevator Company, a division of the F. H. Peavey Company.

The incorporation took place on September 12, 1894, under the laws of the State of West Virginia. The Globe Elevator Company was valued at nine hundred thousand dollars. George Peavey was appointed president. His Board of Directors included Samuel Arthur Harris as general manager and treasurer.[175] Harris was president of the Northwestern National Bank of Minneapolis and later became president of the National Bank of Commerce.

The move by Peavey from the background to the forefront of grain handling in Superior continued with the additional purchase of the Belt Line Elevator system in 1896. Albert Harrington sold his shares of stock to George Peavey, effectively giving control of the elevator system to the F. H. Peavey Company.[176]

On August 24, 1896, the Belt Line Elevator Company reincorporated. The new Board of Directors reflected the control issuing from the Peavey interests. Melvin Phelps was retained as president and manager. The Globe Elevator Company operated the Belt Line under an annual lease agreement.[177]

\* \* \*

In 1895, the newly formed Globe Elevator Company started to upgrade the deteriorating foundation at House No. *3*. Only two years earlier, the *Superior Leader* boasted about the stability of the elevator.

> **Although situated on the edge of the water, the earth on which they stand is of such a character that while one end of these houses is built on piles, and the other end on stone wall resting on clay, neither roof nor floor**

---

175 Peavey Company: Globe Elevator Minute Books, pp. 1–3 (MHS Archives, 145.K.20.11 (b)).

176 Peavey Company: Globe Elevator Minute Books, August 13, 1896, pp. 1–2, and September 1, 1896 (MHS Archives, 145.K.20.3 (b)).

177 Peavey Company: Belt Line Elevator Company minute books, November 4, 1901, initial agreement with Belt Line and Duluth Terminal Elevator and Globe Elevator Company. (MHS Archives, 145.K.20.11 (b))

has ever settled out of line, notwithstanding No. *3* was stored at one time in 1888 with 2,170,000 bushels of wheat—a weight of over 65,000 tons.

The elevator finally began sagging. In 1895, the No. 3 house was nearly eight inches out of line. Work began at Globe to place a new stone foundation under the timber frame. The elevator was jacked to a height sufficient to complete the support work. Timbers were also placed inside the elevator and a new boiler was installed along with machinery to clean and handle flax and barley,[178] which had both been introduced in the Twin Ports market during the 1886-1887 shipping season, edging in on the dominance of wheat on the market.

\* \* \*

The decade of the 1890s saw intense competition for the Duluth elevators from the Superior side of the harbor. With an infusion of capital from its incorporation, the board of directors of Consolidated voted to embark upon a major renovation to one of its existing elevators. To continue competing with increasingly older facilities and outdated technology would not be prudent, so the firm hired Barnett & Record to rebuild Elevator *E*.

Postcard view of Consolidated Elevator *E* loading grain into the *David Z. Norton*. Mailed 1915. Postcard: author's collection.

---

178 "Will Elevate the Elevator," *Evening Telegram*, August 22, 1895.

In 1899, an addition was put on Elevator *E* (Union Improvement, 1884), and the old section was virtually rebuilt, with new equipment upgrading its outdated loading and handling capability. At the time of its construction in 1884, Elevator *E* did not receive the volume of grain brought into its competitors' Elevator *D* (on the Northern Pacific line), but as the flow of grain increased on the Eastern Minnesota, Omaha and St. Paul and Duluth lines, it became necessary to increase the capacity of *E* and upgrade the equipment.

> **The machinery had to be crowded to its utmost, and the house to be worked nights and overtime when it should not have been necessary. With this addition, and the new machinery which has been added, it is equal to all that will be demanded of it and the company now has a finely balanced system, and one that can be operated at the minimum in expense.[179]**

A major emphasis was placed on fire prevention. The drive belts used to run the elevator machinery were located inside a new brick tower situated at the end of the elevator. Previously, belting was housed inside the wooden flues, which ran bottom to top inside the elevator proper. If a fire broke out, the flues would only serve to aid the fire by providing an easy pathway of travel throughout the elevator.

> **On the top floor is a tank 6 feet in diameter and 24 feet long, which supplies the water for the sprinkling plant with which the entire building is fitted. These sprinklers are set at a distance of about eight feet, and are made so that at a certain temperature, not a very high one either, the soft capping melts and the water flows. Just as soon as one of these sprinklers begins to flow a warning is given in the engine room by means of an electrical apparatus.[180]**

---

179 "Is A Great Elevator," *Duluth Evening Herald*, August 25, 1899.
180 Ibid.

In addition to the brick tower, the numerous wooden spouts inside the elevator were replaced with a smaller number of metal spouts, eliminating another potential cause for fire. A new boiler system was installed at the eastern end of the building. Prior to the renovation, Elevator *E* was powered from a 500-horsepower steam plant in the adjacent Elevator *H*. The new boiler system was designed to power Elevators *E* and *H*, having a steam capacity double the old one.[181]

> The new engine was made by S. F. Hodge & Co., of Detroit, Mich., and is a fore and aft vertical compound engine. The high-pressure cylinder is 24 inches in diameter, with 42 inches stroke and the low-pressure cylinder 52 by 42 inches stroke. The number of revolutions is 85 to the minute. It is so designed that it will work as a two-cylinder compound engine, either condensing or non-condensing, using either high or low-pressure cylinders. In all essential features except the valves and valve motion it is the Colgate Hoyt engine. It can never run away, for whenever speed is increased about 8 percent more than it ought to be the steam is closed off automatically.[182] The engine provides power for the rope driving gear, of which there are eleven ropes driving the cleaning shaft, six ropes driving the shovel shaft, and twelve ropes driving the upstairs machinery.

The *Duluth Evening Herald* reported that the Consolidated Elevator Company had "more houses in the city of Duluth and more electrical apparatus than all of the private plants in the city put together."

Fireproofing at the turn of the century was a concern for not just Consolidated but all the elevator concerns in the city. The construction of new plants or the renovation of houses like Elevator *E* gave the companies the added security they needed to keep insurance costs in line. For the older plants, a higher concern of fire would remain.

---

181 Ibid.
182 Ibid.

The Grain Terminal Elevators of Duluth-Superior

\* \* \*

The general contracting firm of Barnett & Record was kept busy throughout the harbor during the last year of the decade. In May, the Imperial Mill, now under the ownership of Thomas McIntyre's conglomerate the United States Flour Milling Company, authorized the construction of a new elevator with a storage and capacity of one million bushels. In early summer, Barnett & Record was awarded the contract and began driving the first of thirty-five hundred wooden pilings soon after.[183] Some of the timber for the elevator was imported from Washington state.[184] Unlike its first elevator, this structure would have,

> ...an independent engine and cleaning machinery and will be so arranged that it can receive from cars and ship out grain in boats. Included in the plans for the new elevator was a new power house, designed to power the two elevators as well as the flour mill. An electrical engineer from the East toured the site and determined the current steam plant was not "properly adapted for the creation of electric power to be transferred to the elevator.[185] The old Imperial elevator is not designed to ship out in boats. The new house will be so arranged that grain may be received in it from the old house. The latter has a capacity of 750,000 bushels...[186]

This "latter" figure seems to be a high number. Capacity for the elevator was noted as 700,000 on the Sanborn Map Company fire insurance map in 1908, but the figure varied within the Duluth Board of Trade's annual reports beginning in 1889 at 350,000 bushels

---

183 "Contract Let," *Duluth Evening Herald*, June 22, 1899.

184 Note: The once abundant supply of local white pine had been virtually exhausted by the end of the century. Imports of western timbers began arriving in the port during the construction of the Duluth iron ore docks in the mid-1890s.

185 "A Bold Assertion," *Duluth News-Tribune*, June 21, 1899.

186 "More Grain Room," *Duluth News-Tribune*, August 29, 1899.

and then rising to 600,000 during its operation as Capitol 5 in 1905 until 1928 before being re-listed at 350,000 bushels from 1929 to 1953 before its totals were reported in combination with Elevator 4.

Capitol 4, built in 1899, was the site of a fist fight on its upper floors while under construction. Photo: Lake Superior Maritime Collections, UW-Superior.

Incidental to the main work on the elevator was a news-grabbing fistfight that occurred 120 feet above ground between two carpenters, James DeYoung and Louis Rivet.

> DeYoung claims that the other man struck him on the ear with his chisel and tried to cut the ear off. Rivet says that his chisel slipped. It is said the men fought fiercely for a few minutes on their dangerous battleground and those below fully expected to see one or both of them fall to the ground. Rivet was knocked out with several hard blows and almost fell over the edge, but grasped a timber and hung on until his friends from below came to his rescue.[187]

---

187 "Battle in Midair," *Duluth News-Tribune*, October 26, 1899.

During the years these elevators operated in support of the flour milling enterprise, there does not appear to be any name or number assigned to the elevator. The Elevator *4* designation first appeared when it came under the operation of the Capitol Elevator Company in 1905. In addition to supplying the milling grain, it was reported that the new elevator would also store wheat for sale on the open market for the New York firm of McIntyre & Wardwell, the commission agents who purchased grain for McIntyre's flour milling enterprise.[188]

---

188 "A Terminal Elevator," *Minneapolis Journal,* June 21, 1899.

# 7
# 1900–1910: The Era of Concrete

The turn of the century saw an explosive boom in new elevator construction. The years spanning the decade were one of the most turbulent eras in Twin Ports grain elevator construction. In addition to the growing market, the rapidly escalating costs for fire insurance in the old wooden structures began forcing the elevator companies to explore alternative construction designs, techniques and materials. It was a period marked by innovation and change. Engineers and architects were challenged to provide a structure with not only enlarged capacity and lower operating costs but also a fireproof capability to protect their investment. The activity that began in 1899 with the renovation of Elevator *E* for the Consolidated Elevator Company continued throughout the Duluth-Superior harbor.

\* \* \*

The growth of the F. H. Peavey Company at Duluth-Superior continued at a seemingly unlimited rate. In 1899, the company announced its intent to add a new elevator at the lakehead on the Owen Fargussen sawmill property at the end of Rice's Point in Duluth. The new elevator was expected to fall under the management of the Peavey Grain Company, which had formed in Chicago on June 24, 1898.[189] That firm was incorporated to control only the elevator interests of

---

189 "A New Peavey Company," *Boston Evening Standard*, June 24, 1898, 4.

the F. H. Peavey Company, according to a statement issued by Frank Peavey. Terminal elevator locations for the Peavey Grain Company, in addition to Chicago, were listed as Duluth, Minneapolis, Kansas City and Omaha.

One of the driving forces behind the new elevator was the increased corn market. The era of "King Wheat" was ending. The development of the corn market was also seen as a major influence in the almost simultaneous construction of a third Great Northern elevator in Superior.

The selection of Duluth by Peavey for his new elevator was cause for celebration by the political and corporate interests of the city. This marked the first new elevator construction in Duluth for over a decade, ending the dominance of Superior in recent elevator construction. The often-bitter rivalry between the two communities was magnified during the competition for a larger industrial base.

Work on the site, including the foundation, began the previous summer with the arrival of large timbers from the Pacific Coast state of Washington. The once readily available supply of local white pine had been virtually exhausted by the end of the century. Imports of western timbers had begun arriving in the port during the construction of the Duluth iron ore docks in the mid-1890s. The erection of a wood-frame workhouse for Peavey started in May 1899 and rapidly progressed throughout the summer. The workhouse was expected to be completed by October in time to store incoming grain over the winter. Along with its timber frame, the elevator was designed to have an exterior fireproof shell of galvanized iron.[190]

The plans drawn up by the Barnett & Record Company for the Peavey elevator were nothing out of the ordinary for the day.[191] They reflected the successful designs utilized in many previous construction efforts. What would make the new Peavey elevator unique in the harbor would be the storage tanks being designed to supply the workhouse.

---

190 "Big Peavey Plant," *Duluth News Tribune*, April 25, 1899.
191 Plans for Peavey Elevator: Barnett & Record on file at Northwest Architectural Archives, Minneapolis.

Instead of using wood, Frank Peavey was considering using innovative, fireproof materials. One of the options available was steel. The Great Northern Railway had recently built a steel elevator at Buffalo and had announced the intention to build a second one at West Superior. Peavey officials were uncertain about the ability of steel to withstand the stresses caused by temperature variations, especially during the winter months. The escalating costs of acquiring steel also contributed to Peavey's decision to continue looking for another alternative.

Another option for Peavey was the use of hollow ceramic tile. This material had been introduced to Minnesota elevator construction around 1898. The ceramic tiles were reinforced with steel rods to give the cylindrical tanks more support.[192] Peavey officials were not totally sold on this idea either. There were two patented tile construction systems, one by the Witherspoon-Englar Company of Chicago and the other by the Barnett & Record Company of Minneapolis.

The Barnett & Record Company had cornered the market for ceramic tile elevators after acquiring the rights to the technology developed by Ernest V. Johnson with some modifications. The most basic premise for using the tile was to make the elevator fireproof. The adaptations made by Barnett & Record improved upon the Johnson design. Francis Kowsky's survey of grain elevators in Buffalo, New York, drawing from disparate sources, summarized the use of tile during this phase of experimentation.[193]

> **Some bins were constructed on a rectangular plan, but most ceramic bins were cylindrical with internal steel bands for reinforcement. Those built by the Barnett-Re-**

---

192 Robert Frame III and Jeffrey Hess, "History of the Saint Anthony Elevator Company," Historic American Engineering Record, 1992.

193 Francis R. Kowsky, "Monuments of a Vanished Prosperity: Buffalo's Grain Elevators and the Rise and Fall of the Great Transnational System of Grain Transportation," in *Reconsidering Concrete Atlantis: Buffalo Grain Elevators*, ed. L. Schneekloth (Buffalo, NY: The Urban Design Project and the Landmark Society of the Niagara Frontier, 2007), 17–42.

> cord Company also captured the space between the bins for storage by constructing linking walls of arched tiles reinforced by metal tie rods. This innovation would be important for the later design of concrete elevators, which would usually adopt this practice of reducing wasted space by linking cylindrical bins with intermediate walls.

> There were several advantages to ceramic tile bins. Not only were they completely fireproof and heat resistant, but their hollow walls were better than steel at insulating grain from the extremes of heat and cold. For this reason, tile silos did not need to be protected from the weather by an enclosing structure; the cylinders could be left exposed to the elements. And the lighter weight of ceramic bins reduced the load that foundations were required to bear...

> Despite tile elevators' many advantages, when compared to concrete elevators, which were becoming practicable at about the same time, tile structures were expensive to build and maintain. The large number of mortar joints needing to be dressed slowed the process of construction and afterward required constant vigilance to prevent leaks. And because tiles were normally produced in pre-fabricated sizes geared for large bins, it was often difficult to obtain materials with which to build smaller elevators.

The firm Barnett & Record was founded by Lewis Barnett, a native of Kentucky, who attended college in Iowa City and shortly afterward was involved in the grain business in northern Iowa around 1870. By 1881, Barnett had moved to Minneapolis, where he was heavily engaged in the construction of elevators. (Advertisements in 1901 for Barnett & Record boast of building over a thousand elevators.) Among his early accomplishments was constructing an elevator on the Fox River in Green Bay, Wisconsin, for W. W. Cargill. Barnett's connection with Cargill probably led to the contracts for the Superior Terminal Elevator and the Belt Line Elevator in Superior in the early 1890s.

In Minneapolis, Barnett partnered with James L. Record, the collaborator with Ernest Johnson, in the development of the tile elevator in 1885. Record was born in Franklin, Vermont, in 1857 and moved to Lake City, Minnesota, in 1874 to work as a custom thresherman. In 1885, he helped found the Barnett & Record Company. Later, in 1902, Record founded the Minneapolis Steel & Machinery Company.[194]

As noted, Barnett & Record ultimately purchased the rights to Johnson's tile elevator methodology. "In 1899 a single test tank was constructed in Minneapolis on the Osborne-McMillan Elevator Company property. Following the successful completion of the experiment in early 1900, the system was turned over to the Barnett & Record firm in Minneapolis."[195]

Concrete was the third material under consideration by Frank Peavey and the choice he would eventually make for his elevator. Using concrete to construct railroad bridges gave Peavey the initial idea to consider it for his elevators. It was his contention that concrete was certainly fireproof, leading to less repair and maintenance and, most importantly, decreased insurance costs.[196]

The F. H. Peavey Company did extensive research into the use of concrete in storing grain. Peavey sent his partner and son-in-law Frank Heffelfinger to Europe to investigate the use of grain storage structures built primarily or wholly of concrete. The history of the trip is well documented in the annals of the F. H. Peavey

---

194 "J. L. Record, of M.-M., Dies," *Minneapolis Star*, March 3, 1944.

195 Historic American Engineering Record: St. Anthony Elevator No. 3. Denver, CO: National Park Service Rocky Mountain Regional Office, Department of the Interior.

196 Kenneth D. Ruble, *The Peavey Story* (Minneapolis: Peavey Company), 46.

Company. In a news release that made the rounds of major and minor newspapers, Frank Peavey was confident he had found the solution to his insurance woes in the form of the concrete elevator and increased efficiency with the use of an electric power plant. As reported in *The Gazette* of Montreal,[197] Peavey made the following statement regarding the new Duluth elevator annexes,

> We are aiming to secure the very best and most advanced method of grain handling in this house, and if the cement elevator proves the best, as we think, we shall use it and have the most up-to-date and complete storage for grain in the world. My experts have been on the Danube for weeks looking into this system and have made exhaustive reports thereon. Electrical experts are now being consulted on plans for operating the entire system at Duluth, 12,000,000 bushels, by electricity derived from some central plant. The most distant of these houses will be five miles apart. The old plan of operating an entire elevator by one steam engine will be thrown aside with us and electric motors set where they will be needed. Each leg, each belt, each platform, etc., will be run by an independent motor, and the cost of power will be greatly reduced in consequence.

Minneapolis contractor Charles F. Haglin accompanied Heffelfinger on his trip to Europe. The two found one elevator as far away as Romania, which operated successfully and was built completely of concrete. Heffelfinger and Haglin returned to Minneapolis and made plans to construct an experimental tank at Peavey's Interior Elevator in St. Louis Park. The skeptics dubbed the silo "Peavey's Folly."[198]

---

197 "Cement Grain Elevators: A Honeycomb of 3,600,000 Bushels Capacity to be Built at Duluth," *Gazette*, May 3, 1899, 15.

198 Ibid, 46; and Ruth J. Heffelfinger, "Experiment in Concrete," *Minnesota History*, March 1960.

The experimental tank succeeded in storing wheat over the winter. The information gathered, along with data collected in Europe, was used by Haglin to plan the construction of thirty large storage tanks at the Duluth elevator site.

The importance of the single, stark tower in St. Louis Park cannot be underestimated. It is the first successful construction of a circular grain elevator built of concrete in North America. The elevator still stands today in testimony to the pioneering work of Haglin and his slipform process of construction that allowed the replication of silos of uniform size and shape. In 1978 the structure was placed on the National Register of Historic Places, and in 1981 became a National Historic Landmark, followed two years later with its designation as a National Historic Civil Engineering Landmark in Work.

Work on the first fifteen storage silos began in September 1900. They were completed in the incredible span of only ninety days and were ready to be filled with grain on December 7. The silos were 33 feet, 6 inches in diameter with a height of 104 feet. The walls were a foot thick at the bottom, tapering to six inches at the top, with reinforced steel hoops wrapped around the silos at intervals from bottom to top.[199]

Haglin devised a method of construction called "slip form" to build the tanks. The slip form method, patented in 1900, became the standard in building subsequent concrete silos for many years to come. The patent describes the method,[200]

> **This new mold, which is made up of steel angles with wood lining held in place by yokes, is of such a character that when it is filled it is readily freed from concrete and raised by means of screws and is again readily adjusted for refilling... As soon as the cement has sufficiently hardened or set, the entire mold is raised until**

---

199 Charles S. Clark, "Grain Elevators of North America," *Grain Dealers Journal*, 5th edition (1942): 7.
200 Ibid, 47.

the lower end of the boards overlap only the extreme upper portions of the section of the bin thus formed. To accomplish the above adjustment or raising movement, it is necessary to loosen the section of the mold from the section of the bin thus formed.

On December 12, 1900, a week after the first grain was poured into the tanks, a break occurred, providing one last chance for the critics to laugh at Peavey's concrete silos. The cause of the failure was determined but was not sufficient to cancel the project. Repairs and corrections began almost immediately. Frank Peavey came to Duluth in April of 1901 to personally inspect the silos. He was reportedly anxious to have a first-hand look at the damage before repairs were completed.[201]

The original Peavey concrete annex at Duluth, the first large-scale usage of concrete for grain elevator construction. Photo: author.

The second section of the storage annex was completed in the summer of 1901. It consisted of an equal number of fifteen bins, the

---

201 Ruble, 42; and "Peavey is Here," *Duluth Evening Herald*, April 20, 1901.

same size but built with thicker walls. The Peavey Annex in Duluth became the first expansive, practical use of concrete grain silos built in the United States, following the St. Louis Park prototype, revolutionizing the building of grain elevators in the United States and the world.[202]

Frank Peavey was duly proud of the Duluth elevator. In his address to the Grain Dealers' national convention in Des Moines in October 1901, Peavey declared, "...we shall not carry any insurance on building or contents. We are justly proud of our undertaking, believing it to be in advance of any known elevator construction."[203]

The success of the concrete storage tanks was undeniable. Peavey had found a way to significantly reduce the cost of insurance for the grain stored in the elevators and greatly increase his ability to make a profit. However, the Duluth Peavey Terminal headhouse, erected with Washington state timber, remained as much at risk as any other wooden elevator. It was sad to note that Frank Peavey died unexpectedly in 1901, shortly after his triumph.

Under terms spelled out in his will, Peavey's partners were given a five-year period to reorganize and reincorporate. The new organization continued under the name F. H. Peavey Company. Included in the firm were two sons-in-law of Peavey's—Frank Wells and Frank Heffelfinger—and Peavey's son George. The Peavey Grain Company was retained as the overseer of the firm's terminal grain elevators.

---

202 Clark, 7.
203 "Elevator in Duluth," *Duluth Evening Herald*, October 3, 1901.

# 8
# The Great Northern Elevator *S*

During this period, the next two elevators were built at Superior, each erected by a railroad interest on the opposite side of town.

Elevator *S* would be the third elevator built in Superior for the Great Northern Railway. It was not built as a replacement for Elevator *A*, as has been suggested by historical sketches. The sustained growth of the grain market alone was reason enough to expand. Rival Duluth interests speculated further as to the controlling factors in the expansion. An article in the *Duluth News Tribune* at the end of March 1898 quoted an unnamed "prominent grain elevator man of Duluth" saying, "The Great Northern interest does not require this additional capacity to handle any possible, or rather probable, increase in the receipts of northwestern wheat, oats, flax, and barley. It is King Corn that will build this great steel house if it is built." The businessman was basing his comment on the large amount of corn in store at Elevator *A* and other local elevators that winter. Corn was first introduced on the market at Duluth in 1878, and its future as a major commodity was on the horizon.

The Great Northern's decision to store corn over the winter was contrary to the generally held belief that the winter climate was harmful to the crop. The newspaper's source also expressed doubts about the ability of a "steel" elevator to properly house corn compared to a conventional wooden elevator. "It is a question in my mind whether the steel elevators will be as great a success in this latitude as the wooden elevators as far as successfully storing grain is concerned...," yet he did concede that success in this area would necessitate definite expansion. "It is equally certain that with a normal increased movement of corn that is expected there will be additional elevator capacity required in the not very distant future. I look to see Mr. Hill put his elevator's plans in the hands of a contractor before long."[204]

As predicted, plans for the new elevator were soon prepared. The Great Northern's elevator superintendent, Albert D. Bellinger, was placed in charge of the project. The designer, Max Toltz, a mechanical engineer for the railroad, also supervised the construction. From its inception, the elevator would be unique to the harbor because of its use of steel as the primary material. Milo Ketchum, a noted structural engineer, noted, "The Great Northern Elevator at West Superior, designed by Mr. Toltz, is an excellent example of a modern steel elevator of the working house type."[205] It had been designed with square bins instead of circular bins. The use of steel was first used in Philadelphia as early as 1859, followed years later in elevators erected in Montreal, Buffalo, and Winona, Minnesota.

The spout or distribution floor of the Great Northern Elevator S.
Photo: author.

---

204 "Elevator for Corn," *Duluth News Tribune*, March 28, 1898.
205 Milo Ketchum, *The Design of Walls, Bins and Grain Elevators* (1907), 300.

Mechanical Engineer Max Toltz was born in Germany and graduated in 1877 from the Royal Academy of Science and Engineering in Berlin. Historian William J. Brown described Toltz in *American Colossus* as the "engineering genius" of the railway's golden age.

> Toltz emigrated to the US and arrived in St. Paul in 1882. He became the Chief Engineer for James J. Hill's Great Northern Railway... Among his many projects with Hill, he designed the huge steel grain elevator and the Allouez Bay Dock No. 4 at Superior, Wisconsin, which were owned for many years by Great Northern Iron Ore Properties.[206]

Actual construction commenced in the spring of 1898. General contractor Charles Barker of Superior began the removal of the old coal dock that had previously operated on the site. In late March, Barker sank the first of 4,570 pilings to support the foundation of Elevator S.[207]

Barker first arrived in Superior in 1886 and was soon engaged in harbor improvements, primarily dredging, the spoils he was often accused of illegally dumping. He gained lasting notoriety over a dispute in which he accused the city of Superior of non-payment of services. In protest, beginning in 1892, Barker deposited the odorous muck in front of the house of Martin Pattison, then mayor of Superior, to ruin his view of the harbor. Barker's Island is the lasting result of his retaliatory actions.

---

206 "Maximilian ("Max") Toltz," Great Northern Iron, April 7, 2020, https://bit.ly/43fYMWx.

207 Great Northern Railway Archives, correspondence file 359A (MHS Archives, 133.L.12.1).

**At the very top of the cupola in Elevator *S* is the machinery floor, where the receiving legs enter the elevator.** Photo: author.

The Great Northern elevator in West Superior had many standard layout features associated with elevators, even though the actual construction material differed. In general, the lower half of the structure, resting on a pile and concrete foundation, contained the storage bins, with the upper half cupola housing the machinery, scales, transferring belts and spouting equipment. At its inception, Elevator *S* was the talk of the town. It was as much an engineering marvel as it was a terminal elevator. Mr. Hill's steel elevator was heralded as "… the most advanced specimen of elevator architecture extant…"[208]

The elevator foundation is set on piling sunk by a water jack and a 4,200-lb hammer through the sand and clay to depths of twenty-five to forty-five feet before striking hardpan. Ketchum described the construction of the elevator in detail. "The lower timbers of the grillage are 8" x 12" white pine timbers spaced 2' 6" center to center, while the upper layer are of 6" x 6" timbers spaced close together. On top of the grillage were built the concrete pedestals to carry to columns."

---

208 "The Largest Steel Grain Elevator," *The Iron Age*, April 25, 1901.

> **Steel Framework:** The rectangular bins are carried on girders, which are in turn carried by 280 Z-bar columns about forty-two feet long. The Z-bar columns rest on cast bases which are anchored to the concrete pedestals. The bin corners are directly above the columns and carry the columnar structure to the level of the bin floor where the columns supporting the upper part of the house begin. To the height of the bottoms of the bins the exterior walls are of brick, and above this level they are of corrugated iron.

The bins within the elevator vary in dimension and capacity. In total, there were 505 rectangular bins, 85 feet in height.

| 8 | Shipping bins | 13' 6" x 27' 0" | 24,000 bushels |
|---|---|---|---|
| 91 | Standard bins | 13' 6" x 13' 6" | 12,800 bushels |
| 54 | Large bins | 16' 10½" x 13' 6" | 15,600 bushels |
| 28 | Small bins | 6' 9" x 13' 6" | 6,300 bushels |
| 324 | House and cleaner pocket bins | 6'9" x 4' 6" | 2,100 bushels |

**Photograph showing the erection of the elevator bins for Elevator S, 1900.** Photo: author's collection.

One of the revolutionary features of Elevator S was its square steel bins rising vertically above the main floor. There was controversy as to whether the square bins could withstand the pressure exerted by the grain. As part of the design, the bins were reinforced by steel tie bars to alleviate strain.[209]

> The bins were constructed of plates and angles, there being seventeen courses of plates five feet wide. On every second seam, or at intervals of ten feet the lower end of these butt straps is bent out toward the center lines of the bin. This construction was adopted for the purpose of arching the grain so that the pressure would be transferred directly to the corners of the bin, thus relieving the pressure on the bin bottom.

**Main floor car dump area of Elevator S, Superior.** Photo, author.

Grain entering the elevator via rail car was dropped below the main floor into nine receiving hopper pits in the basement floor

---

209 Ketchum, 327.

of the main workhouse. The pits are concrete lined and into them "extend the hopper-shaped boot legs of steel plates. The receiving elevator legs extend up through the bins and are then continued in steel frame towers to the level of the top floor of the cupola."

> Cupola Floors: The cupola floors contain four floors… (1) The bin floor…(2) The spout and conveyor floor with two 40-in. conveyor belts…(3) The scale floor, containing 18 scale hoppers having a capacity of 1,000 bushels each, and 18 Fairbank's scales with a capacity of 120,000 lbs. each. Above the scale hoppers are 18 scale garners and 9 cleaner garners. The capacity of the garners is 25 per cent larger than the capacity of the scale hoppers. (4) The machinery floor, which contains all the motors which drive the 9 receiving, 9 shipping and 9 cleaner legs. The capacity of the receiving and shipping legs is 12,000 bushels per leg hour, and the capacity of the cleaner legs is 3,000 bushels per leg per hour.

> Operation: When wheat is brought into the elevator in cars, of which nine can be pulled in by a grip cable at one time, it is pushed by the automatic shovels out of the car onto a grating over one of the nine receiving hoppers. Running to the bottom of these are endless belts carrying small buckets which scoop up grain and hoist it to the very top of the house, the upper part of each belt running in one of the nine steel towers. Dumped from the belt the grain is shot into a spout and directed across the top of the building to the garners, from which it falls to into the scales. It then drops into a swinging turn-head into any one of numerous spouts and conducted perhaps to a belt conveyor by which it can be handled longitudinally of the building, perhaps by way of another series of turn-heads and spouts to

> its bin...If it is to be shipped it is sent a second time to the scales and thence to the shipping bins, which have a capacity sufficient to load a ship of 160,000 bushels at one draft.

The work on the elevator began May 1, 1899; the erection of steel January 1, 1900; the first car of grain was received on Tuesday, February 26, 1901.

\* \* \*

On the outskirts of Superior, along the isolated Allouez Bay, a fourth elevator was leaving the design stage behind and entering construction, supposedly modeled after the new Peavey elevator at Duluth.[210]

The Itasca Elevator was built for the Chicago, St. Paul, Minneapolis & Omaha Railway. The Omaha line had a large tract of land in Superior's Itasca neighborhood, which was used for development of the elevator site. The Itasca was the most remote elevator in relation to the Duluth-Superior harbor proper, but its location just inside the Superior entry made it readily accessible to ships.

Official announcement of the railroad's intent to build came in the spring of 1899, although it would be August before the contract was let to the Barnett & Record Company of Minneapolis to perform the construction. A finished capacity of 1,250,000 bushels was expected from the design.[211]

The Omaha elevator was constructed of wood with an iron-clad exterior for fireproofing. Typical of elevators of the day, a separate building housed the steam plant to power the elevator and its machinery.

The C. St. P. M. & O. railroad retained ownership of the property.[212] Duluth Board of Trade records indicate the Itasca Elevator

---

210 "Operations Begin Today," *Superior Evening Telegram*, April 23, 1900.
211 "Contract Let for Elevator," *Inland Ocean*, August 5, 1899.
212 "Ibid.

Company owned the elevator, but the Nye-Jenks Company, a large grain commission house, managed the daily operation of the plant. The word ITASCA covered the dock side wall of the elevator in large, white lettering.

**The Omaha Railroad Itasca Elevator in Superior, early 1900s.** Photo: Lake Superior Maritime Collections, UW-Superior.

The Nye-Jenks & Company joined the Duluth Board of Trade in early 1900. Raymond Nye and James Messer Jenks founded the company in Fremont, Nebraska. Jenks started in the grain business at Port Huron, Michigan, before moving to Chicago, where he became engaged in the grain commission business. Nye-Jenks was a large grain exporter with offices in Chicago, New York, Boston, Milwaukee and Minneapolis. It was the first commission house to introduce the trading of coarse grains in the Minneapolis market around 1890.[213] Martin Lane Jenks, brother of James, was placed in charge of the Duluth commission office, moving to the Twin Ports from Milwaukee in 1900. [214] In its initial year in the harbor, many years before the port was established as an international marketplace, Nye-Jenks and the Globe Elevator Company brokered a deal with the United States government to send two hundred thousand bushels of oats to China via the Pacific Coast.[215]

\* \* \*

Midway into the first decade of the new century, the Grain and Warehouse Commission was organized in Wisconsin. One of the primary purposes of the commission was to inspect, weigh and certify all grain handled at the port of Superior. Along with Superior, the commission was also appointed to service warehouses at Green Bay and La Crosse.

For elevator operators, it was the middle of a decades long battle over nothing more than the sting of wounded civic pride in Superior over being left out of a well-run and efficient operation. The grain inspection was operated by the state of Minnesota, through the Board of Trade, also in line with the Minneapolis Grain Exchange trading regulations. The introduction of a second, redundant service simply because the elevator was situated on the Superior side of the harbor, was deemed an unnecessary demand. The inspection controversy also displayed the power the railroads and elevator owners wielded in the harbor when used as a collective voice.

The entrance of the Grain and Warehouse Commission at Superior met with mixed reactions from both sides of the harbor. For Minnesota officials, it meant an end to nearly ten years of on-again, off-again inspection and controversy at Superior.

---

213 Note: coarse grains are grains where the surface of the millet is rough. These grains included corn, barley, oats and rye.

214 Helen Clarke Jenks Cleary, "A Jenks Genealogy with Allied Families," no date.

215 "Oats for China: Government Takes 200,000 Bushels in This Market for Use There," *Duluth Evening Herald,* July 20, 1900.

Ten years earlier, in 1885, the Wisconsin legislature enacted its first effort to regulate the inspection and weighing of grain in Superior. This initial effort was spearheaded by Superior Board of Trade members who wished to separate the Minnesota and Wisconsin grain affiliations. Enforcement of the new inspection regulations was left in the hands of the Superior Board of Trade but restricted to the port of Superior only.

The initial attempt at inspection and weighing of grain by Wisconsin officials in Superior did not go as smoothly as hoped. By 1896, after several ill-fated attempts, the Superior Board of Trade authorized the Railroad and Warehouse Commission of Minnesota to resume its inspection and weighing at Superior.[216]

The return of Minnesota inspectors to the Wisconsin port did not bring an end to the troubles between the two commissions. In 1902, the animosities again took center stage in the Twin Ports. Albert C. Clausen, chief inspector for Minnesota, described the latest incident in the ongoing dispute in his annual report to the Minnesota Railroad and Warehouse Commission.

> The work proceeded without further friction or incident until the fall of 1902 when several of our inspectors were summarily arrested and brought into a Superior court on the charge of trespass preferred by one Homer T. Fowler, a member of the Superior Board of Trade, and a vindictive enemy of the Minnesota system, and who is chiefly responsible for the many gross misrepresentation which has been so industriously circulated that they even found temporary credence in Wisconsin courts and the Senate of the United States.[217]

---

216 Railroad and Warehouse Commission: Grain Inspection, *1896 Annual Report*, 11th Annual Report for the Year Ending 8/31/1896, pp 59–63. (MHS Archives 120.I.3.7B).

217 *Brief History of Minnesota Inspection at Superior, Wisconsin*, Railroad and Warehouse Commission: Year Ending August 31, 1906, pp 6–11 (MHS Archives, 120.I.3.7B).

The court ruled quickly in favor of the Minnesota inspectors and criticized the actions of the Superior Board of Trade. The fact that the Board had invited the return of the Minnesota inspectors was the primary cause for the dismissal of all charges.

New inspection and warehouse laws enacted by the Wisconsin legislature in 1905 divested the Superior Board of Trade of its former authority. The new Wisconsin commission was comprised of representatives not only from Wisconsin but from New York and North Dakota as well. In early July, the Railroad and Warehouse Commission of Minnesota announced it would again discontinue the inspection of grain at Superior. A dispatch from St. Paul issued the following statement:[218]

> The Minnesota commission has inspected grain at west Superior since 1885. The inspection has been made at the request of the shippers of the Northwest, and with the consent of the Wisconsin authorities. The Minnesota commissioners have never maintained that they had legal authority to make legal inspection outside of Minnesota.
>
> We are ready at any time to discontinue the inspection in West Superior,' said an official of the railroad and warehouse commission today. We have no interest in the matter other than a desire to comply with the request of the grain shippers of Minnesota.

On August 1, 1905, the Wisconsin system of inspection was again put in place in the port of Superior. Inspector Clausen remained skeptical of the new system's viability. As expected, the operators of the elevators in Superior, all Minnesota-based companies, requested a continuation of inspection from the Minnesota Railroad and Warehouse Commission. They believed their status as private houses allowed the Minnesota inspection to continue. "It is said there is

---

218 "Will Keep Out: Minnesota Inspection May Be Withdrawn From Superior," *Duluth Evening Herald*, July 8, 1905, 2.

nothing in the Wisconsin law to prevent Minnesota inspection in private warehouses. Minnesota accords this privilege to Wisconsin and all other states," read a statement from the Minnesota Railroad and Warehouse Commission.[219]

The *Duluth Evening Herald* was happy to report on the wrath of "Superiorites" over the grain inspection issue with these words:

> **Things have not turned out exactly as they expected when they induced the Wisconsin legislature to pass a bill permitting them to establish a Wisconsin grain inspection across the bay. They thought that with the passage of this law they were going to deal a deadly blow at the Duluth board of trade and build up the weak and wobbly institution that has masqueraded under the name of a board of trade in Superior. Their expectations have not been realized, and they are very sore and talk in bitter tones and indulge in threatening language."**[220]

By late summer, the matter had gained national attention when grain cars from North Dakota destined for Superior were allegedly held up and inspected in Minnesota without any authorization. North Dakota Senator George Young referred the matter to the United States attorney general as a violation of the Interstate Commerce Act as interference with the rights of shippers.[221] At the time, there were no federal regulations regarding the inspection of grain, so the appeal to the attorney general did not gain traction. What did was the growing animosity between the officials at Superior toward the Duluth Board of Trade and Minnesota inspection. The only way to resolve the issue was to pursue it in the federal courts.

---

219 "They Are Wanted: Elevators and Mills at Wisconsin Want Minnesota Inspection," *Duluth Evening Herald*, August 3, 1905.
220 "Angry Superiorites," *Duluth Evening Herald*, August 6, 1895.
221 "Is Without Basis: Rumored Appeal to Federal Authorities In Inspection Matter," *Duluth Evening Herald*, August 25, 1905.

In February 1906, the Globe Elevator Company filed suit in the United States court in Madison, Wisconsin, testing the legality of the Wisconsin inspection law and asking for a temporary restraining order preventing the Wisconsin grain commission and railroads from interfering with its business. The Great Northern and Northern Pacific railroads were made parties to the suit for allegedly placing cars of grain out of the reach of Minnesota inspectors.

In April, amidst the disaster of the great San Francisco earthquake, a federal court judge ruled that Wisconsin could not regulate Minnesota commerce with its grain inspection bill. The bill, passed in 1904, was ruled unconstitutional by Judge Arthur L. Sanborn of the United States Court for the Western District of Wisconsin. In his ruling, Sanborn wrote:

> **The purpose to destroy the Minnesota inspection for the purpose of selling grain, and substituting the Wisconsin system, was, I think, the dominant purpose of the statures in question, without which they never would have passed. Believing that such statutes constitute a regulation of commerce between the states, they must be held invalid.**[222]

As a result, officials in Madison gave the word to the grain inspectors at Superior to not interfere with the business of the elevator companies until the suit by Globe was decided at the federal level.[223]

---

222 "Inspection Is Killed: Judge Sanborn Holds That Wisconsin Law Is Invalid," *Duluth Evening Herald*, April 21, 1906.

223 "Order's Scope Is Increased," *Duluth Evening Herald*, April 14, 1896.

# 9
# The Capitol Elevator Company

Amidst the grain inspection controversy, a new elevator company was preparing to enter the Duluth market. The Capitol Elevator Company was incorporated in Duluth in 1905. It was by no means the largest elevator system to operate in Duluth. The importance of Capitol in the Twin Ports elevator business lies in the fact that it was really the last independently owned and operated elevator system at Duluth. Capitol was founded by McCarthy Bros. & Company along with Duluth elevator owner and grain merchant James Graves.[224]

The McCarthys operated a successful grain commission business out of the Duluth Board of Trade, and they managed Interior Elevator in Minneapolis as well as several line elevators in North Dakota. They were certainly familiar with the Twin Ports market and its opportunities. Capitol took over the flour mill and elevator property originally operated by the Imperial Mill, purchasing the land from the Standard Milling Company, a New Jersey corporation. A restriction on the sale required that no flour mill could be built on the property.

The McCarthy brothers, Thomas G. and John, were small-town merchants in Oakes, North Dakota. When the railroad came to town, Oakes was proclaimed "The Coming Marvel of Dakota" and a rail center for the region. Thomas and John were involved in the mercantile trade and, in anticipation of the coming economic boom, formed the McCarthy Bros. Grain Company. The boom

---

[224] Hollis Graves, Jr., interview with author, February 13, 1994, Duluth.

never happened in Oakes. The McCarthy brothers closed their mercantile business in 1890 but held onto the grain business, heading to Minneapolis as grain commission agents.

Co-owner Jim Graves moved to Duluth from southern Minnesota in the mid-1890s. At Duluth, Graves founded the Railway Express Delivery Agency. In addition to this business, Graves operated a small grain mill along Rice's Point. Hollis "Holly" Graves, Jr. recalled his grandfather's mill operation as a small one. "He built a little elevator down by where Goldfine's was years ago, there on Garfield. He built a little elevator which was operated by a horse. The horse walked around in a circle. That lifted the legs for the elevator. He unloaded one car of grain a day."[225]

Jump ahead in time for a moment, a half a century later and we find that man's grandson operating a 1,750,000-bushel elevator. A document in the Capitol elevator archives listing the labor costs for a single day (May 22, 1946) of operation at Capitol Elevator No. 6 provides a stark contrast to the one-horse operation of Jim Graves. On that day, the crew at Cap 6 unloaded seventy-four cars totaling 124,622.20 bushels. "Six men in car—one on car puller."

The document listed forty-two employees on the payroll for that day, their rate of pay, hours worked, total paid and job classification. The highest-paid workers were Axel Grenvall and Hollis F. Graves, Jr., assistant superintendents at $1.75 per hour. Jean Carr, Millwright, earned $1.57, the highest non-management wage. Examining the job classifications, in addition to the two superintendents, the elevator employed two inspectors, four weighers, an annex man, two oilers, two millwrights, two floormen, two sweepers, one prober, one assistant prober, one annex man and twenty-one laborers.

The lowest paid employees were the laborers, annex men, probers and sweepers at .87 per hour—a total of $6.96 for an eight-hour shift. The total cost for labor that day was $326.16. An additional hundred dollars was expended for power.[226]

---

225 Ibid.
226 "Labor and electrical consumption," document, Capitol 6 elevator, May 22, 1946, collection of author.

The Capitol elevators were located along Rice's Point between the Peavey Terminal and the Consolidated elevators. Capitol Elevator No. 5 (a.k.a. Cap 5) was located off the water. The shipping elevator, Capitol No. 4, was situated just north of Cap 5 at the head of the pier. The Two Harbor's firm, Minnesota Mining and Manufacturing, subsequently leased the former Imperial Mill building for use as a sandpaper production plant.

The Capitol Elevator's 4 and 5, seen from the Garfield Avenue rail corridor. The Imperial Mill building is in the background.
Photo: Lake Superior Maritime Collections, UW-Superior.

"My grandfather, Jim Graves, and the McCarthy brothers, they started this up," explained Hollis Graves about the start of the Capitol Elevator Company. "He was working for Salyards (Salyards Grain Co.) out in North Dakota, in little country elevators. Walter McCarthy asked him to come down and operate this here little elevator (Cap 4); operate the plant and that's what they did," recalled Hollis, the grandson of Jim Graves.[227] During their lifespan in Duluth, Capitol developed a strong customer relationship with the Minneapolis-based International Milling Company. International used the Duluth elevator for years to transfer grain to the firm's East Coast millers.

---

227 Ibid.

\*\*\*

On February 17, 1906, ten months before the F. H. Peavey Company was reincorporated, the Peavey Duluth Terminal was struck with disaster. The wood frame workhouse, built in 1899, was destroyed by fire. The fire was first reported at a quarter past seven in the evening in the cupola. Within a half hour, it had spread to other floors in the workhouse. "When seen, the fire was far beyond the capacity of any fire department, no matter how much water they had at its command," wrote Dwight Woodbridge for *The Northwestern Miller*.[228]

The volume of grains stored in the workhouse at the time of the fire was listed as 600,000 bushels of wheat, 174,000 bushels of oats, 100,000 bushels of flax and 64,000 bushels of rye "valued at about $690,000 and insured for within $25,000 of full value. The house was valued at some $300,000 and was insured for within $25,000 of that sum," added Woodbridge, who wrote "the heat was so intense that the engines and boilers cannot be reached, and it is feared these are seriously injured, if not destroyed."[229]

"The origin of the fire is unknown," reported the *Wausau Pilot*. "Fortunately, there was no wind blowing toward other improved districts on the harbor front or the loss would have been tremendous. The fire department had much difficulty in getting streams on the fire, as there were no hydrants within half a mile and it was necessary to cut holes in the ice six feet thick in the slips to get water."[230]

The destruction of the workhouse was a devastating blow to the F. H. Peavey Company. The lone bright spot was the ability of the concrete storage tanks to withstand the fire.[231] "The concrete building went through the fire intact and does not show the slightest injury from the terrible heat it was subjected for hours. The two buildings are about 35 feet apart, and the heat from the millions of feet of dry timber in the wood house was so great that steel rails between the

---

[228] Dwight E. Woodbridge, "Peavey Elevator Fire," *The Northwestern Miller* 65, no. 8 (February 21, 1906): 474.

[229] Ibid.

[230] "Duluth Elevator Burns," *Wausau Pilot*, February 27, 1906.

[231] "Losses By Companies," *Duluth Evening Herald*, February 19, 1906.

two were subjected to a welding and fusing temperature, while for hundreds of feet away it was so hot that men could not live in the glare," said Woodbridge with a dramatic flair.[232]

Peavey officials were impressed with the ability of the concrete to withstand the intense heat generated by the fire. The only reported damage to the concrete tanks occurred on the two easternmost tanks. "Aside from one or two holes in the tanks, caused by the I-beams being dragged out when the galleries fell, and an old crack or two of no consequence and above the storage part of the tanks, which are slightly enlarged, there appears to have been no damage whatever to the tanks,"[233] reported the industry journal *The American Elevator and Grain Trade* in their coverage of the fire.

Within a week, the Duluth Board of Trade declared the concrete annexes "irregular" because there was no means of conveying the grain into or out of the silos. A series of portable conveyors eventually moved the grain out of the annexes to other local elevators for shipment. A replacement of the Peavey headhouse was expected to be built quickly because of the approaching shipping season and heavy demand, but by September, it was progressing slowly due to difficulties in obtaining the materials.

\* \* \*

News of a second major fire in the Twin Ports would soon claim the headlines of the day. Attention this time was focused on Superior and the loss of its original Great Northern Elevator *A*.

The workday came noisily to a close along the West Superior waterfront on Saturday, November 9, 1907. As another day of loading concluded, the crisp November air, earlier clouded with grain dust, slowly cleared while the voices of the longshoremen faded into the distance.

At the Great Northern elevator, the steamers *S. A. Parent* and *W. A. Rogers* were tied securely to the dock and settled low in the dark water.

---

232 Woodbridge, 474.

233 "Grain Storage in Reinforced Concrete Tanks," *The American Elevator and Grain Trade* 25, no. 3 (1906): 128.

The glow of lights in the ship's cabins mingled softly with the warm light spilling out from the doorways and windows of the elevator. Great Northern Elevator *A*'s dock was narrow. The vessels were tucked up tightly beneath the loading spouts. It was time to brush off the grain dust and follow the tracks into Superior's North End tavern district. Constructed of wood, *A* had proudly displayed the Great Northern name across its exterior planking for over twenty years.

This was a busy time of year. Across the slip at the Great Northern merchandising dock the steamer *Chili* had shifted over from *A* earlier in the afternoon to finish off its loading before leaving port. At the flour sheds along with the *Chili* were the steamers *Alva* and *Utica*. The season at the head of the lakes wouldn't last more than a few more trips before ice would seal up the harbor.

Behind Elevator *A*, across the tracks and a half-block south, stood the less stylish Elevator *X*. By every means a contemporary in age, Elevator *X* was designated as an intake and storage elevator. It did not have the status of an export terminal. Grain held there was shuttled forward via an overhead conveyor to *A* for shipment. Elevator *X* was an unimaginative rectangle with an extra set of floors at the south end for the intake and weighing of grain. Up the slip to the north, the timber wharf widened under the expanse of Elevator *S,* touted as the "World's Largest Grain Elevator."

As Saturday night began settling in, the watchmen made their rounds to the various stations inside each elevator while night crews continued moving grain into shipping bins in preparation for the next day's loading schedule. To trained eyes and ears, the buildings had their own ways of talking. The sound and rhythm of motors and gears amid the rushing of grain along conveyors was a distinct sound to the well-tuned ear. There were many things to look for. The risk of fire in an elevator was very real. Shortly past seven, the dreaded cry of "fire" went up along the dock near the older Great Northern *A*. The daily routine of the Great Northern docks was to change rapidly and forever in the next eight hours.

The fire, discovered in the basement of Elevator *A*, spread quickly through the wooden structure. Men working on the top floor ran downstairs in a race against flames coming up from below. All but one would make it out alive. As the building caved in on itself, the airborne sparks, propelled by a strong west wind, leaped across the bayfront, igniting everything in their path. The spectacular blaze was easily seen from a thirty-mile radius encompassing Cloquet to the west and Two Harbors up the North Shore. Newspapers reported seeing the fire as far away as Ashland, Wisconsin, some seventy-five miles down the Wisconsin shore.

When it was all over and the flames had been suppressed, one man was dead. The property loss was estimated at over $2.5 million. In addition to Elevator *A,* the fire consumed several elevators and flour mills along the Tower and Hughitt Avenue slips. Among the casualties were the Grand Republic Mill and elevator, the Freeman Mill and elevator (owned by Sterling, Illinois, grain merchant A. A. Freeman), and the Minkota Mill and elevator. All were considered total losses. Along with partial damage to other businesses just beyond the mills, a total of eight houses were destroyed on Connors Point, rendering numerous people homeless.

At the height of the fire, the exterior walls of nearby Elevator *S* were said to have glowed white-hot, yet the steel structure withstood the fire. New design techniques at Elevator *S* gave the men working inside confidence that it could withstand a fire of major magnitude. One of the key fire prevention features of *S* was a series of water discharge pipes ringing the top of the elevator. The pipes were positioned between the outside bin walls and a second wall of galvanized iron. The idea was to open the pipes to pour water down the wall in case of a fire. The heated metal, when contacting the water, would form a vapor curtain, protecting the exterior shell of the structure. Elevator *S* had backed up its fireproof claim and continued functioning after the ashes of destruction had disappeared.[234]

The three wooden houses of the Globe Elevator Company adjacent to the Great Northern were saved by their respective

---

[234] "Superior Waterfront Is Devastated By Flames," *Duluth Evening Herald,* November 10, 1907; and "Great Elevators and Mills Are Laid In Ruins By a Two Million Dollar Fire," *Superior Telegram,* November 9, 1907.

sprinkler systems. It could be speculated, however, that had they been closer to the fire's origin, they would also have perished. Ironically, though the buildings stood, the grain inside suffered more damage from the water sprinklers than the fire itself. As for the Great Northern's Elevator *A*, it was a total loss and never replaced. This single fire event forever removed its visage from the West Superior waterfront.

Despite the fire, the year closed positively for Superior when a long-awaited agreement was reached in December over the issue of grain inspection. Attorneys for both sides brokered a two-year agreement allowing the Wisconsin commission to "inspect and weigh all coarse grain, including barley, rye, corn, and oats in and out until January 1, 1910. The inspection of wheat and flax by Wisconsin officials will occur only when requested by the owners." It was agreed that the elevators would issue warehouse receipts under the general warehouse law of Wisconsin. The Wisconsin warehouse commission was given $16,000 in compensation for monies they expended two years earlier in their battle for inspection rights.[235]

\* \* \*

The opening of the 1908 shipping season was a difficult one for the city of Superior. The charred remains of the buildings destroyed by the winter fire dotted the waterfront, a grim reminder of the devastation caused by the fire.

The concern placed upon the prevention of elevator fires and the need for changes in construction materials was well-founded. Still, there were many wood-frame elevators in the Twin Ports. It would be prohibitively expensive to replace them with new technology. For the Consolidated Elevator Company, the afternoon of June 25, 1908, would be an unwelcome reminder of the flammable combination of wood and grain.

Consolidated Elevator *D* became the fourth Duluth elevator to be destroyed by fire. This blaze began just before lunch hour, quickly engulfing the wooden structure and its contents. A dollar value of

---

235 "End Grain Inspection War," *Ladysmith News-Budget*, December 5, 1907.

$750,000 was assessed as the value of the burned elevator.[236] Debris flying from the fire ignited the Northern Pacific Freight Shed No. 1, located a scant 160 feet to the north of the elevator. The wooden shed burned as quickly as the elevator and was a total loss. The major firefighting effort was concentrated on watering down the surrounding structures and assisting in removing a steamer docked near the elevator.

A period of rebuilding followed the destructive fires. In Duluth, the ceramic-tile structures designed and built by the Barnett & Record Company of Minneapolis replaced the Peavey and Consolidated workhouses.

The rebuilt Peavey Terminal Elevator workhouse came shortly after the reincorporation of the F. H. Peavey Company as part of the disposition of Frank Peavey's will. The new Board of Directors were Frank Heffelfinger, Fred B. Wells and George S. Peavey.

The replacement workhouse, built in 1907, was completed for Peavey on the same footprint as the original wooden structure. It is uncertain why Peavey chose tile instead of concrete since the company had pioneered the use of concrete for storage silos.

The new workhouse was constructed of hollow ceramic tiles reinforced with steel rods. The use of tile had begun nearly a decade earlier. The company of Barnett & Record was granted a series of patents for the use of hollow tile in elevator construction starting in 1895. Following the successful completion of an experimental tank in Minneapolis in 1900, the company went on to complete several tile elevators in Minneapolis and Buffalo. In the construction of its concrete silos in 1900 and 1901, Peavey rejected the idea of using tile, being unsatisfied and uncertain of its ability. Barnett & Record had a considerable track record in building and designing tile elevators and finally convinced Peavey officials of its merits. The contractors were meticulous in the application of their patented tiles in the Peavey elevator.[237]

---

236 "Big Conflagration on Duluth Water Front," *Superior Telegram*, June 26, 1908.

237 "The New Peavey Elevator Building at Rice's Point," *Duluth Evening*

The new workhouse was built on the foundation of the previous workhouse with some modifications to the support pilings. Additional care was given to designing the lower section of the elevator to withstand flooding. The location of the elevator was barely above sea level, and in the great storm of November 1905, the previous wooden elevator had suffered substantial flood damage.

The physical dimensions for the exterior of the workhouse were 227 feet in length and 128 feet wide, with a maximum height of 170 feet. There were seventy tile bins with a total capacity of 650,000 bushels. Together with the concrete storage silos, the Duluth plant had an overall capacity of 3,650,000 bushels. As it had done prior to the fire, the Peavey Duluth elevator continued operating under the management of the Globe Elevator Company.[238]

\* \* \*

After reincorporation, the Consolidated Elevator Company was in a position of strength and let contracts to construct a new elevator to replace Elevator *D*. The foundation from the original wooden structure would provide the base for this replacement elevator as well. The original Elevator *D* was built in 1884 as part of the agreement between the Northern Pacific and Lake Superior Elevator Company.

The recent widespread experimentation in elevator construction gave Consolidated's owners much to consider. Various methods and materials were the subject of vigorous debate in industry circles. Consolidated's board of directors was unanimous in the belief that the era of the all-wooden elevator had come to an end. In early August 1908, the contract was let to Barnett & Record to build a tile elevator. The decision made by the board of Consolidated was perhaps influenced by the recent completion of the tile elevator for F. H. Peavey Company by Barnett & Record at the opposite end of Rice's Point.

---

*Herald*, January 19, 1907; and Rayner Banham, *A Concrete Atlantis* (Cambridge: MIT Press, 1986), 133–137.

    238 "The New Peavey Elevator Building at Rice's Point," *Duluth Evening Herald*, January 19, 1907.

**Consolidated Elevator *D* with ceramic tile headhouse and concrete annex.**
Photo: University of Minnesota Duluth, Kathryn A. Martin Library, Northeast Minnesota Historical Collections, on loan from the St. Louis County Historical Society.

The price tag for the replacement elevator was estimated to be a half-million dollars. The tile headhouse was expected to hold approximately 600,000 bushels, with its 32-bin concrete annex (including interstice bins) adding another 798,000 bushels.[239] The main tanks had a capacity of 21,000 bushels, and the smaller interstice bins were rated for 6,000 bushels each.[240] Completion of the headhouse was slated for June 1909, with the annex ready by August, nearly a year after the contract was signed.

Work on the new tile headhouse was carried out over the winter months. By early April of the following year, it was near completion just as construction began on the series of concrete tanks, work that could not occur during the winter when the concrete could not set properly.

---

239 Note: In elevators with multiple rows of silos, the void between where the exterior concrete bin walls meet leaves a smaller bin, hidden from the outside, called an interstitial bin. These spaces have hopper openings on the bottom like the regular bins, and are also filled with grain.

240 *Sanborn Fire Insurance Map from Duluth, Saint Louis County, Minnesota* 1 (Sanborn Map Company, 1909, Republished 1955): 47.

The acceptance of tile was limited, and the use of tile in construction did not gain much popularity. The rapid ascent of reinforced concrete overtook all the other materials in use at the turn of the century. The two new elevators built for Consolidated and Peavey would be the only tile elevators to be built in Duluth. Barnett & Record did go on to build more tile elevators at locations other than the Twin Ports.

\* \* \*

The Great Northern did not replace Elevator *A*. It was the original elevator at West Superior, but the significant changes in design, construction and capacity incorporated within Elevator *S* made replacing the structure unnecessary.

Instead, an annex would be added to the east side of Elevator *S*. There had been talk of an annex as early as 1901, shortly after the elevator's completion. The talk never came to fruition. After the destruction of Elevator *A*, these plans were discussed again, with a final design prepared by Great Northern's Chief Engineer Albert H. Hogeland.

The Barnett & Record Company was hired as the main contractor for the new annex. Work commenced in January 1909 and completed by October. The annex was constructed of reinforced concrete. The overall capacity of the new annex was about 2.4 million bushels. Milo Ketchum provided the following general description of the annex.[241]

> **In building the storage annex eight circular bins were placed opposite each of the nine south units of the steel elevator. The storage units thus formed have no connection with each other except through the longitudinal conveyors and partial system of cross spouting in the main elevator The storage annex consists of 72 reinforced concrete bins 19 ft 7 ins. Inside diameter,**

---

[241] Milo Ketchum, "The Great Northern Concrete Annex," *The Designs of Walls, Bins and Grain Elevators* (New York: McGraw-Hill Book Company, Inc., 1919), 441.

> and 110 ft. height, and 51 interspace bins. The circular and interspace bins have a capacity of approximately 2,400,000 bushels.

The technical nature of the construction was of keen interest for Ketchum. He further describes how they were constructed.

> The outer walls were made 7 ins. thick, while the inside walls, having grain pressure on both sides, were made 7½ ins. thick. The walls were made the same thickness from bottom to top to permit the use of sliding forms in the construction. The circular bins were reinforced with plain round 5/8-in. and ½-in. diameter bars, spaced to carry the bursting pressures. The circular bins were tied together at the corners by corrugated bars bent into U shape, and placed in the intersections of the bins... The bottoms of the bins were hoppered with a very lean concrete.

> The cupola consists of a steel frame-work resting on the bin walls, which carries 6-in. reinforced concrete side walls. The roof consists of reinforced concrete tile resting on steel T's and covered with 4-ply pitch and grave roof. The roofing tiles were 18-in. span, 24 ins. Long and 1 ½ ins. thick, reinforced with woven wire.

Two layers of concrete were put in daily. The night crew got the forms ready for the day's runs, putting the tops of the forms about thirty inches above the top of the concrete placed the day before. The morning crew placed, on average, about sixteen inches of concrete before noon. The afternoon run began several hours later, about half-past two, to give the concrete time to set and the form to be raised a few more inches. The process of building the silo is known as the slipform process, developed by Haglin. This method made the erection of concrete silos universal in North America.

> Excavation for the foundations began January, 1909, and the storage house was practically completed by September 15, 1909. The bins were filled about October 1, 60 days after the concrete was placed.

> The work was designed and constructed under the direction of Mr. A. H. Hogeland, Chief Engineer, Great Northern Ry. Mr. Max Toltz was consulting engineer on design and construction. The construction was under the direction of Mr. O. B. Robbins, acting under Bridge Engineer Mr. George A. Casseday, and his successor, Mr. John A. Bohland. The contractors were the Barnett & Record Company, Minneapolis, Minnesota.[242]

Annex No. *1* is located directly to the east of the main workhouse. The two structures were connected by a series of horizontal conveyor belts intersecting with the longitudinal belts in Elevator *S*.

> The upper conveyor belts are 42 ins. wide and the lower belts 46 ins. wide. These belts are made of solid woven canvas with a thin rubber coating and are spliced with copper belt fasteners. The lower belts are driven by new 15-H.P. alternating current motors, while the upper belts are driven by eight 15-H.P. motors of an old type and one new 20-H.P. motor."

The rapid pace at which the annex was constructed caught the attention of industry insiders. An article in the *Engineering News-Record* reported the concrete walls were raised "… at an average rate of 30 in. in height per day of ten hours. During the latter part of the work a rate of 36 to 40 ins. per day was usually attained. Each inch of height required about 9 cu. yds of concrete for the whole group of bins."[243] When the

---

242 Ibid., 447.
243 Ibid., 446.

concrete work was completed, the exterior surfaces were coated with a cement and alum wash as a partial waterproofing and as a finish.

* * *

Since its inception as a grain shipment port, the elevators have been under the control of, or worked with, three major railroads for switching cars in and out of the elevators—Jay Cooke's Northern Pacific, James Hill's Great Northern, and the Chicago, St. Paul, Minneapolis & Omaha Railway. In 1909, that changed with the arrival in the port of the Soo Line for its first full season. The Soo Line recently purchased the Wisconsin Central Railway in 1908 and was making great strides into grain country. In a history of the Soo Line, authors Steve Glischinski and J. David Ingles write:

> Soo Line history dates to the Sept. 29, 1883, incorporation of the Minneapolis, St. Paul & Atlantic. It was the brainchild of Minneapolis milling interests anxious to find a way to ship their products east without going through the expensive and congested Chicago terminal. The millers' answer was a direct 500-mile line from Minneapolis to a CP connection at Sault Ste. Marie, Ontario.

The Wisconsin Central Railway was incorporated Feb. 4, 1871. The railroad reached Ashland in 1877, Chicago two years later, and eventually Superior in 1908. The railroad's first year of shipping to Superior and Duluth got off to an auspicious beginning with a bumper crop. "The Soo road will be hauling wheat into Duluth this fall, and already preparations are being made. All along the Soo line throughout North Dakota reports indicated that there is an unusually heavy yield of wheat. Much of this wheat will find its way to the Head of the Lakes,"[244] contributed the *Duluth Evening Herald* in its coverage of the grain prospects for late summer and fall.

The entrance of the Soo Line into the wheat fields brought some heat as the Northern Pacific and Great Northern levied a track

---

[244] "Ready for Bumper Crop," *Duluth Evening Herald,* July 12, 1909.

crossing fee of one dollar per crossing. Between the two, the Soo would have to cross over an estimated twenty-eight tracks. Tariffs for both grain and coal were established for the Soo Line at Duluth. The Northern Pacific would handle all switching into the elevators. One of the behind-the-scenes but not secret caveats about the Soo Line was that its majority owner was the Canadian Pacific Railway.

While lawyers were arguing over the legality of the crossing tariff, nineteen carloads of steel rail arrived via the Wisconsin Central, with work commencing around June 1. There was already tension when the Soo Line sent a branch line down from Manitoba into North Dakota to connect with the Soo Line, giving the Canadian Pacific a direct route to ship to Minneapolis from Brandon, Manitoba. The line was to run "between the two Hill lines which now run into Manitoba, one ending at Brandon and the other at Portage La Prairie," came the news out of Winnipeg.

Speculation ran swiftly in Duluth about whether the Canadian Pacific would use the rail connection with the Soo Line to ship through Duluth, with the possibility it would build a new elevator in the port. The rumors were quashed in early June when William Whyte, second vice president of the Canadian Pacific, denied that the Canadian Pacific would use the cut-off at Thief River Falls to the Soo Line rails to Duluth. "The Canadian Pacific has no intention of erecting elevators at Duluth." The railroad would continue using the terminals at Fort William.[245] Whyte conceded that if the lines from Winnipeg to Fort William were congested, he'd consider the option of shipping directly to Duluth.

At the end of October, Soo Line track crews finished laying new switching tracks to two of the three big elevators in Duluth with the Capitol elevator expected in another week. "It is believed that the Soo will be hauling wheat some time the present week to elevators *E* and *H* of the Consolidated line, and to the Peavey elevator."[246] The arrival of the Soo Line at Duluth was greeted with enthusiasm.

---

245 "Says no elevators will be built here," *Duluth Evening Herald*, June 10, 1909.

246 "Haul wheat this week," *Duluth Evening Herald*, October 25, 1909.

# 10
# 1910–1920: A Decade of Growth

Three years into the 1910s decade, the Consolidated Elevator Company made another addition to its Elevator *D* complex with twenty-one concrete tanks connected to its 1909 annex. The 101-foot-high tanks added an additional 870,000 bushels of storage capacity to the elevator system.

Since the completion of the Duluth Terminal Elevator, the Peavey operation had remained relatively unchanged until 1914, when Peavey sold its Belt Line Elevator to rival Cargill. Several years after the completion of its Duluth workhouse, the Peavey Company began seeking a buyer for its Belt Line Elevator in Superior. The stockholders of the company voted not to renew the annual lease agreement with the Globe Elevator Company, authorizing the plant manager to begin searching for an interested party.[247]

The Cargills, owners of the Superior Terminal Elevator Company, became the primary focus of the search. Negotiations started, and in January 1914, an agreement was reached on the sale of the elevator system.[248] The Cargill Elevator Company itself was

---

247 Peavey Company: Belt Line Elevator Company minute books: Director's Meeting, June 10, 1907, p 89. (MHS Archives 145.K.20.3).

248 Peavey Company: Belt Line Elevator Company, minute books, Stockholders' Special Meeting, January 29, 1914, p. 181; and Directors' Meeting, July 10, 1914, p. 191–193 (MHS Archives, 145.K.20.3).

undergoing some internal restructuring at the time in response to debts it had incurred. Despite this financial trouble, its subsidiary, the Superior Terminal Elevator Company, purchased the Belt Line elevators for a price of $250,000.[249]

Ironically, a short time later, on April 25, 1914, the Belt Line Elevator *M* was heavily damaged by fire discovered shortly after midnight by the night watchman. The arrival of the fire department shortly afterward made no difference in the outcome. By morning, Elevator *M* was a total loss.[250]

An interesting story has survived about the origins of the fire at Elevator *M*. Jay Van Horn, former superintendent at *M*, recalled the version the old timers told him:

> There was a weigher and a foreman that worked for Peavey and they were in cahoots with a train crew that worked on the Northern Pacific railroad. Every once in a while, to make a little extra money, they'd go down there in the middle of the night and they'd take a boxcar and they'd load it up with grain. They'd get the railroad crew to help them switch it over to a little feed mill that was east of Daisy Mill. They'll sell that grain to this feed mill. They'd evidently been doing this for a period of time, and when Peavey sold to Cargill these guys knew that when Cargill weighed up to see what they'd have to settle on, there'd be a shortage of some kind. So their only out was to burn the elevator down. And it burned down the night before Cargill was to take possession.[251]

Peavey and Cargill reportedly struck a deal to conclude the sale after the fire. Peavey agreed to share the insurance money if Cargill

---

249 Wayne Broehl, Jr., *Cargill: Trading the World's Grain* (Hanover: University Press of New England, 1992), 192.
250 "Big Elevator is Destroyed," *Duluth Herald*, April 27, 1914.
251 Jay Van Horn, interview with author, Superior, 1994.

agreed to take the property and rebuild on the site. Cargill officials estimated the loss at about $150,000. The F. H. Peavey Company still owned the grain stored at the elevator. It estimated a loss of $250,000. Both the elevator and its contents were fully insured.[252]

The rebuilding of Elevator *M* began almost immediately. "The house is to be rebuilt of wood for the reason that there is not sufficient time to erect one of fireproof construction between now and next fall," noted a spokesman for the project. The only change to the design was that Cargill put in an overhead conveyor between *M* and its annex instead of feeding the annex through a tunnel. "It will be modern in every particular and will have a capacity of unloading eighty cars of grain a day, and with their other house it will afford the Cargill interests a total holding capacity of 160 cars daily, and a total storage capacity of nearly 4,500,000 bushes at the Head of the Lakes."[253] Barnett & Record were hired as general contractors. The rebuilt Elevator *M* opened the first week of October 1914.

\* \* \*

In 1917, the Chicago, St. Paul, Minneapolis and Omaha Railroad sold the Itasca elevator operation to Julius Barnes. The Itasca Elevator Company reincorporated at this time under the leadership of Barnes. Enrollment at the Duluth Board of Trade listed the elevator capacity as 1,250,000 bushels.

James M. Jenks, president of the elevator at the time of the sale, continued in that role under the new ownership. Jenks was born in New York in 1850 but spent his formative years living in Chicago. He remained in the role until his death in 1925.[254]

Julius Howland Barnes was born in Little Rock, Arkansas, and was ten years old when his family moved to Duluth in 1883. "Barnes' life was characterized by remarkable achievement, extraordinary generosity, exemplary public service and bad luck," wrote a biographer, adding:

---

252 "Big Elevator is Destroyed," *Duluth Herald*, April 27, 1914.
253 "Elevator Will Be Rebuilt," *Duluth Herald*, May 14, 1914.
254 "Omaha Busy Too," *Superior Telegram*, August 8, 1908.

Barnes dropped out of high school (10th Grade) after only two months (his father died in 1890) and went to work as an office boy for the Ames-Brooks grain trading firm (headed by Ward Ames, Sr.). He eventually became wealthy on the trading floor of the Duluth Board of Trade. He was a partner or sole owner of many business enterprises. Barnes-Ames Company (with Ward Ames, Jr.) was at one time the largest grain exporter in the world, operating elevators and ships with offices in Duluth, New York, and Winnipeg.[255]

\* \* \*

Activity slowly returned to the Hughitt Avenue slip area of Superior following the great fire of 1907. The flour milling companies that operated there did not rebuild, although some continued holding lease agreements on their parcels. In 1908, the American Milling Company of Peoria, Illinois, purchased property along the slip, operating a stock feed processing operation in conjunction with the Marsden Company.[256]

**Spencer Kellogg headhouse, built in 1912. The two flax storage tanks at the left were known as the "Republics."** Photo: Lake Superior Maritime Collections, UW-Superior.

---

255 Mike Zionis, "Notes on Julius Barnes," https://bit.ly/48W0jlX.

256 Note: Marsden Company was an East Coast-based feed processing company involved in the international agricultural feed products industry, processing corn stalk into cattle food, among many other uses. The company was absorbed into the American Milling Company when they became financially distressed.

In 1912, American Milling converted the site to process linseed oil, constructing a wood-frame, iron-clad structure on a reinforced concrete foundation for an estimated $30,000. It housed thirty-three wood-cribbed bins with a total capacity of 134,535 bushels. A small brick dryer building stood along the north side of the elevator, and further up at the northern end of the slip, a one-story wood-frame warehouse was erected. Directly west of the elevator were two 76,680-bushel iron tanks (the Republics) for flax screenings, typically imported via ship from Port Arthur, Ontario. The tanks were connected to the elevator via an elevated conveyor mounted atop steel-frame trusses. Vessels were unloaded with a marine leg on the side of the elevator.[257]

The mill continued operation until 1915, when it closed and stood dormant but intact. In 1917, an agreement was made with Spencer Kellogg & Sons, Inc. of Buffalo, New York, to purchase the site. The property was transferred for a monetary consideration of $175,000. Spencer Kellogg was in the linseed oil business at Superior, and its takeover of the American Milling property did not at the time directly change the face of the grain export business in the port.[258]

\* \* \*

Across the bay in Duluth, a major change took place in 1916 with an addition to the Capitol Elevator system. The McCarthy's were finding it hard to compete with the small, outdated milling structures they had started with. To remain in business, expansion was a necessity. As early as 1901, prior to the formation of the Capitol Elevator Company, the McCarthy brothers considered building a 400,000-bushel steel elevator, along with a 1.6 million-bushel steel annex on Rice's Point[259], but those plans never came to fruition.

---

[257] Note: The two storage tanks were commonly referred to as "The Republics" as late as the 1980s by personnel at CHS, according to Dick Carlson, Terminal Manager. This refers to the Grand Republic Mill, which likely built the two silos as part of their flour mill.

[258] "Oil Mill Purchase Involves $175,000," *Superior Telegram*, January 5, 1917.

[259] "Erect New Steel Elevator," *Minneapolis Star Tribune*, September 22, 1901.

A combination concrete workhouse and concrete storage was erected, adding an additional 1,750,000 bushels to the Capitol system. The new headhouse was called Capitol Elevator No. 6, following the numbering sequence of the two wooden elevators. The annex was named Capitol No. 7. The state weighmaster reported that Cap 6 received its first load of grain on January 2, 1917.[260]

This new workhouse and annex were located on the east side of the pier, with the old Imperial Mill sandwiched between it and the wooden elevators. Included was a rail car dumping shed and a steam power plant.

**Capitol Elevator *6* and annex, built in 1916, and 1928 era annex at end.**
Photo: Lake Superior Maritime Collections, UW-Superior.

On the next slip over, across the coal dock from Capitol, the last major expansion for the Consolidated Elevator Company closed

---

260 Railroad and Warehouse Commission: Grain Inspection, *1917 Annual Report*: 32nd Annual Reports for the Year Ending 8/31/1917 (MNS Archives, 120.I.3.7B).

out the decade. Consolidated announced plans in May 1919 to erect a 1.25-million-bushel annex to Elevator *H*. The new Elevator *I*, consisting of a headhouse and a series of cylindrical concrete storage silos, would cost an estimated $250,000.[261] The machinery for the elevator was placed in a 138,000-bushel headhouse facing the wood-framed Elevator *H*.

The contractor was Barnett & Record. The firm's two most recent elevators in the harbor were made of ceramic tiles. For Consolidated, Elevator *I* would be made of concrete, the material now recognized as the dominant fireproof material on the market. Delays in completing the elevator pushed its opening back to November.

By the end of the decade, the Duluth grain trade had changed considerably. The Federal Trade Commission published Volume III of its report on the grain trade in December 1921, providing a good summary of the trade at Duluth from its inception until 1897 "or thereabouts..."[262] [See the Appendix for more information.]

The first decades of the century saw the transition from wood-framed elevators to experimentation in construction materials ranging from ceramic tiles to concrete, then to steel. The elevator operators placed a premium on having fireproof structures and paid a hefty price for the wooden elevators of the past after several major fires occurred along the waterfront. Despite these setbacks, Duluth-Superior continued growing as a grain export destination for commodities from the Upper Midwest farms of Minnesota, the Red River Valley and North Dakota.

---

261 "Consolidated to Build Big Annex," *Duluth Herald*, April 9, 1919.

262 U. S. Government. Report of the Federal Trade Commission on The Grain Trade, Vol. III Terminal Grain Marketing. December 21, 1921. Minneapolis Public Library, FT1.2: G7622 Vol 3.

# 11
# The 1920s: The Occident Terminal Sets the Standard

As the end of the 1920 shipping season drew to a close, the Twin Ports elevators geared up for the usual late-season rush. Train cars were unloading the grain from the final harvest as quickly as the elevators could load it back onto lake boats.

In Superior, the Itasca Elevator had operated a relatively uneventful existence in the first twenty years. An event at the start of the 1920s threatened to put an end to its short life. The brush with disaster occurred in October 1920 when a conveyor belt broke and cut an electrical line, triggering a grain dust explosion that rocked the elevator. A fire quickly built inside the main workhouse. Several workers unloading cars in the building were temporarily trapped by the flames and smoke but worked their way to safety.

Unlike the results of many past Twin Ports elevator fires, the conclusion to this one was good. The fast response by workers at the elevator was credited with saving the structure. In fact, the fire was well under control by the time the fire department arrived on the scene. The monetary loss was listed as three thousand dollars, well under the estimated million-dollar worth of the elevator.[263]

\* \* \*

---

263 "Flames Peril Big Elevator," *Superior Evening Telegram*, October 6, 1920.

## The Grain Terminal Elevators of Duluth-Superior

The decade of the 1920s saw some of the largest volumes of grain ever handled in the Twin Ports. By mid-decade, cargo records were set that would take nearly a half-century to break. A contributing factor in the setting of these tonnage marks was the building of another new elevator at Duluth in 1923.

Early photo of the Occident Terminal and the water-lot acreage it was built on. Photo: Lake Superior Maritime Collections, UW-Superior.

The Occident Terminal Elevator at Duluth was built and operated by the Occident Elevator Company, a division of the Minneapolis-based Russell-Miller Milling Company. The Russell-Miller Milling Company was founded in North Dakota. The scope of its operations grew with the development of the Dakota wheat fields. In 1907, the company shifted its base of operations to Minneapolis. During this period, the Occident Elevator Company was incorporated with an operating capital of fifty thousand dollars, authorized by the Russell-Miller organization.[264] William F. P. Converse was the local manager and Charles L. Bostwick was assistant treasurer.

---

264 Herman Steen, *Flour Milling in America* (T. S. Denison & Co., 1963).

William "Bud" Freeman Converse was involved in the Minneapolis grain trade many years before assuming the job as manager of the Occident Terminal. He came to Duluth in 1923 to manage the Occident, but only three years into his tenure, he passed away unexpectedly just shy of his forty-eighth birthday. "Mr. Converse was active in the grain marketing industry in Minneapolis for many years. He was associated with Hallet & Carey for a considerable time and took part in the war time of the northwest grain industry," memorialized the Minneapolis *Star Tribune* years later.[265]

As a grain commission agent for Hallett and Carey, Converse was credited with being "the largest exclusive handler of durum wheat in America."[266] He was known as an excellent horseman and led an adventurous life from living along the Rio Grande in southwest Texas during the reign of Poncho Villa to dogsledding over four hundred miles across "the frozen wastes of Northern Canada" with Gabriel Campell, brother of Canadian "folk hero" musher Albert Campell[267] while employed as a prospector for an iron mining concern.

The Duluth elevator became the link in the Russell-Miller operations, receiving grain in boxcars sent from any number of their Red River Valley line elevators before sending it onward via ship loaded at Duluth to the American Elevator in Buffalo. The Buffalo elevator was constructed about the same time as the Duluth site.

The Occident Terminal Elevator was constructed on a site across from the Northwestern Fuel Company dock on Rice's Point. The location was considered a "water lot," which required a tremendous amount of preparation before building could begin. An average depth of twenty feet of water covered the site. An enclosing

---

265 William F. Converse, "Grain Man Is Dead," *Minneapolis Star Tribune*, April 11, 1926.

266 "Converse Knew Judge Would Win," *Fargo Forum and Daily Republican*, July 26, 1917, 8.

267 "Albert Campell (dogsled racer)," Wikipedia, October 13, 2023, https://bit.ly/48Td6FF.

barrier was built using 6,200 pilings covered with 140,000 cubic yards of fill before the foundation could begin.[268]

The workhouse for the elevator was 184 feet 6 inches high, 110 feet 6 inches long and 78 feet 6 inches wide with a capacity of 373,000 bushels, containing "35 circular bins and 43 interstice bins. The storage proper is made up of 34 circular bins and 82 smaller ones and covers an area of 82x497 feet."[269] Three shipping spouts were located on the dock side for transferring grain to waiting vessels. Each spout could load ships at a rate of twenty thousand bushels per hour.

The storage annex consisted of 135 concrete tanks with an overall capacity of 2,140,000 bushels. An unloading "marine leg," located midway along the storage annex, had an intake capacity of fifteen thousand bushels per hour. The first vessel was unloaded on December 10, 1923, to inaugurate the new elevator.[270]

The 2.5-million-bushel elevator was built by the Barnett & Record Company. At the time of its completion, the Occident Terminal Elevator became the largest single elevator ever built in the Twin Ports. The main workhouse and the storage tanks were all built of reinforced concrete. The use of concrete as a material in elevator construction had become dominant by this time, even though Barnett & Record were pioneers in the use of ceramic tile. An innovative feature was the electrical plant that provided power to the building. The huge steam power plants used at other elevators were being replaced with the more efficient electrical substations.[271]

> The elevator is operated by electricity throughout, and separate motors are used for driving the various elevator legs, conveyors, cleaners, power shovel and car

---

268 Charles S. Clark, "Occident Terminal Elevator at Duluth, Minnesota," In *Grain Elevators of North America*. Chicago: *Grain Dealers Journal* (1942): 180–183.

269 "Occident Terminal Elevator," *The Northwestern Miller* 137, no. 5 (January 30, 1924): 475.

270 "New $1,000,000 Elevator Opened Here: Stores 2,500,000 Bushels of Grain," *Duluth Herald*, January 11, 1924.

271 Ibid.

pullers. There are two receiving elevator legs, three shipping legs, three cleaner legs and one screening leg. Five receiving scales are used with garners, each with a capacity of 2,000 bus. There are two spouts for car loading and three for vessel loading, the latter leading from six vessel shipping bins. The elevator is equipped with a marine leg with a rated capacity of 15,000 bushel per hour for unloading the grain from vessels. It is also equipped with Monitor grain cleaners and Carter disc separators.

## 12
## 1925–1935: A Time for Expansion

The period from the mid-twenties to the mid-thirties could be classified as an era of plant expansion. This ten-year stretch was launched by record-setting volumes of grain handled on both sides of the port. These increased levels initiated a level of expansion affecting nearly every grain operation in the Twin Ports.

The first of several stages of expansion began in 1926 at Cargill's Elevator *M*. A total of twenty-one concrete silos were built for Cargill by the Barnett & Record Company. The new silos were located between the main workhouse and the storage annex, increasing the capacity of Elevator *M* by 725,000 bushels. This marked the first major work on the elevator since the rebuilding of the workhouse in 1914.[272] Jay Van Horn talks of the changes this way:

> They shut the elevator down for a season. They took the metal gallery and moved that over to Elevator *K*, and put that up between the workhouse and the annex over at *K*. Then they built the new concrete tanks at *M* and they had one belt that could go out and hit that belt that was in the wood annex and fill the wood annex also.

---

272 *Grain Dealers Journal* (May 25, 1936): 604.

The steamer *S. H. Robbins* takes a load of wheat at Cargill's Elevator *M*. The concrete annex was erected in 1926.
Photo: Copyright Cargill, Incorporated. Used with permission.

During the same year, the Spencer Kellogg Company of Buffalo announced plans to expand its linseed oil plant in Superior with the construction of ten new concrete tanks. The Fegles Construction Company of Minneapolis was hired for the project, which eventually expanded to fourteen total grain tanks along the Hughitt Avenue slip when completed.[273] Ten concrete grain tanks (Section *J*), ninety feet in height with a capacity of 25,000 bushels each, and four intermediate tanks, each with a 7,500-bushel capacity, were erected on the north side of the headhouse. On the south side of the headhouse, four 32,000-bushel flax seed tanks (Section *I*) were constructed, also of concrete, including one intermediate tank of 1,800 bushels. These four tanks were 84 feet in height.[274]

To keep up with the competition, the Itasca Elevator Company announced that it, too, would add to its elevator on Allouez Bay. Itasca contracted with Barnett & Record for a fifteen-tank expansion scheduled to begin on April 1, 1926. When completed, the concrete silos added an additional 567,000 bushels to its Superior plant.[275]

---

273 *Grain Dealers Journal* (January 25, 1926): 113.
274 Sanborn Fire Insurance Map, page 7, 1914, republished 1955, https://bit.ly/3TC5q6x.
275 *Grain Dealers Journal* (March 25, 1926): 358.

Two years after the Superior expansions, the Duluth-based Capitol Elevator Company added a 40-silo annex. The 100-foot-high concrete tanks became part of Capitol 7. Annex *A-3* added a capacity of 750,000 bushels, pushing the overall capacity at the Capitol system to the four-million-bushel mark by the end of the 1928 season.[276]

\* \* \*

During the addition to Capitol's operation at Duluth, the Great Northern embarked on erecting a second annex to Elevator *S*. Annex No. *2* was located to the north of Annex No. *1*, separated by forty feet. In the older wood-frame systems, a larger distance between buildings was maintained. The theory behind this was that in case of fire, the distance would lessen the likelihood of the fire spreading.

Annex No. *2* was 478 feet 4 inches in length, 86 feet wide and topped out at 110 feet in height. There were 135 bins with an additional 104 interstice bins, giving the annex a storage capacity of three million bushels, surpassing the overall capacity of many of the existing elevators in the harbor.[277]

On the opposite side of Superior, a second phase of expansion was underway at the Itasca Elevator. Excavation began in late July 1929 for an additional fifteen concrete silos to complement the fifteen built in 1926. When combined with the Itasca's existing plant, the new silos raised the elevator's capacity to over two million bushels.

The Barnett & Record Company was placed in charge of the construction in both Itasca expansions. The silos were 95 feet in height and 24 feet in diameter. Erection of the silos was accomplished using the slip-form method for raising concrete silos, the system developed by C. F. Haglin at the Peavey site a quarter of a century earlier.[278] Charles F. Haglin was an architect and engineer who gained renown

---

276 Marsh & McLennan: Fire Insurance Map, Capitol Elevator System, June 1954. Note: The first section of concrete tanks was now labelled as Annex *A2*, as part of Capitol 7.

277 ADM Company: Elevator Report: 1. Collection of Bill Hoffer.

278 "Workmen Getting Site Ready for New Grain Tanks," *Superior Evening Telegram*, July 19, 1929.

after moving to Minneapolis. He was involved in the first concrete storage silo built in St. Louis Park, Minnesota, for Frank Peavey.

On the Duluth side of the harbor, equally impressive and large capacity annexes were built onto both the Peavey and Occident terminal elevators. These additions would add another two million bushels each to their respective plant capacities. Construction on the annexes in Duluth began in 1930 and completed the same year.[279]

Phase three of the Great Northern Elevator S expansion took place in 1930 with the construction of Annex No. *3* directly north of the main workhouse. The Great Northern elevator system at Superior was recognized as the largest grain-handling system in the world. Storage capacity at Annex No. *3* was rated at just under 3 million bushels.[280]

\* \* \*

Reinforced concrete was the primary construction material for all the annexes. The universality of cement as a fireproofing agent was no longer questioned. Along with its relatively low cost and low maintenance, concrete became the material of choice for grain-handling firms and their contractors.

The movement of grain within the elevators had also undergone significant changes. Primary among them was the use of full-hopper bins in the annexes. The hoppers were designed to aid in the rapid and efficient discharge of grain from the bins. The tapered bottom of the silo simply allows gravity to empty the grain. Flat-bottomed silos usually required an auger of some sort to remove the grain, requiring electricity, manpower and maintenance. Once discharged to a conveyor system, grain could easily be moved anywhere in the house or annex. The conveyor systems were all operated with electric motors and designed to carry capacities, in some instances of 60,000 bushels per hour, to the shipping legs. These modern conveyor systems greatly increased the efficiency

---

279 Clark, "Peavey Annex at Duluth" and "Elevator Work Progressing Rapidly," *Duluth News Tribune*, July 25, 1930.

280 ADM Company: Elevator Report: 1. Collection of Bill Hoffer.

of the elevators and spared the companies the higher labor costs associated with belt maintenance.

The last annex built during this expansion era was for Spencer Kellogg & Sons. For the Buffalo-based company, it was a significant move, representing a shift away from their oil processing business at Superior to a more traditional grain handling enterprise. By 1933, its Superior linseed oil-crushing plant had been idle for about three years. The fourteen existing storage tanks added in 1927 were now being used to store wheat. Included in the proposed build-up of the Spencer Kellogg mill were twenty-one new storage silos designed to load vessels on the water side and rail cars on the track side.

The Barnett & Record Company completed the pouring of concrete for the new bins in mid-June 1934. When completed, the new tanks (Section *H*) added approximately a half-million bushels to the Spencer Kellogg site.[281] The tanks were 110 feet high with a capacity of 500,000 bushels. In 1939, a new concrete headhouse was added onto the south side of these grain tanks.

The Spencer Kellogg addition marked the end of expansion for the grain business at the Twin Ports for several years. The Globe Elevator at Superior and the Consolidated Company in Duluth were the only elevator systems that did not expand their storage capacities. Overall elevator capacity between the two cities had increased from 38,825,000 in 1925 to 50,875,000 bushels by the end of 1933, according to the Duluth Board of Trade's annual reports.[282]

\* \* \*

Over the past decade, the expansion that had been so prominent gave way to a period of change encompassing nearly every aspect of the grain business, from ownership and operation to the physical elevators themselves. The first major change took place at the beginning of the decade amidst the building boom. The

---

281 "Contract Let for Elevator," Spencer Kellogg & Sons archives, F3, Box 25: Dec. 22, 1933, Buffalo & Erie County Historical Society.
282 Duluth Board of Trade, *Annual Report*, December 31, 1933.

second phase of expansion at the Itasca Elevator was completed in time to see a change in ownership. In the summer of 1930, Julius Barnes retired from the grain business and began disposing of his holdings.

On July 31, 1930, the Superior newspaper announced the purchase of the Itasca Elevator Company by Cargill, including the grain in storage at the elevator.[283] A purchase price was not specified but believed to be somewhere around $1 million. At the time, Cargill had major plants in Minneapolis, Buffalo, and Omaha, as well as their Superior sites. The acquisition of the Itasca Elevator gave Cargill ownership of over half of Superior's export terminals. It was noted in the Cargill history by Wayne Broehl, Jr., that the Itasca acquisition was somewhat unusual for Cargill.

> **Cargill wanted it, but the restrictions in the company's certificate of incorporation relating to the mortgaging of property while preferred stock was outstanding would have made direct purchase difficult. Thus, it was decided to establish a separate corporation, with the stock subscription to be offered to the holders of the Cargill Elevator common stock. The subscription price was $120 per share. Most, but not all, of the common stockholders accepted, and the 2.4-million-bushel terminal was added to Cargill's Duluth-Superior capacity, which now stood at 7.2 million.**[284]

Six years later, the Cargill Elevator Company was reorganized, bringing all of Cargill's various subsidiaries under one consolidated enterprise. Included in the reorganization were the recently acquired Itasca Corporation and the holdings of the Cargill Grain Company, which controlled the Superior Terminal Elevator and the former Belt

---

283 "Cargill Buys Itasca Elevator," *Superior Evening Telegram*, December 31, 1930.

284 Wayne G. Broehl Jr., *Cargill: Trading the World's Grain* (Hanover, New Hampshire: University Press of New England, 1992), 382.

Line Elevator. Effective November 30, 1936, all the Superior properties would operate under the business name Cargill, Incorporated.[285]

\* \* \*

In Duluth, the Consolidated Elevator Company, as noted, was the only organization that had not made a major expansion in recent years. Consolidated struggled during the Depression and did not participate in the growth its neighbors experienced. Aside from the new concrete Elevator *I* and the rebuilt Elevator *D*, made of tile, its older wood-framed buildings were showing their age.

In 1937, Consolidated razed Elevators *B* and *C*. These were the first structures built within the harbor for the Lake Superior Elevator Company in the early 1880s and the first to be removed without being destroyed by fire. The two elevators, built as part of the original deal with the Northern Pacific, had served well beyond their best years in the Duluth trade. Prior to demolition, *B* and *C* stood vacant for several years. Removal of the structures was a harbinger of things to come for the Consolidated organization.

\* \* \*

Concurrently, the Works Progress Administration (WPA) in Superior was placed in charge of the removal of two former flour mills as well as the Cargill Annex *N*. By the time of the 1936 demolition, the flour industry in the Twin Ports had greatly declined, leaving only two active mills in the port. The bricks salvaged from the Anchor and Listman Mills were used along with timbers from the Cargill annex to construct a municipal ballpark in Superior. Cargill Annex *N* had been built in 1893 as part of the Belt Line system and survived a fire in 1914 that destroyed the original workhouse.[286]

In West Superior, the end of another era was taking place at the Great Northern elevator. Since the opening of Elevator *A* in

---

285 "Reorganization of Cargill Companies: New Name, 'Cargill Incorporated,'" *Cargill News*, October 1936.

286 Harry E. Babcock, *WPA Accomplishments in Superior* (Superior, WI: Superior Regional Center, 1939).

1886, the grain commission firm of A. D. Thomson and Company operated the elevators for the Great Northern.

Alexander Douglas Thomson was born in Scotland in 1855 before emigrating to Montreal, where he was engaged in the grain business with his brother. He next moved to Duluth around 1887, where he became a prominent member of the grain community with various iterations of the firm A. D. Thomson and Company, including a partnership with Charles Pillsbury. He was a close friend of James J. Hill, whose elevator he managed at Superior.

This long and successful relationship ended with the transfer of operations to The Archer-Daniels-Midland Company. ADM embarked on a major expansion of its grain handling business with the management of the Superior elevators as well as a site on the West Coast in Vancouver, Washington. It was the beginning of a relationship that would last for many years.

ADM took control of Superior's largest grain elevator system in 1937, inheriting a handling capacity for the elevator rated as the largest in the world and offering ship and train loading capability for 12,500,000 bushels. The physical plant at Superior consisted of a unique combination of concrete, steel and wood-frame construction.[287]

The decade of the 1930s closed with the formation of a new cooperative movement that would quickly change the face of the elevator business at Duluth-Superior, as well as across the country. The idea of a farm cooperative was not a new one. As early as the 1880s, Northwest growers had been trying to find an avenue in which they could fight against perceived injustices brought about by the controlling grain merchants.

In 1907, farmers organized a cooperative in St. Paul called the Equity Cooperative Exchange. They intended to use this as a vehicle to control the sale of their grain on the market. The Exchange lasted sixteen years before collapsing in 1923.[288]

---

[287] Marion Cross, *From Land, Sea and Test Tube: The Story of A.D.M. Company* (Minneapolis: Archer-Daniels-Midland Company, 1957), 47.

[288] Clifford E. Clark Jr., *Minnesota In a Century of Change* (St. Paul: MHS Press, 1989), 269–270.

The decline of the Equity Exchange was popularly attributed to unscrupulous allegations and tactics sponsored by officers of the Minneapolis Grain Exchange to prevent the cooperative from buying and selling grain on the open market. Federal courts eventually ruled on the side of the cooperatives after hearings were opened by the Federal Trade Commission.[289]

Fifteen years later, in 1938, the farmers again had their chance. On June 1 of that year, the Farmers Union Grain Terminal Association incorporated with an operating capital of $30,000.[290] In the FUGTA, the farmers were direct partners in the ag business economy with direct access to trading on the commodity exchanges. The Board of Directors of the FUGTA authorized the building of a new elevator at Superior adjacent to the Spencer-Kellogg property. It was located on land formerly occupied by the Superior Manufacturing Company.

---

289 Ibid., 269.
290 Farmers Union Grain Terminal Association, *1940 Annual Report*, collection of Harvest States Cooperatives.

# 13
# 1940–1950: The Farmers Union Grain Terminal Association

Along the Tower Avenue slip, construction commenced in March 1941 for the three-million-bushel Farmers Union Grain Terminal elevator, which had an estimated price tag of over $233,000. Over 500 workers were employed, laboring in shifts twenty-four hours per day toward the scheduled October completion.[291] Before completion of the headhouse for the elevator, a third section was added to the plans, increasing the expected capacity to 4.5 million bushels. The headhouse was a record 265 feet in height, the tallest in the world.

Two ten-tank sections were erected on the north side of the main headhouse on the Tower Avenue slip. Sections *A* and *B* had a total capacity of 3,008,000 bushels. To the south of the headhouse, Section *C* consisted of twelve concrete tanks with a capacity of 1,103,000 bushels. The design of the silos is such that where the round bins meet, the interstice space between, also known as a "star bin," which iss also filled with grain. The Farmers Union Grain Terminal Association was very proud of its new elevator, which graced the cover of its 1941 annual report. The completed facility was valued at $1,598,928 according to the cooperative's annual report.[292]

---

291 "City Boasts Tallest Elevator In World," *Superior Evening Telegram*, March 26, 1941.

292 Farmers Union Grain Terminal Association, *1941 Annual Report*, collection of Harvest States Cooperatives.

**Construction photo showing headhouse and footprint for concrete silos, July 1941.** Photo: author's collection, courtesy of Farmers Union Grain Terminal Association.

As construction continued along the Tower slip to the west, the working life of the Globe Elevator Company came to an end. At a meeting on July 15, the board of directors led by Fred B. Wells voted to liquidate all property and assets to the stockholders effective at the end of July. The property was duly distributed to the F. H. Peavey Company. A final September meeting by the board adjourned the Globe Elevator Company.[293] Globe had reincorporated under Minnesota laws in November 1915. Its predecessor, the Duluth Elevator Company, was dissolved in August 1915 as part of a reorganization by Peavey centered around the Monarch Elevator Company.[294]

Globe would now be managed and operated by the Globe Elevator Division of the F. H. Peavey Company. The elevator would see the arrival of the diamond logo with the letters PV painted on

---

293 Director's Meeting, F. B. Wells presiding... to adjourn Globe Elevator Company shareholders. September 18, 1941. (MHS Archives, Peavey Company 145.K20.11, Bob 33. Pp. 169–171 and 177–179).

294 Peavey Company: Globe Elevator Company minute books, pp. 203–215. Directors Meeting, August 16, 1915. (MHS Archives, 145.K.20.10).

the outside walls. Over time, it became simply known as the Peavey Globe Elevator.

Construction of the Farmers Union elevator culminated on May 11, 1942, when the whaleback steamer *South Park* entered the Tower slip to take the first load of grain. Directors and dignitaries from the FUGTA were on hand to welcome the boat. The *South Park* loaded 45,000 bushels of durum wheat before departing for Buffalo. The *South Park*, initially named *Meteor*, was built in Superior in 1892 by the American Steel and Barge Company. The *Meteor* currently resides in Superior as a museum ship.

The 1942 shipping season operated at full tilt despite the entrance of the United States into World War II. The bins were filled, and the grain moved down the lake at a steady pace. The Farmers Union was a welcome addition after the lean years of the Great Depression.

\* \* \*

As the Farmers Union celebrated the start of its new business, the Great Northern elevators, under the guidance of the Archer-Daniels-Midland Company, were sizing up the loss of Elevator X the previous year.

January 10, 1942, proved to be more than just another subzero day along the waterfront. The negative ten-degree weather played havoc on the machinery at the elevators. Nothing wanted to work in those temperatures.

The fire started a little past midnight at X. Workers investigating a broken conveyor belt in the elevator's upper story smelled smoke and notified the fire department. As employees desperately sought the source of the fire, a grain dust explosion rocked the elevator. The force of the blast lifted the roof twenty feet into the air, turning the fire into an inferno. The blast occurred just as Superior firemen were entering the building. Two elevator employees on the 110-foot-high upper level were blown out of the building. The blast could be felt several miles away, rattling dishes and doors.

Remarkably, no one was killed, although there were numerous injuries. The cause of the broken belt that started the fire was blamed on a combination of static and friction due to the extremely cold weather. Even so, the fire was investigated by the FBI because of the possibility of sabotage during the war. The loss of the elevator and contents was estimated at more than 2 million dollars.[295]

Superior fire officials were fortunate that a strong southwest wind prevented the fire from spreading across the harbor as the 1907 fire had. Instead, the wind spread the embers harmlessly onto the ice in the bay. The conveyor connecting Elevator *S* with *X* was cut to prevent the fire from spreading to the steel house.

At the time of the fire, ADM officials admitted that plans had been discussed between the railroad and ADM to build a new elevator at Superior but had been discarded due to a lack of available space. After the January fire, the issue of available space became a moot point.

On April 20, 1942, the *Superior Evening Telegram* marked the 100th day since the start of the fire with an article on the grain pile that continued to burn since the January blaze. Activities to salvage the remaining grain were contracted to private parties while the fire department maintained a water line on the smoldering grain pile. Residents of Superior had reportedly grown somewhat accustomed to the stench of the burnt grain.[296] It was also tough to sell for feed because it was believed that if a farmer bought burnt grain and fed it to his chickens, the eggs would often retain the smokey taste.

\* \* \*

The roller coaster ride of the Twin Ports grain industry continued during the following two years. The board of the Consolidated Elevator Company of Duluth voted in July 1943 to sell the company to Twin Cities-based General Mills, Inc. Included in the sale were all Consolidated elevators and storage facilities at Duluth. The site where Elevator *D* was located was owned by the Northern Pacific,

---

295 "$2,250,000 Blast, Fire Destroy Great Northern Elevator 'X,'" *Superior Evening Telegram*, January 10, 1942.

296 "100 Days Old, Elevator X Fire Still Burns-Strong!" *Superior Evening Telegram*, April 20, 1942.

with the value of its properties placed at $672,446. General Mills hired George Barnum, owner of Barnum Grain Company, to operate its new Duluth Elevator Division. Cecil Blair and many other Consolidated employees were retained by General Mills.[297]

Barnum was born in Buffalo, New York, and like many of his era, he was a veteran of the Civil War. He came to Duluth in 1867 "as a member of the first survey party. He first was involved in the railroad and lake shipping industries before joining the grain trade as an incorporator of the Duluth Board of Trade and owner of the Barnum Grain Co."[298] The town of Barnum, Minnesota, is named in his honor.

In May 1944, almost a year after the acquisition of the Consolidated holdings, General Mills sold most of the elevators to the Norris Grain Company of Chicago. General Mills retained Elevator D and Annex G, renaming them A and B, respectively. General Mills planned to use the 3,750,000-bushel facility to service its Eastern, Central and Purity Oats divisions as well as for the general handling of wheat and other grains.[299] Some speculated that Norris purchased the Duluth elevators in desperation in the aftermath of the fire at the Rosenbaum and Norris elevators in Chicago in May 1943, but there is no direct evidence to corroborate this.

The sale of the Consolidated Elevator Company was the end of Duluth-owned elevator systems operating at the Twin Ports. The loss continued a slowly evolving shift from small, independent grain companies to larger, commodity-diverse agricultural corporations.

*\*\**

James Norris, a Canadian grain merchant, founded The Norris Grain Company. His father was reportedly a grain merchant as

---

[297] "Mill City Firm Purchases Duluth Elevator Concern," *Duluth News Tribune*, July 9, 1943.

[298] "George Grenville Barnum II," Veteran's Memorial Hall, http://www.vetshall.org/stories/civil-war/george-barnum

[299] "New Division Formed at Duluth," *The Modern Millwheel* (General Mills, December 1944), 2.

well. Following college, Norris began working in the grain export business in 1895 at the firm of Hugh McLennon of Montreal. In 1898, Norris emigrated to the United States, arriving in Chicago to work for Richardson & Company. "During 1904–05 he was with Harris, Scotten & Co., Chicago, and in the latter year organized the grain merchandising firm of Norris & Co. In 1909 the firm was incorporated under the laws of Illinois, and in 1914 its name was changed to the Norris Grain Co."

**Norris Grain Company Elevators *I*, *H*, and *E*. Elevator *I*, was built of concrete in 1919.** Photo: Copyright Cargill, Incorporated. Used with permission.

James Dougan Norris, heir to the Norris Grain Company, joined his father's grain firm in Chicago in 1928 and became a member of the Chicago Board of Trade. A business association formed in 1932 between Canadian shipping agent Gordon Leitch, and Norris gave the Norris Grain Company access to a fleet of lake carriers to complement the grain business. This association became the storied Canadian fleet called the Upper Lakes Steamship Company. The steamer *James Norris* was launched in 1952, shortly after Norris passed away.

In addition to his grain interests, James Norris was heavily involved in sports, particularly boxing and hockey. His interests drew him to owning numerous sports arenas and the Detroit Red Wings hockey club. Norris was followed in the grain business by his sons, James Norris, Jr., and Bruce Norris, but it seems the Norris family's interests in the sporting world competed against their grain interests.[300]

At Duluth, the Norris Grain Company represented little more than a name change on the side of the elevators for the next fifteen years. The Chicago-based company turned the operation of its Duluth elevators over to Cecil Blair. Superintendent Blair had formerly been associated with Consolidated until its sale in 1943. He stayed on at *E, H* and *I* in the brief time General Mills owned them and was left to run the Norris interests pretty much as he saw fit.

In late August 1949, a fire inside a conveyor tunnel beneath one of the Norris Elevators got some brief notice, but the fire was contained and put out quickly. The structure had been put up in 1888 and was valued at $100,000, Blair told reporters.[301]

Cecil Charles Blair was from Decatur, Illinois. He arrived in Duluth in 1919, where he became active in the grain industry. Blair was "an early member of the Grain Committee on National Affairs, which was set up in 1934 to administer a code for grain exchanges, and headed the wheat export section of the federal surplus commodity corporation in Washington prior to World War II."[302] Blair was also a musician and contributed to the founding of the Duluth Symphony Orchestra.

\* \* \*

Four years after the fire that leveled the Great Northern's Elevator *X*, construction began on a replacement. The new Elevator *X* would be built on the site of the previous elevator with an estimated

---

300 *National Cyclopedia of American Biography*, 466.
301 "Damage $50,000 In Elevator Fires," *Winona Republican-Herald*, August 30, 1949.
302 "Cecil Charles Blair," *Minneapolis Star*, December 1, 1960.

capacity of 1.5 million bushels. The James Stewart Corporation, a noted Missouri elevator contractor, was hired by the Great Northern for the project. Preparation began in the fall of 1945 for the foundation. The biggest challenge would be an attempted winter pouring of concrete. This would be the first time pouring concrete in freezing weather had been attempted in the Twin Ports. The elevator would consist of two sections—a storage annex and the workhouse. Over 46,000 cubic feet of concrete were required for the elevator foundations.[303]

For the concrete to set properly, a steady 70-degree temperature would need to be maintained. The *Duluth News Tribune* reported that James Stewart's superintendent, Harry Zachau, planned to place steam coils beneath the stock piles. The steam coils would keep the sand and gravel 100 percent heated. A large tent was being prepared to cover the foundation's surface. Once the concrete was poured, the tent would be heated with steam radiation until the concrete cured.

The new Elevator X would have 36 bins, each 22 feet wide and 108 feet high, and expected to hold 1,348,000 bushels of grain. One of the elevator's modern features would be an automatic rail car dump similar to one installed at the Farmers Union. When operational, a train car could now be unloaded in about eight minutes, roughly one-fifth the time of conventional unloading systems.[304] The first hydraulic truck dump in the harbor was installed at Elevator M later that year.

Testimony in a lawsuit between the Great Northern and the United States provides an idea of the volume of business at the Great Northern during this time.[305]

---

303 "Big Elevator Concrete Job Is Unique," *Duluth News Tribune*, January 6, 1946.
304 "Mechanical Hand, Heart of New Grain Unloader," *St. Paul Pioneer Press*, January 11, 1948.
305 United States v. Great Northern Ry. Co., 103 F. Supp. 889 (W.D. Wis. 1952).

**The principal work in the Superior Yard is the handling of grain cars for Great Northern Railway Company's elevators "X" and "S", which are located at the northeast end of the Yard, as show on Exhibit 1. These elevators are operated as a unit and as such constitute the largest elevator in the United States. 25,857,254 bushels of grain (15,364 cars) in 1948 and 34,643,310 bushels of grain (19,356 cars) in 1949 came into the Superior Yard for unloading at these elevators. These elevators are "fast" elevators in respect to unloading grain from cars and loading grain onto boats for trans-shipment on the Great Lakes. During the peak movement in the fall of 1948, 5,765 cars were unloaded in the month of September at these elevators. Elevator "X" is equipped with an automatic car dumper which picks up loaded grain cars and tilts them in several directions dumping the grain into an open pit.**

\* \* \*

The announcement of the sale of the Capitol Elevator Company came on Halloween 1947. Walter McCarthy announced the sale of Capitol to Minneapolis-based International Milling Company. The signatures at the end of the sale document included Charles H. McCarthy, Louis A. McCarthy, John R. McCarthy, J. V. McCarthy, Hollis F. Graves and Walter R. McCarthy.[306]

Walter McCarthy was president at the time of the purchase. International Milling Company "completed purchase of outstanding stock of Capitol Elevator Company Dec. 19, 1947. (The purchase agreement was made up Oct. 31, 1957)."[307]

---

306 Sale agreement between Capitol Elevator and International Milling Co International Multifoods Corporation corporate records, Box 143.J.9.3 (B), Minnesota Historical Society, p. 11.

307 Minnesota Historical Society Archives 112.H.11.6F, Secretary of State: Index to Incorporations 1858 – 1906, Capitol Elevator Company, Book J3, p 145.

"The elevator was originally purchased in 1947 to meet the mounting requirements of grain for our eastern Great Lakes mills at Detroit, Buffalo, Baldwinsville and Cleveland," stated a transcript of a speech given by an International Milling executive to employees in the mid-sixties.[308]

For many years, International Milling relied heavily on the Capitol Elevator for the shipment of its grain. A close working relationship developed between the companies. A rapid expansion in International Millings' mills in Detroit and Buffalo, as well as other Eastern locations, were driving factors in the purchase of the Duluth elevator.[309] Hollis Graves, Sr., the lone Duluthian with interests in the company, served as the manager-owner's representative in Duluth, continuing the Graves' family link to the Capitol elevators.

Within a year or two of the sale, Robert "Bob" Beck, of Cromwell, Minnesota, began working at the International Milling elevator after graduating from high school. Beck would remain at the elevator another forty-two years before retiring as superintendent in 1989. His tenure at International Milling/Multifoods spanned all but the last few years of the firm's ownership of the elevator in Duluth.

\* \* \*

Buoyed by its success, the capacity of the Farmers Union Grain Terminal Association elevator in Superior could not keep pace with the growth of cooperatives. In a 1947 tenth-anniversary address to the cooperative's members, general manager Mark W. Thatcher set the table for the future, stating, "We have one of two choices we can make. We can try to stand still, be complacent and shrink, or we can determine to understand the problems that lie ahead of us and go beyond."[310] One of the problems Thatcher foresaw was the capacity

---

308 "The Role of International Milling in Duluth, Minn." Speech notes, Box 143.J.8.4 (F), International Multifoods Corporate Records, Minnesota History Center.

309 "Duluth Grain Elevator Sold," *Duluth News Tribune*, October 31, 1947.

310 FUGTA, *1947 Annual Report*, Collection of Harvest States Cooperatives.

to handle and store the growing volume of the cooperative's grain. "Immediately in the next few years we need to double the elevator capacity of the big Superior terminal."

In September 1940, two announcements were made regarding the future expansion at Superior. In Buffalo, New York, a special meeting of the Board of Directors of Spencer-Kellogg and Sons, Inc. was called to report on the negotiations underway to sell its Superior plant to the FUGTA of St. Paul. The Farmers Union made an offer of $800,000 for the property and its contents. The members of Spencer Kellogg voted in agreement to the sale at that price, and the deal was finalized in October, although Farmers Union began operations in the elevator earlier that summer.[311]

After negotiations were completed with Spencer Kellogg, Farmers Union officials announced plans for expansion along the Tower slip. The addition would extend the line of concrete silos south along the slip, on property once held by U. S. Gypsum and Morton Salt. Two sections consisting of thirty-three concrete tanks (Sections D and E) were built in 1950, adding a combined total of 2,206,000 bushels to the elevator's capacity.

The board also authorized the construction of additional concrete tanks continuing along a line south from the newly acquired Spencer Kellogg headhouse (Workhouse No. 3)[312] on the Hughitt Avenue slip. The overall increase in capacity for the additions would be 5,700,000 bushels. The firm of McKenzie, Hague Company of Minneapolis were again hired as general contractors. The two-year project, scheduled to be completed in August 1951, would give the Superior terminal an overall capacity of 11,500,00 bushels.[313] At some point between 1949 and 1951, a 400-foot catwalk was erected to connect the two main elevators.

---

311 Minutes for Director's Meeting: Spencer Kellogg and Sons, Inc., September 12, 1949, Erie County & Buffalo Historical Society, F 4, Box 2, minute book #6; and FUGTA, *1949 Annual Report*, 43, collection of Harvest States.

312 Sanborn Fire Insurance Map, 1956, https://bit.ly/3TC5q6x.

313 "Farmers Union Elevator Job of Expansion is Completed," *Superior Evening Telegram*, August 8, 1951.

The scope of the project included the construction of a new headhouse on the Hughitt Avenue slip (Head House No. 2) with a large locker room and inspection office between it and the former Spencer Kellogg headhouse (Head House No. 3). Attached to the new headhouse, the first section of twenty-four tanks (Section *F1*) 160-feet high contained 741,000 bushels, the second, or middle section (*F2*) consisting of thirty-three tanks had a capacity of 1,103,000 bushels and the final section (*G*) at the south end of the Hughitt Avenue slip held 1,362,000 bushels within forty-four concrete tanks.

The Hughitt Avenue side of the Farmers Union opened the 1952 shipping season on June 18 when the *Penobscot* took on 190,000 bushels of wheat. From June 18 through July, the new addition loaded 4,805,000 bushels. Among the numerous vessels taking grain were the *John J. Boland (2), Fred E. Taplin, James E. Davidson* and *J. P. Wells*.[314]

\* \* \*

The mid-1950s were a time of transition for several long-standing Superior structures. Elevators *K*, *L*, and *M*, all long-time Cargill operations, were sold. The new owners were the Osborne-McMillan (O&M) Elevator Company. Like Cargill, the Osborne-McMillan Company originated in La Crosse. Edward Osborne and John McMillan both worked as accountants for W. W. Cargill before starting their merchandising business in 1887. Two decades later, in 1907, Osborne-McMillan officially incorporated its business.

Elevator *M* was purchased by Osborne-McMillan in 1952. Cargill held onto Elevators *K* and *L* for two more years. In 1954, they were also sold to the O&M Elevator Company.[315]

---

314 Ship Loading Records: Superior Farmer's Union Terminal (collection of Harvest States).
315 Jay Van Horn, interview with author, Superior, WI, 1994.

**Osborne-McMillian Elevators *K* and *L* (later changed to *O*), and *M* and annex in background, circa 1962.**
Photo: Copyright Cargill, Incorporated. Used with permission.

The Osborne-McMillan Elevator Company changed the names of their new Superior holdings. In most cases, the elevator names remained the same even after changes in ownership. Elevator *K* became Elevator *O* in honor of Edward Osborne. Elevator *M* across the slip was not changed because it fit the bill for the McMillan side of the system.

In September 1958, O&M Elevators began expanding the Elevator *M* site. No new additions had been made to this elevator since the construction of the concrete grain tanks during the mid-1920s. The addition of new tanks was noteworthy because they were to be built of steel instead of concrete.[316] The use of steel in elevator construction had not been used in the port since the building of Elevator *S* by the Great Northern at the turn of the century. Four storage tanks would be added to Elevator *M*, increasing the overall storage capacity of the elevator by 1 million bushels.

---

316 *Superior Evening Telegram*, September 12, 1958, with photo, and November 8, 1958, with photo.

## The Grain Terminal Elevators of Duluth-Superior

In 1954, sandwiched between the expansions of the Osborne-McMillan elevators, the Farmers Union completed a final section of forty-four concrete tanks along the Tower Avenue slip, increasing capacity by 1,366,400 bushels.

\* \* \*

A major change in the Great Lakes maritime industry was ready to explode at the end of the 1950s. The completion of the long-awaited St. Lawrence Seaway system was finally at hand. The grain distribution funnel at the western end of Lake Superior was gearing up for the 1959 shipping season. From Thunder Bay down to Duluth-Superior, the Seaway provided the key to unlocking the Northwest grain market to direct worldwide distribution.

Nowhere was the impact of the Seaway more important than at the ports of Duluth-Superior and rival Buffalo, New York. As the opening of the Seaway lit up the lights of commerce in the Twin Ports, it began the slow extinguishing of Buffalo as the Great Lakes' major grain terminus. The development of ports along the upper stretches of the St. Lawrence River soon replaced Buffalo as the end of the line for the new 730-foot Canadian lakers carrying grain down the Welland Canal and beyond, bypassing Buffalo.

Anticipation was high at the head of the lakes in late 1958. The elevators experienced a brief flurry of modernization in preparation for the arrival of the ocean-going vessels. The "salties," as they were soon dubbed, rode higher in the water than the "lakers" when unballasted, and they were generally wider in girth. To accommodate the vessels, the elevators were forced to raise their loading spouts. In some cases, such as at the Cargill Itasca elevator, new pipes were installed high up on the wall. The slips in front of the elevator were dredged to a Seaway depth of twenty-four feet.[317]

"The Seaway makes head-of-the-lakes facilities particularly important, for it makes possible export and domestic shipping

---

317 "Improvements Made at Cargill Superior Elevator," *The Northwestern Miller*, July 28, 1959 (MHS Archives: Donald M. Gregg Flour Milling Collection, 149.I.16.3 (B)).

unavailable before," said John Cole, Cargill's northwest regional grain manager. "I anticipate that Cargill will someday expand or add to its storage and loading facilities in this area."[318]

Cargill had recently set a record by handling 12 million bushels at the Itasca Elevator between June 1956 and the end of that year. "In a stepped-up effort to move grain to eastern lake ports before the freeze-up of the Superior-Duluth harbor, the elevator unloaded 2,328,854 bushels from 1,290 rail cars and loaded 3,665,293 bushels to fill eighteen lake boats." They couldn't wait for the Seaway and its potential to open new markets for their grain.

\* \* \*

The winter of 1958–59 saw another elevator expansion in the use of cylindrical steel tanks. The Farmers Union Grain Terminal Association was at it once again. It seemed as if there was hardly ever a pause in the expansion and growth of the Superior elevator system. Fifteen steel tanks were built on the ground between the Tower Avenue and Hughitt Avenue slips. It was the only available space left to the Farmers Union for expansion.

Western Knapp Engineering Company of San Francisco, with a local office in Hibbing, designed and erected the steel bins. Each tank was eighty-six feet in diameter with a wall height of sixty-four feet. The tanks were expected to add approximately 400,000 bushels of capacity and were located between the main elevator, Farmers No. *1*, and Farmers No. *2*, on the Hughitt Avenue slip. An overhead conveyor system connected the tanks to either of the No. *1* or No. *2* houses.[319]

> A special feature of the steel bins is that they can be erected in a much shorter period of time than would be necessary for construction of similar storage capacity in standard concrete elevators. The project at Superior was started early this summer and all bins will be avail-

---

318 Ibid.
319 *Skillings' Mining Review*, September 27, 1958, 22–23.

> able for service this fall... Another interesting aspect is the great capacity of the steel bins as compared with the concrete tanks in the main elevator – which is an advantage when large quantities of a single grade of grain are to be stored. A standard concrete elevator is made up of numerous tanks, some of full circular shape and others convex, and triangular shape to take up the in-between spaces. The largest tanks in Farmers No. 1 elevator are 160 ft. high by 30 ft. in diameter and these can hold approximately 30,000 bushels of grain. The in-between tanks are of 40,000, 20,000, and lesser bushel capacity...

The new steel tanks added an additional 6 million bushels, giving the Farmers Union elevator complex an overall capacity 19 million bushels. When broken down, the capacity at House No. *1* was rated at 7.5 million bushels and House No. *2* at about 5.5 million bushels.

\* \* \*

Everyone looked forward to the arrival of the first ocean-going ship to call at Duluth via the St. Lawrence Seaway. On a blustery May 3, 1959, the British motor vessel *Ramon de Larrinaga* arrived at the Peavey Duluth Terminal to officially open the Twin Ports to ocean shipping. Trailing right behind was the *Herald*, heading to the Globe Elevator in Superior. All indications pointed to a successful entrance into the direct export market.

*The Northwestern Miller* reported on the early season activity generated at Duluth. "In the first few weeks of operation, from May 3 to June 11, 37 foreign bottoms lifted more than 290,000 tons of grain in direct export at Duluth, compared with 26,000 tons loaded by 14 small foreign vessels in all of the 1958 shipping season for direct export."[320] Three days later, on May 6, 1959, another historic milestone was reached—the electrification of Elevator *M* and the end of its steam engine. Jay Van Horn remembered this in these words:

---

320 Ibid.

> I got called back in January and put in the millwright crew. After a couple days the fellow that was in charge, the superintendent of maintenance for the company, he was a travelling maintenance superintendent in charge of the job. He made me a foreman then. We had myself and three other fellows, we worked the upstairs on the legs, stripped out the old legs, the old drives, modified the leg heads and put new drives on.
>
> There was a steam engine down in the engine room; three boilers. Old "Ell" Johnson, he used to fire the boilers. He was the engineer, and he'd run the engine. There was a line shaft going in the elevator and then rope drives going to the top floor, and then a line shaft up there. All the legs were driven off this line shaft. The shaft would run the length of the workhouse and everything was driven off the same drive, by ropes, and they drove the cleaners and house belts downstairs and that sort of thing. They had done some electrification in 1948 when they put in a truck dump. It was the first hydraulic truck dump in the city of Superior. Cargill put that in. That was electrified.

In May, the inbound voyage of the motor vessel *Saint Remi* was captured in newspaper stories and photographs transiting the Seaway en route to Duluth. As the "largest vessel" yet to call at the Port of Duluth, the 20,000-ton tanker *Saint Remi* arrived at Capitol 6 to load grain for International Multifood's Venezuelan flour mill. The vessel had launched in Bordeaux, France, the previous November and stopped in downtown Duluth, where the general public were encouraged to view the ship in the slip where the Pier B Inn is located prior to shifting over to Cap 6. The sleek, raked bow and gleaming white deck cabins midship and aft was an ideal picture of the dream of the St. Lawrence Seaway turned into reality.

**The *Saint Remi* docked in Duluth for tours in May, 1959.**
Photo: author's collection, courtesy International Multifoods.

Hank Mulaner, general manager of International Milling's flour mill in Caracas, flew to Duluth to inspect the cargo. In Duluth, he met with Paul Callaghan, general export manager for the International Milling Company, at the elevator. Callaghan and his wife, Sofie, then rode the *Saint Remi* from Duluth to Caracas on a combination vacation-business trip.

The arrival of the ocean ships brought glamour and excitement. Parents brought their children down to the docks, posing them on bollards for photographs at the base of rope mooring cables. From a labor perspective, the arrival of the salties caused big changes in how grain was loaded in the harbor. Prior to the 1959 season, there was no labor union in the port for loading. That was all about to change.

Before the Seaway opened, a group of men, known collectively as the twelve apostles, were the workers hired by the elevators to load the ships. When the work became unionized with the International

Longshoremen's Association (ILA), the workers became the first gang of longshoremen in the local union. "They were paid by the bushel or by the ton, probably by the bushel back then, when a ship came in to unload, for example, because several of the elevators had marine legs to discharge," recalled veteran Ceres stevedore Chuck Ilenda. "Yet they were being paid by the ton. That's how Thunder Bay still works for the most part."[321]

In 1959, Ceres Terminals of Chicago entered Duluth, becoming the port's first stevedore in the modern era of the Seaway. "At that time, the loading was not necessarily paid for by the elevators. It may have been an owners' load, or it may have been the owner of the ship, for example." Afterward, Ilenda said, the grain companies themselves began contracting with the various stevedores to do the loading. "For example, Bunge, who at that time never really had an elevator up here, they would contract with the various stevedores to do the loading… they didn't have an elevator, but they were buying the grain from the elevators." Once the Seaway came in," Ilenda said, "the ILA really gained a foothold in the elevators."[322]

---

[321] Note: Thunder Bay is a Canadian port on Lake Superior northeast of Duluth. At one time it was two cities, Port Arthur, and Fort William. The port has long established history with the Canadian grain export business and continues as Canada's largest grain shipping port on the Great Lakes.

[322] Chuck Ilenda, interview with author, Duluth, MN 2024.

## 14:
## The 1960s: New Growth with the St. Lawrence Seaway

In 1960, another notable operational transition took place in Duluth. The Occident Terminal was taken under the wing of Peavey's Globe Elevator division. Peavey purchased the Russell-Miller Milling Company in 1954, although the Occident Terminal continued operating under the Occident Elevator management until the 1960 change.[323]

Peavey connected the Occident Elevator to its tank farm via an overhead conveyor, providing the ability to move grain in either direction from storage to dock. The additional bins gave the Peavey operation an overall capacity of 14 million bushels at Duluth alone.

In the summer of 1960, the F. H. Peavey Company erected a new ship-loading gallery next to its headhouse. Zenith Dredge of Duluth was hired to install 776 feet of interlocking steel sheet piling before the slip could be dredged for a Seaway depth of thirty feet. A 700-foot loading dock was created for the gallery, eliminating the need for vessels to shift along the wharf as they did when loading alongside the headhouse.

Three rigid, steel-framed towers supported the 114-foot-high conveyor gallery. A total of six high-level loading spouts and two low-level spouts were installed. The new gallery was expected to be fully

---

323 Kenneth D. Ruble, *The Peavey Story* (Minneapolis: Peavey Company), 66.

operational by July 1960. The maximum anticipated loaded speed would range from 75,000 to 100,000 bushels per hour depending upon the grain.

It was fast. Long-time Peavey man Charles B. Green, vice president and general manager of Peavey's interests in the harbor, said, "Loading time of vessels will be reduced as much as 50 percent, and as many as four different kinds of grain can be loaded at the same time, doubling the elevator's efficiency."[324] The Canadian steamer *T. R. McLagan* was the first vessel to load under the new gallery, followed that week by the Liberian-flagged *Atlantic Baroness*.

Many of the elevators were adapting to the arrival of the ocean ships. ADM added three high spouts to Elevator S. Installing spouts higher up on the walls of the elevators helped to load the saltwater ships more efficiently, which rode higher out of the water without ballast.

All the elevators were having their loading berths dredged. In a somewhat awkward moment, superintendent Russell Johnson of the Farmers Union GTA had to dance around how they loaded the Greek motor vessel *George Manolakis* to a depth of twenty-four feet in a slip that only had about twenty-two or twenty-three feet of water. On Thursday, July 8, 1960, with the help of four tugs, the vessel was freed from its bed of mud in the Hughitt Avenue slip, finally departing the harbor with a load of 450,000 bushels of barley.[325]

Just a few months earlier, on May 7, the Canadian steamer *Murray Bay* took on a split load of corn, rye and oats bound for Montreal, the largest single shipment of grain ever loaded on the Great Lakes. The vessel loaded 800,000 bushels of an overall 850,000-bushel cargo on the Tower Avenue slip side of the Farmers Union elevator before sailing to the Canadian lakehead to complete its load.[326] Because of local interest in news about the cargo, elevator superintendent Johnson made accommodations for the public to view the loading.

---

324 "Peavey Port Facilities Improved," *The Minneapolis Star*, February 15, 1960.

325 "Grounded Freighter Freed in Superior," *Minneapolis Star Tribune*, July 8, 1960.

326 "Big Lake Ship Loading Grain," *The Minneapolis Star*, May 7, 1960.

## The Grain Terminal Elevators of Duluth-Superior

The summer of 1960 also saw a brief interruption in grain shipping when members of the American Federation of Grain Millers Local 112 and 118 went on strike in late August. Within a couple days, eleven ships were waiting to load. Roughly four days later, negotiators reached an agreement, and work resumed along the waterfront.

The year concluded with the Farmers Union Grain Terminal Association announcing plans for a million-dollar investment in its Superior elevator before the start of the 1962 shipping season. Foremost in the plans would be the installation of a new ship-loading gallery. The gallery, also known as 'the bridge,' is 450-feet in length, with five loading spouts. The dock on which the gallery sits was dredged to a depth of 32 feet.[327] "The Superior elevator has raised its water grain shipments from 11 million bushels in 1958 to nearly 27 million this year," read a statement from elevator superintendent Johnson. "The deepening of the harbors in the St. Lawrence Seaway to 27 feet will bring bigger ships, and the Superior elevator will be enlarged to handle them."[328]

\* \* \*

The sale of its East End holdings in the 1950s left Cargill with only the Itasca Elevator in Superior to handle its Twin Ports grain shipping business. The Itasca elevator was certainly an adequate facility but not as modern as several other local elevators and had no room for expansion. Word on the street in the late 1950s had Cargill looking for a new location in Superior, which seemed unlikely. Since Cargill already owned land on Rice's Point, there was little incentive to build in Superior.

---

327 Note: The bridge had five loading spouts, but because loading was controlled by the ILA, and because of the size of the loading gang, they typically only used two spouts, sometimes three, and never four, according to Dick Carlson, Terminal Manager at Harvest States and later CHS. "They had a crew of six all the time, and then walking boss; it was actually seven guys. And they wanted to make sure they had two guys per spout so nothing got away on them. One on one side with the rope, and one on the other side with the rope."

328 "State Grain Elevator to Be Improved," *Marshfield News-Herald*, December 14, 1960.

The possibility of expanding in Superior was out of the question. The Itasca elevator was confined to a peninsula-shaped dock with limited rail and truck access. Another strike against the Superior location was a lack of water depth for the deep-draft ocean vessels soon to be coming as well as any sizable turning basin for maneuvering ships. Dredging would be costly, and the length of time to obtain permits would be prohibitive.

Superior city officials had unsuccessfully made offers and concessions to entice the company to relocate in Superior. As recently as 1953, Cargill had been trying to work out an expansion with the city, but the two parties could not reach any conclusive agreements.[329] With the coming of the St. Lawrence Seaway, Cargill looked to develop a new facility on Rice's Point. In addition to the physical space, the Garfield Avenue corridor had a well-developed rail system to handle the number of cars that would come into the elevator and easy access for truck traffic.

In April 1960, Cargill took its first step in a shift to Duluth with the acquisition of the Norris Grain Elevator Company holdings. As quietly as Norris had come into the port, the Chicago firm left.[330]

Cargill inherited a series of older elevators such as Norris had when it acquired the property. Some dated back to Duluth's pioneer Union and Improvement Elevator Company, while others were remnants of the Consolidated empire. The Norris Elevator Company made no significant changes to the elevators during its tenure at Duluth.

Before any development was announced, Cargill, Inc. was rocked by the unexpected death of John MacMillan, Jr. on December 23, 1960. MacMillan's tenure with the firm had begun in 1919. When the Cargill Elevator Company became Cargill, Inc. in 1932, he became vice president and general manager, succeeding his father as president in 1936. His influence in the company was significant. "Mr. MacMillan took a leading role in the design of large elevators

---

329 "New Cargill Building Looms as Council Clears Street Routes," *Superior Evening Telegram*, November 18, 1953.

330 "New Dock and Grain Bins Due," *Duluth Herald*, June 16, 1961.

for efficient storage and handling of grain and was responsible for two developments that revolutionized the grain handling business—temperature control inside huge storage bins and equipment for rapid unloading of the bins."[331] MacMillan's cousin, Howard, the president of Osborne-McMillan, had died a month earlier on November 22. It was a difficult time for the MacMillan family.

Cargill wasted little time in announcing plans for a major renovation of the Duluth elevators. In June 1961, the elevators were closed for the season to begin the rebuilding process. Included in the plans were the razing of wooden Elevators *F* and *H* as well as their old steam power plant building;[332] the construction of a new steel-framed, concrete exterior headhouse and steel tanks to replace Elevator *H*; a new office building; and a maintenance shop/lunchroom. Dredging along the slip was also done to a Seaway draft of twenty-seven feet. The firm of Western-Knapp Engineering, a San Francisco-based company with a satellite office in Minnesota's Iron Range, was awarded the contract.[333]

Steamer *Alexander Leslie* loading at Cargill Elevator *H* in 1962. Photo: Copyright Cargill, Incorporated. Used with permission.

---

331 "Chairman of Cargill Dies at 65," *Minneapolis Star*, December 23, 1960.
332 Ibid.
333 "Contract Awarded," *Minneapolis Star Tribune*, August 7, 1961.

Elevator *F* was built in 1885 for the Union Improvement and Elevator Company, followed by Elevator *H* in 1887. Both elevators used the timber-frame construction technique developed in the 1860s. Elevator *E* would be salvaged but stripped of nearly all the internal machinery to increase its storage capacity. When the remodeling was completed, the gutted Elevator *E* had "numerous and expansive" open areas between the floors of the cupola, with the top floor basically empty.

The second level down from the top of the cupola—the separator floor—housed the cleaners and leg, which straddled the next floor down, the conveyor floor. Beneath it was the drive floor and then the bin floor. The stairway access to all the floors was on the east side of the elevator. An inclined conveyor at ground level connected Elevator *E* to the new headhouse, running along the south side of the office and shop buildings. The maximum storage capacity of Elevator *E* in August of 1962 was a million bushels.[334]

A series of sixteen steel tanks were built on the site formerly occupied by the wood-frame Elevator *H*, with a total storage capacity of 1,040,000 bushels. There were five shipping spouts operated from a control cab in the new loading gallery named Cargill *B2*. The garners, scales and loading apparatus formerly housed in Elevator *E* were relocated to the headhouse, now the "new" Elevator *H*.[335] Steel grating separated each of the inside floors of the new headhouse. In descending order, the floors housed the elevator heads, followed by shakers, screens, cleaners, garners, scales, garners and the elevator boots at ground level. A 5,000-bushel steel screening and dust tank stood next to the headhouse. Grain was sent to the steel tanks via an overhead conveyor system to the wood storage house Elevator *E*, or to the steel tanks at *H*, or to the headhouse and or concrete tanks of Elevator *I*.

The headhouse at Elevator *I* had a capacity of 138,000 bushels and the concrete tanks portion of Elevator *I* were rated for 1,062,000 bushels. Two hydraulic truck dumps were put in to the north of the

---

[334] Note: Information derived from Marsh & McLennan Inc. fire insurance plan for Cargill, Inc. Elevators *E*, *H*, *I* and *I* tanks, August 1962.

[335] "The Midwestern Link," *Cargill News*, 52, no. 4 (September 1988).

concrete tanks and headhouse, and a grain drier was located at the extreme east side of the concrete tanks.

On May 9, 1962, Cargill president Erwin E. Kelm arrived in Duluth to dedicate the remodeled facility. He was flanked by dignitaries such as Minnesota governor Elmer Anderson, Duluth mayor E. Clifford Mork and Robert Smith, director of the Seaway Port Authority of Duluth. In Kelm's remarks, farm politics were at the forefront. He pointed to the increased efficiency of the elevator as a necessity in a changing global grain market[336] and was critical of proposed farm legislation he believed would increase domestic grain prices, which in turn would lead to reduced exports.

The first week in May saw the arrival of the Canadian vessel *Canadoc* to take the first load at the new Cargill *B2* ship loading gallery. About 180,000 bushels of soybeans and corn were loaded into the *Canadoc* bound for Cargill's new Baie Comeau facility on the St. Lawrence River.

During the 1950s, Cargill conducted extensive research on several Atlantic coast locations in anticipation of the Seaway, which they considered as "a linchpin for a new era in ocean shipments from North America. Huge oceangoing ships would now be able to dock at Baie Comeau to load efficiently and quickly with the grain that had been sent out to Baie Comeau by fleets of lakers."[337] Grain exported from Duluth on lakers could be stockpiled at Baie Comeau to be loaded when the Great Lakes shut down during the winter months.

An online profile of Cargill described the firm's expansion in some detail.[338]

> John MacMillan, Jr., and his brother Cargill were determined to expand the company after the war, but in a cautious manner that minimized risk. Cargill took the

---

336 "Cargill Dedicates Duluth Elevator," *The Northwestern Miller* (May 14, 1962): 10.

337 Wayne Broehl, Jr., *Cargill: Trading the World's Grain* (Hanover: University Press of New England, 1992), 791.

338 Cargill, Inc., accessed June 28, 2023, https://bit.ly/4aiar9U.

> lead among the major grain companies in efforts to combine a network of inland grain elevators with the ability to export large quantities of grain. Two developments in the 1950s helped to establish Cargill in world trade. In 1955 Cargill opened a Swiss subsidiary, Tradax, to sell grain in Europe. Eventually, Tradax grew into one of the largest grain companies in the world. And in 1960, Cargill opened a 13-million-bushel grain elevator in Baie Comeau, Quebec. This facility allowed Cargill to store grain for shipment during the months that winter weather closed the Great Lakes to traffic. The grain elevator also cut the cost of midwestern grain bound for Europe by 15¢ a bushel. In order to maximize profit, the barges that took grain to Baie Comeau hauled back iron ore. Also in the 1950s, barges that carried grain to New Orleans began to backhaul salt. Both practices would lead to profitable new enterprises for Cargill. Before the end of the decade, Cargill's sales topped the $1 billion mark.

Several days later, Cargill officials, representatives of the city and the port, along with the governor of Minnesota, returned to Duluth, welcoming the first ocean vessel to call at the new elevator. The Norwegian motor vessel *Beltana* took the honors with a cargo bound for Hamburg, Germany.[339]

The shortcomings of the Great Lakes/St. Lawrence Seaway System due to the closure of the system during the peak winter season were also a matter of concern for International Milling. Getting product to its mills was a critical part of its supply chain. In Duluth, the company developed a system for loading rail cars during the winter months. The transcript of a speech described an early development of the unit train.[340]

---

[339] "First Grain Cargo Loaded from New Elevator," *Duluth News Tribune*, May 8, 1962.

[340] "The Role of International Milling at Duluth," February 23, 1966, Min-

The Grain Terminal Elevators of Duluth-Superior

> International introduced a new concept into grain handling at Duluth when it introduced the "Unit Train" concept into the grain and milling industries. In January 1964, "shuttle service" featuring two 95-car trains carrying entirely grain moved from Duluth and Buffalo, each train making three round trips a month and continuing through April.
>
> International moved some 3,000,000 bushels of wheat from Duluth to Buffalo that winter via this method and has continued to do so each year since. During the winter when the Great Lakes are frozen this new concept enhanced Duluth as a grain center because of the additional activity which it brought to the city.
>
> Under previously normal conditions, International shipped much of its grain from Duluth to Buffalo via the Great Lakes and all grain activity ceased when the Great Lakes were frozen. Now the company keeps grain moving the year round.

\* \* \*

January is usually a bitterly cold month at the head of the lakes. The Northeast winds that brought cool air off Lake Superior in the summer now sweep the port with frigid wind chills. On the night of January 19, 1962, the air temperature dropped to -31 F, cold even for the hearty residents. Wisps of white smoke trailing upwards from chimneys all over the Twin Ports were swallowed that night by the dark, cold sky. As Sunday night eased into Monday morning, the stillness was shattered by the explosive sound of metal being rent apart.

Along Superior's East End waterfront, one of Elevator *M*'s new steel tanks, Tank *A*, had exploded. It was improbable— unbelievable

---

nesota Historical Society.

to some—yet here it was. It took an estimated one-hundredth of a second to split a single tank into three large fragments. The kinetic energy that had built up within the tank was so great that the explosion forced the metal shell out in three directions. The silent Superior night was interrupted by the sound of grain rushing out on the frozen ground.

In a few moments, sirens pierced the midnight quiet. Emergency response crews were summoned to the scene along with elevator personnel to survey the damage. A section of the ruptured tank was blown across the train tracks, taking out the power substation for the area. A second piece of metal partially caved in a neighboring tank, as a third piece traveled north and dropped through the thick ice of the elevator slip. This section, measured by superintendent Jay Van Horn, was found over 173 feet from the tank's concrete pad.[341]

For the next five days, laborers at Elevator *M* worked around the clock cleaning up the grain and debris. As disastrous as the explosion had been, it had luckily occurred during the off-season when repairs could be made without impacting the shipping season.

Several court trials were later held to determine the cause of the rupture. Insurance adjusters claimed that no explosion had occurred because they could find no evidence of fire. It was determined that the combined effects of expansion and contraction of the metal tank under the extremes of temperature over several years had placed stress on a faulty weld. The extreme cold on the night of January 18 caused the metal to contract by as much as seven inches, providing the final catalyst to the explosion.[342]

> "When they built the tank, they cut pieces of steel to mirror the circumference of the tank; three-quarter-inch steel plate, and they were laid down on anchor bolts in the concrete and when they welded these plates together, they didn't 'V' out the material, so it was a solid weld," explained elevator superintendent Jay Van

---

[341] Jay Van Horn, interview with author, Superior, WI, 1994.
[342] Ibid, 1994.

> Horn. "Now that tank, 80 feet in diameter, meant that it was almost 250-feet in circumference... between 30 degrees below and 90 degrees above, that tank will expand and contract almost seven inches around that perimeter.[343]

Osborne-McMillan replaced the metal tank with four smaller concrete silos having interstice bins. Each of the steel tanks had a capacity of 50,000 bushels. Construction on the replacement silos was completed by late August of the 1962 shipping season. Elevator *M* also had a combination of wood, concrete and steel in its construction history, showing a willingness to adapt new technology in expansions occurring over decades while retaining the elevator's original wooden headhouse.

\* \* \*

The loss of Cargill to Superior was a big one. The firm had operated on the East End since 1893. Efforts had failed to entice the Minnetonka-based company to stay. City and port officials sought new developers to fill the void created in their grain economy. Even though the former Cargill site continued operating under the Osborne & McMillan Company, the prestige of being home to a large corporation such as Cargill was not easily replaced.

Superior officials looked to the Connors Point area to develop additional elevator sites. Speculation about new industrial development on Connors Point moved closer to reality during the summer of 1964. The city of Superior prepared to purchase the property formerly occupied by the Youghiogheny & Ohio (Y & O) coal dock, alternately known as the Northern coal dock. After the city purchased the site, the parcel would then be sold to the Chicago and North Western Railroad, which proposed to build an elevator there.

At the time, the Chicago and North Western Railroad negotiated with the Continental Grain Company, a firm headquartered in New York City. Continental agreed to operate a 5-million-bushel elevator

---

343 Jay Van Horn, interview with author, Superior, WI, 1994.

on a twenty-year lease arrangement with the railroad's North Western Leasing Company. The railroad would provide all rail access to the facility.[344] The official announcement came on January 4, 1965. The project was estimated to cost six million dollars.

"We are especially pleased to be coming to the Superior area to further serve the grain farming community in the upper Midwest. Continued access to these markets is essential," stated Michel Fribourg, president of Continental, from his office in New York City. "The Seaway will certainly continue to play an important part in the United States' grain export effort, which is a vital contribution to maintain our country's balance of payments with foreign countries."[345]

Within months of announcing the Superior elevator project, Continental Grain and Cargill, Inc. both closed their respective elevators in Buffalo, New York,[346] citing unfavorable railroad mileage rates and government policies for the closures. Cargill officials also cited the decline of export grain handled in Buffalo since the opening of the St. Lawrence Seaway.

Fabrication of steel tanks for the Continental Grain elevator on Connors Point, 1965. Photo: Lake Superior Maritime Collections, UW-Superior.

---

344 "Terminal Grain Elevator In Prospect For Superior," *Superior Evening Telegram*, July 16, 1964.

345 "Grain Elevator Being Built at Superior Port," *Green Bay Press-Gazette*, January 5, 1965.

346 "Rail Rates, U.S. Blamed for Elevator Closing," *Star Tribune*, June 10, 1965.

Construction on the new elevator in Superior got underway in early 1965. Foley Brothers, Inc. of St. Paul, was retained as the general contractor. The St. Paul-based construction company had a long history dating back to the 1880s. It had performed work for all the major railroads in addition to constructing an ocean terminal in Halifax. Among its many accomplishments, Foley Brothers was the company of record for the building of the St. Paul Cathedral, in Minnesota.

Preliminary designs by Continental for the elevator called for an overall capacity of five million bushels. The main section of the elevator would consist of thirty-one concrete silos on the north side facing the dock. Additional storage would consist of twelve cylindrical steel tanks built directly behind the concrete silos.

The capacity of the steel tanks was perhaps the most unusual feature of the new elevator. Each of the twelve tanks would hold 25,000 bushels of grain. This was four times the amount of grain held in a conventional concrete silo. Fabrication and erection of the steel tanks and concrete bins began simultaneously in early July 1965. It was anticipated the elevator would be completed around February the following year, in time for the 1966 shipping season.[347]

The Continental Elevator was built with ease of operation in mind, as well as for high-capacity movement of grain. One of its unique features was the placement of the receiving legs on the outside of the elevator. The prevention of fire or explosion within the elevator was an obvious consideration in this design.

Two receiving legs were built, one to handle rail cars and one to accommodate trucks entering the facility. Ship loading was controlled from the deck of a vessel via a remote-control box located in the glass-paneled loading booth high on the elevator wall overlooking the ship. The automated control eliminated the need for the dock man, who typically ran the winch from the dock to raise or lower the grain spout over the deck of the vessel. Cap 6 in Duluth is believed to have been the last elevator to use a dock man.

On May 11, 1966, the *Paget Trader* arrived at Continental to load the first cargo—140,000 bushels of oats and 250,000 bushels

---

347 "Moving Skyward," *Superior Evening Telegram*, July 13, 1965.

of barley destined for Italy. The 1966 shipping season proved to be a successful inaugural year for Continental. 18,300,000 bushels of grain were moved through the elevator in its first year, mainly on the sixty-five vessels that called on the Connors Point elevator.[348]

Continental grain superintendent John Parrington stressed that the operational approach to business at the elevator was one of teamwork. It was a chain that involved everyone from commodity traders to vessel agents and stevedores. Included in the formula was the key cooperation of the Chicago Northwestern Railroad. Parrington explained, "We were able to do what we needed to do because of the CNW giving the service we needed when it was needed."[349]

\* \* \*

In December, the Farmers Union elevator shipped its 50 millionth bushel of grain. A brief celebration commemorating the event took place on the deck of the steamer *Joe S. Morrow* with elevator superintendent Russell Johnson and his son Russell, Jr. holding a paper sign while posing for a photograph.

The late 1960s saw Cargill's continued shift away from Superior with the closing of the Itasca Elevator. The Itasca plant had been in Cargill's hands since the 1931 purchase. The facility had worked well for Cargill. In 1956, the elevator enjoyed a banner year in the shipment of grain. During a two-week stretch from late November to December 7, the *Superior Evening Telegram* reported that the elevator "unloaded 2,238,854 bushels from 1,290 rail cars and loaded 3,665,293 bushels to fill 18 lake boats."[350]

The Itasca Elevator was idled in the mid-to-late 1960s. In 1969, after several years of being shut down, the elevator was razed by the firm of Carl Bolander & Sons of St. Paul. The demolition ended

---

348 "Elevator Meets All Expectations," *Superior Evening Telegram*, January 31, 1967.

349 John Parrington, interview with author, Minneapolis, MN, 1993.

350 "Cargill Hits Grain Record," *Superior Evening Telegram*, January 11, 1957.

nearly seventy years of grain moved through the port via the Allouez-Itasca connection. Ending with it was Cargill's seventy-five years of operation at Superior.

# 15:
# The 1970s: The Soviet Grain Trade and Embargo

The move by Cargill to Duluth coincidentally occurred at a time when the Peavey Company was shifting its operations in the opposite direction toward Superior. Peavey sold its Duluth Terminal and Occident Elevator to Cargill in 1970. This was not the first time that two competitors had bought or sold elevators from each other. The Peavey-owned Belt Line Elevator was sold to the Cargill-owned Superior Terminal Elevator Company in 1914.

For the Peavey Company, the two Duluth elevators simply had become too old for them to operate without investing a substantial amount of money and effort toward modernization, which included expensive dust collection systems. In Peavey's judgment, the costs of updating electrical and mechanical aspects of the plant exceeded their value.

Cargill evidently felt that, for the interim, the acquisition could help their operation at Duluth until a new facility could be built. The former Peavey Duluth Terminal was renamed Cargill D. The former Occident Elevator was designated Cargill C. They, too, would soon be under the same pressure to update the dust collection systems.

In Superior, Elevator O was last used in the summer of 1972, according to the *Superior Evening Telegram*. The property was closed and later passed into the ownership of Douglas County, which sold the property and elevator to the City of Superior for ten dollars in

May 1979. A Duluth organization, Elevator O, Ltd., proposed to develop the property into condominiums, but neither side could come to an agreement over the proposal.[351] The city sold the timber salvage rights to Tri-State Wreckage and Salvage for three thousand dollars.

On January 16, 1970, the International Milling Company changed its name to International Multifoods Corporation, a reflection of its increasingly diverse portfolio.[352] There was no change in operation at Duluth, which remained known locally as Cap 6 from its days with the Capitol Elevator Company.

\* \* \*

The early 1970s were good years for the Twin Ports grain economy. Most of the elevators were running wide open. Transactions with the Soviet Union led to an upswing in trading activity and grain movement. High-level tonnage marks were achieved from 1973 through 1976.[353] Continental Grain became a pioneer in shipments of sunflower seeds from its Connors Point elevator. John Parrington, a longtime superintendent, recalled the early efforts to handle the oil seed commodity.

> The farmers out in the valley had marginal land, and they were looking for a crop to put on the marginal land. Fortunately for them, sunflower seeds were a product that they could grow on the marginal land... consequently it was a product that came into high demand. It was a good product for us to move.[354]

In 1977, the US had grown 1.18 million metric tons of oil-type sunflower, according to agriculture reporter Don Lilliboe from

---

351 "Torches Blamed for Elevator Fire," *Superior Evening Telegram*, August 27, 1984.

352 "Milling Firm Now International Multifoods Corp," *Minneapolis Star Tribune*, January 17, 1970.

353 Seaway Port Authority of Duluth: tonnage figures, 1973–1976.

354 John Parrington, interview with author, Minneapolis, MN, 1993.

Fargo. "More than 900,000 tons were exported during the 1977–78 marketing year, most of them through Duluth-Superior."

**Continental Grain in the late 1970s was a leader in the shipment of sunflower seeds to overseas markets.** Photo: author.

Between 1973 and 1979, Jim Koski worked just about every job in the elevator. He was the twenty-first employee hired at the elevator. A half-century later, he still recalled his first day on the job. He was going to school to learn to be a machine tool operator when his brother-in-law told him one of the elevators was hiring. Continental Grain was looking for utility men to clean the elevator when it was operating.[355]

> My brother-in-law said to be down early. So, I punched in early. I guess I was one of six people that got hired. At that time, I was the 21st employee, at Continental. When I got there, the first morning, they're giving us a little orientation, and orientation back then was grab

---

355 Jim Koski, interview with author, St. Paul, MN, November 21, 2023.

> the shovel and go. So I walked into the office, and they give me a timecard and I punch in and the superintendent says, "Where you're going you're going to need this," and he pulls the drawer open and here's a bottle of whiskey. I'm 20 years old at this time, and I'm going, this is a hell of an orientation. So anyway, he pours me a shot, and he says, "If you can't drink this you're not a man." You're not, you know, whatever. He was giving me a hard time. Well at 20, I had had a few beers already so I had been around it. So anyway, I did it and I said, now where do I go and he says, "I'll take you out there," and I went to the top of the headhouse, that's where the grain goes to be loaded in the boats. And there is a man-lift up there. And he said, "You go to the top, and there's five layers there. You clean all the dust up, you sweep it up, and you dispose it."

Koski took whatever the superintendent threw at him. "I had various positions. I'd be on the boats, as a weigher." Continental paid him to be trained as a federally qualified weigh man. He said it was a great job.

> As a weigher, I would be on the ships and I would just tell them to start the grain up there, whatever grain they were going to do in certain holes. I mean, hell, all you do is you stand around and you hold a radio and tell them to start the grain. In 1973 I was at vocational school there, and I was living off about $35 a week. So, when I started the grain elevator, my pay was $8.13, starting. I went from poverty to eating steak. I was eating Cheerios, and then I was eating steak.

In just a few years, Koski became the elevator's equivalent of the utility man in baseball. "I held just about every position. So, with my seniority, whenever there was an opening in a position, I could get that. If somebody had a crappy job, I could take a better job. If somebody called in sick, I could fill in any position."

For some reason, no one seems to be able to fully explain that in its early years in Superior, Continental Elevator employed a lot of residents from Port Wing down on the south shore. "I tell you what, it was a crazy place," reflected Koski on his six years at the elevator.

> **When the superintendent gives you a drink on your first day, when we were unloading cars say, it was my second year, we're unloading cars and John Parrington would come into the, we were getting done with our shift, and he said, "We have some hot cars with a lot of demurrages." He says, "What would it take for you guys to stay and unload?" I think it was like 40 cars, because of the demurrage that they were paying. I said, "Well, a bucket of chicken and a case of beer." Well, no crap, he'd go get a bucket of chicken and a case of beer for us.**

Koski recalled a lot of card playing, even a craps table made out of three-quarter-inch plywood. "I remember one time I lost my paycheck in about five minutes, so I had to borrow money from my brother-in-law. That was awkward, so I never did that again." He also recalled one guy who really drank a lot and would stumble around. He was a heavy drinker at a time when drinking on the job was common. One night, his drinking almost cost him his life.

"I was dumping cars one time," recalled Koski, "and here he had passed out right on the rail track. I shut everything down and I said, 'Boys, this could have been really bad.' At that point, I never drank again there. I think that was in my third year."

One of the skills Koski learned at Continental was how to load a ship or at least operate the machinery at the command of the longshoreman on the ship.

> **You're up in and it's called the head house, because you're overlooking the whole ship from up there, it's all glass windows. We don't know what kind of grain**

they're gonna get, because the office will tell the people down on the basement, we're gonna be loading corn or wheat or whatever. It's going to get sampled again when it comes out of the bin, so that the people on the ship know what they're getting. What they do is up in the head house, if you have the pipes in there, and the ILA is ready to go you just start opening these gates. And these are automatic gates, you just open the gate, and you can see your amp meter—how much the belt is pulling by the weight that you're actually running into that pipe. You have three belts, because it would be common just to be running one type of grain in a ship, so if they got all the pipes in there and you got six pipes, you have six belts bringing the grain to the pipe. The ILA would tell you when they were ready, and then you just open the gates and, and the grain would come off the hopper that had come up from the basement. There are three elevators in the basement to bring grain up to the head house, or to the scale. It's going into a hopper that's weighing that grain as it goes. Then from that hopper, it's dropping into a holding bin. So it's tallying the grain as it goes into that one. It'll fill up that hopper, it is weighed, and then it's dumped into a holding hopper. So, once all the grain is you empty that whole hopper out.

\* \* \*

The early 1970s marked the official closure of the Duluth Board of Trade. The building was closed and sold in May of 1972. Receipts and shipments were listed on the Duluth Board up to the 1970s, but in essence, all trading was done in Minneapolis and had been for many years before it closed.

The Duluth Board of Trade was founded in 1881 at a time when Duluth was emerging as a major grain market. There were eleven members that first year. The incorporators were Clinton Markell, Andrew J. Sawyer, Owen Fargussen, William T. Hooker, Wilmer W. Davis, Roger S. Munger, Charles H. Graves and Walter Van Brunt. Wheat was the only crop received from 1870 to 1878. During the following crop season, several grain staples were introduced to Duluth.

The Duluth Board of Trade maintained a strong position within the maritime community. Since the organization of the Board in 1881, the elevator capacity of the combined ports increased from 2,660,000 to 32,475,000 bushels. While many of these elevators were located in Superior, the entire business connected with them was done from Duluth.

The promotion and marketing of durum wheat through the port became one of the Board's big success stories after a rocky start. The Board itself was first headquartered on the Metropolitan block between First and Second Avenues West on Superior Street. They eventually would have several locations, one destroyed in a dramatic fire.

At the start, many companies operating on the board were Duluth-owned operations. By the end of the Great Depression, many companies were based in Minneapolis. Futures trading at Duluth was virtually non-existent from the 1930s onward. It was much more convenient to trade on the Minneapolis Grain Exchange rather than compete against themselves at Duluth.[356]

The DBOT was the victim of an unusual quirk in the language of its own incorporation papers. The life of the corporation was listed as only thirty years instead of the indefinite lifespan used by most business entities. This clause meant that every three decades the membership was forced to vote to extend the life of the board. It is unknown why the Duluth membership never reincorporated to extend its own existence. In 1971, with the majority membership shares now based in Minneapolis, the vote to extend the corporation another thirty years failed.[357]

---

356 H. Wilson Watson, Jr., interview with author, Duluth, MN, 1993.
357 Ibid.

## The Grain Terminal Elevators of Duluth-Superior

The closing came at a time when the first wave of Russian grain exports began leaving the port. The first two ships arrived in late 1971, loading grain for Nakhodka, a Russian port on the Sea of Japan. The following season, sixty-nine vessels loaded grain in the harbor for Russia. The business was great for all the elevators, the longshoremen and everyone involved in the grain trade.

In 1973, the first actual Soviet vessel was allowed through the locks at Sault Ste. Marie. Prior to this passage, any vessels registered in a Sino-Soviet Bloc nation were prohibited from passing through these locks. In an arrival as celebrated as the first Seaway ship back in 1959, throngs of people and media descended on the ship canal as the M/V *Zakarpatye* became the first Russian ship to enter the Duluth harbor. It was a record breaker for more than one reason. The April 5, 1973, arrival was the earliest recorded for an oceangoing ship at Duluth, surpassing the old record by seven days.[358]

Turkish-flagged vessel *Günay-A* after a day of loading at Cargill *B2*. The vessel was built in 1981 in Sunderland, U.K. Photo: author.

---

358 "East West Trade, no longer just a phrase," *Minnesota's World Port* 9, no. 2 (Summer 1973). There is also a vessel called *Zakarpatye* that was a well-known Soviet intelligence-gathering vessel (a spy ship).

The biggest year for grain exports from the port would be 1973. Records show that 8,855,681 metric tons were exported overseas, and 38,005,382 tons were shipped domestically on the Great Lakes for a total of 46,861,063 tons. The Soviet Union grain trade and the leap in demand for sunflower seeds led to the record-setting season. The port benefitted from its proximity to the sunflower-growing regions of western Minnesota and North Dakota. Davis Helberg, former executive director of the Duluth Seaway Port Authority, recalled that period:

> I became the port director on January 21, 1979. We started seeing Soviet ships come in and that was still the heart and the depths of the Cold War. There was a tremendous amount of curiosity, fascination, and a little bit of tension in the community at the time when we started seeing not only the Soviet ships, but Soviet bloc ships coming in. CIA people would come in from time to time into the pilot's office and there would always be two of them and they'd be in suits and very smartly attired and they would meet with Tony Rico, or with Tony and me in his office with the door shut. They'd be asking all manner of interesting questions about observations and just what we saw, what we might have seen, what we think we saw, what we heard from the pilots.

Deciding to have a little fun with the agents, Helberg remembered a time when the late Rico pranked the CIA with a story about some strange markings on the Soviet navigation charts, which led to a couple of pilfered charts being sent to the CIA in the Twin Cities knowing there was nothing different about them.

Helberg had his own observations about the Soviet vessels, which he shared in an interview. He expressed his regret at the grain embargo imposed by President Carter and the long-lasting impact of the Twin Ports grain millers strike of 1979, a three-month action from which the port never recovered.

One of the interesting things with the Soviet bloc ships, not just the Soviet ships but those others who were from the Soviet bloc nations, it didn't take too long usually to figure out who the political officer was aboard. Every one of them seemed to have one. Somebody who either had a rank or a title that didn't seem to be common in seafaring, or maybe it was a legitimate position, but whoever the person on the ship was, always made sure that he was present whenever anyone was talking with the captain or with any of the officers. He was sort of the eyes and the ears and behind the scenes and was a link to the party and to the government power.

It was just symptomatic of the times, I suppose, but there was a lot of business. In fact, as the 70s went on, and that market started to develop almost in the way that free markets do, although the market was terribly twisted and stilted because of the way the Soviets did things. But there was a significant amount of traffic that went from here to Baltic Sea ports and also to Black Sea ports. There were size restrictions in some of those ports, as well as into the Black Sea that were very similar to the size restrictions of the St. Lawrence Seaway. So, there was a wonderful compatibility with this great fleet of Soviet and Soviet bloc ships looking for business, and then, of course, here we are on the doorstep almost to the to the Great Plains and the great growing areas, the wheat and barley and corn and soybean country to the west of us.

The business was doing pretty well, and by 1979, even despite that horrifying strike that we had for three months in '79, we were up to something like a million tons a year of grain just moving to the Soviets or to Soviet-controlled nations. And then came the first week of January 1980, and President Carter imposed the embargo on the Russian grain trade, and that was coming on the heels of the devastation of that strike that we had endured in '79. It was an absolute crippler.

I recall that January when John Fedo was installed as mayor. I, in fact, was leaving for India on a trade mission the very next day, and I had a call the afternoon prior to my departure, prior to the day of my departure, from Congressman Oberstar, who was riding I think it was an Air Force II with Vice President Mondale, and they were coming here for John Fedo's installation and Oberstar and Vice President Mondale, I spoke with them and they urged me to come to the installation that night, and I did.

In the receiving line afterward, I told the Vice President, you know, respectfully, but I said, we think that you made a terrible error in embargoing grain to the Soviet Union. I said that, the politics notwithstanding, it's going to cause a great deal of harm to our port. The Vice President said, "No, no, we studied this quite carefully, and you're going to be alright. It won't affect you that much."

Well, it knocked the wind out of that trade. We just didn't see any more Soviet grain. It was a bad double whammy after that strike. That strike occurred in the year 1979 when the world grain market was stronger than it had ever been up to that point in history. Bumper crops throughout the upper Midwest and especially in our region. The grain was flowing out of here as though there were no tomorrow, and came August and everything started shutting down...

**One of the fellows running for governor in North Dakota was talking about mobilizing the North Dakota National Guard to come in here and operate the elevators. We had the crew from the *Today* show in New York come out here to do a story and to interview me and others. It came at the worst possible time that it could have, and it's caused enmity and anger in the producer community to the west and southwest of here that, believe it or not, all these years, a quarter of a century later, we still hear about.**

**There were many producers, as well as some of the grain companies, who said we've got to have options. We just can never again put ourselves in a position of such vulnerability in a port like Duluth-Superior, where the Seaway means there's no other option in moving the grain out. And almost instantly, the railroads made heavy commitments to build new grain cars and new equipment. And the people on the Upper Mississippi started building barges left and right. All of which I mention because then, when the bottom fell out of the world grain market, and we had a recession in 1983 and 84, a lot of those barge companies frankly went under, and there was a retrenchment in the railroads, too, because so many of them had overbuilt partly because of that strike we had here in 1979.**

The firm of Guthrie-Hubner provided the local vessel agents for the Russians. Chuck Hilleren, a young vessel agent at the time, remembers that year as the one in which he never seemed to get any sleep. "It was back-to-back ships," he recalled. "We'd finish loading one, and another would come in from anchor to take its place. A lot of days, I'd get home at two in the morning and go back to work at six. The port had never seen tonnage like that."

From a cultural perspective, Hilleren immediately noticed how the Russians were different from seafarers of other nations. "They employed women on the boats, which was rare. The Greeks or Italians would have never allowed women on board. They thought they were bad luck." And the Russians liked talking politics. Hilleren recalled one late night when he, a local stevedore and the captain of a Russian ship, "solved most of the world's problems" over a bottle of vodka. "Here we were," laughed Hilleren, "sitting on a ship at 2 a.m., arguing with the captain about communism. I didn't think I'd ever get home that night."[359]

Ceres stevedore Chuck Ilenda had similar memories, such as during the 1974 season when they loaded, by his estimation, around 457 saltwater vessels alone.

> **Both Chuck Hilleren and I, we'd go down for an inspection on a Russian flag ship at four o'clock in the morning and get that inspected and start loading it at eight. But the reason we had to go down there is because they didn't have their paperwork done correctly to the satisfaction of the National Cargo Bureau,"** recalled Ilenda. **"Not only that, but they would not even consider looking at the documents until they'd given us maybe two drinks of vodka at four in the morning. That was the norm for them.**

---

359 Chuck Hilleren, interview with author, Superior, WI, 2007.

M/V Merlin, a tanker, loading grain through the circular butterworth hatches on deck, at Elevator S.
Photo: author's collection.

Between Ilenda, Hilleren and the National Cargo Bureau, they all met on the ship to go over the documentation and help them out.

> That's where everybody learned how to do stability forms inside out and backwards, because they [the Russians] didn't know how. Then you'd finish the ship maybe at one o'clock in the morning. You'd go home and you know the old expression, "$%@! shower and shave" and get back there for another four o'clock inspection. This went on all year.

The saltwater vessels added a layer of complexity to the ship loading operation, but their needs also employed a lot of people in the port in a variety of jobs— from being a stevedore to a laborer stitching sections of burlap together with nails in the bottom of a humid cargo hold, to cargo inspectors and longshoremen. Ilenda explained:

> The simplest thing would be, say one lot is 18,000 tons plus or minus 10 percent of Number One wheat, 15 protein. Well, that's pretty simple, but these guys didn't know that you could only load to 26 feet at the time, and you could only have maybe one slack hold, maybe two, but never more than that, to make it from Duluth-Superior to the Welland Canal, which was exactly 26 feet. For instance, the draft could be 26 feet, two inches aft, and maybe 26 feet forward, and the fuel that they're going to consume, and the water they're going to consume will make them exactly 26 feet in two and a half days, or whatever it took to get to the Welland. So, you had to make all those calculations because the mate just did not know how to do it.

In grain loading, a slack hold is one that isn't completely full. This usually occurs when a vessel is loading multiple lots of grain and using separations within the cargo holds to maintain the integrity of each specific lot. If this were the case, a different gang of workers would handle this part of the loading operation. According to Ilenda, "You'd have to hire a special gang to make a separation. You couldn't use the loading gang. So, while that separation is going in, for example, maybe you're loading with the other gang in two other holds, and then once that separation is in and approved, you can load on top of that."

Separations were created by using large sections of burlap forty by eighty feet in size, with additional sections stitched together with nails if needed.

> Let's say that a hold would take 4,000 tons. You might put 500 tons of one lot in there and put a burlap separation over that. The classic example was Bunge. They loved to do separations. They had ships that would have 15 to 20 different lots, and I'm telling you, it would drive you crazy, but they hired Ceres to do that.

> Then, when you start to load over a separation, you couldn't go full blast, because it would just pull that burlap down. You'd have to go very, very slow and build it up and build it up so that once that burlap was covered with grain, then you can go full tilt. You might have to put 200 tons on top of the separation.

\* \* \*

In Superior, the elevators previously owned and operated by Cargill and/or Peavey were undergoing operational changes. The Osborne-McMillan Elevator Company saw a shift in majority interests and reincorporated as the McMillan Elevator Company in 1969, operating in Superior as O&M Elevators.[360]

Following the death of Howard McMillan, Sr. in late 1960, Osborne-McMillan elected Cavour Langdon McMillan as president of the company. C. Langdon McMillan became the third generation McMillan to manage the business, which he did until his siblings decided to liquidate the grain company. Howard McMillan, Jr. wanted to stay in the business and formed the McMillan Company, first acquiring and operating the Shoreham Elevator in Minneapolis.

It wasn't until November 1969 that he could afford to purchase Elevators *O* and *M* in Superior, explained former superintendent Jay Van Horn. "Howard bought both of them at the same time. With both houses full of storage, there was enough income generated so that he could have income, and once he got control of those two elevators, he bought a Thief River Falls terminal at the same time. So, he had three sets of terminals. We sat on the oats." Van Horn explained further:

> In 1970, Peavey came to Howard McMillan, and they made a deal that they would ship all of their milling wheat through Elevator *M*. So, we had to start shipping out the commodity stuff we had. I had to hire crew.

---

360 Duluth Board of Trade, *1969 Annual Report*.

> I hired five people in November 1969. The McMillen Company operated the Superior elevators through O&M Elevators, Inc. of Minneapolis. Starting in May of 1970, now we had to hire about 20 people. We started doing Peavey's mill business through Elevator $M$, and we became quite busy. That led to a contract with Cook Industries... we started handling other grains for Cook Industries... and Peavey wondered, "Why are we shipping our mill wheat through $M$ when we've got our own elevator [Globe] that's not doing anything?" So, they stopped doing business with McMillan, but McMillan was able to get a contract with Dreyfus, so we got all the Dreyfus business. That was 1972, and we became even busier. Between Dreyfus and Cook, 1972, 73, 74, in those years, we became very busy."[361]

By 1972, OSHA safety violations forced McMillan to close Elevator O and concentrate on shipping efforts at Elevator M. The bins in Elevator O and its annex were open on the top floor. Estimates from contractors to deck the tops of the bins far exceeded the value that McMillan placed in the structure. Continuing to operate the elevator would leave McMillan open to OSHA fines if the elevator were to be inspected. In July 1972, Elevator O was emptied and closed.[362]

O&M was actively seeking to add a meal plant at the Superior site and had enlisted support to study the possibility of rebuilding into a large new elevator at the Northern Pacific ore dock location in Superior. The plans never came to fruition. Warren Olson, vice president of the company, said, "The $2.2 million proposed byproduct elevator project at the O&M Elevators will be delayed... At least 20 percent higher construction cost than the originally estimated in late 1972."[363] The City of Superior had previously approved the issuance of

---

[361] Jay Van Horn, interview with author, Superior, WI, 1994.
[362] Ibid.
[363] "Elevator project delayed," *Superior Evening Telegram*, October 31, 1974.

$2.2 million in municipal revenue bonds to the project. O&M officials were now asking for additional funding to make up the deficit.

The issues of dust emission and air quality grabbed the headlines and the attention of elevator operators in the early 1970s. State and federal air quality regulations forced the elevators to install costly dust and filtration systems or risk fines and possible shutdowns. On the Superior side of the harbor, the Great Northern's Elevator S added a new dust control system in 1974. The Peavey Globe Elevator followed in 1976 with a similar system as well as the Farmers Union in the 1980s.

Dick Carlson, former terminal manager at CHS, recalled his start as a laborer in 1978 at the old Farmers Union elevator in the pre-dust collection era.

> You would not believe how dirty the place was at the time, because they're running so hard and everything. In the basement, [beneath the grain bins] it was probably about four to six inches of wet, old dust and grain and everything. For their pathways, they had grain doors. That's what they had for paths in the basement. As you shoveled along, you took them old wet things and hauled them out, cleaned up and everything. If you had a pile that looked dry, you had the guy you were working with—he had what's called a track shovel, which is a small coal shovel that's eight by eight, and one would disrupt the pile, and the other guy would stand there and swat the rats and kill them.

Prior to the installation of dust control systems, rats were a common problem at the elevators. Carlson's father worked over at the Great Northern Elevator S, a facility overrun with rodents. Elevator S was one of the last elevators to install a collection system after OSHA threatened to close them down. It had a reputation for being a dusty workplace. Carlson recalled his teen years when he'd ride down to the elevator to pick up his father when he'd work late.

> That was an absolute shithole. You came around that corner where Midwest Energy is right now, the coal plant, we'd go down to pick up dad, say he's working until eight. You slowed down because so many rats were crossing that roadway. The road was literally moving like rats coming out of the swamp where Midwest Energy was. My dad and them always tied their pant legs off because the rats were so thick they would crawl the guy's pants leg.

The installation of dust collection systems, the cleaning out of old rotting grain, and the arrival of pest control companies that utilized poisonous tracking powder eventually eliminated the rats.

Not all the elevator companies were willing or able to finance the costly filtration systems. The result was evident in the closings and demolitions that took place across the harbor in the 1970s. Notably earmarked for demolition were the older, wood-framed elevators. The year 1977 was particularly noteworthy for the changes involving these older structures.

The demolition of the Itasca and the shutdown of Elevator O were evidence of the changes coming to Superior. In 1977, the trend continued at the Farmers Union plant with the winter removal of the old Spencer Kellogg and Sons wood-frame workhouse built by American Milling in 1912. The elevator had been taken over by Spencer Kellogg for their linseed oil plant in 1917. The frozen Hughitt Avenue slip became littered with rubble as the razing took place over the winter.

On the Duluth side, another former flour milling elevator would be next on the list. International Multifoods' Elevator No. 5 was razed in 1977. This elevator was built in 1889 as a storage house for the Imperial Mill. In 1905, it came under the control of the Capitol Elevator Company and, subsequently, the International Milling Company. Workers at the elevator had expressed fears about the structural integrity of the elevator. It was fast deteriorating into an unsafe workplace.

\* \* \*

Cargill, Inc. became the last company to build a new facility in the Twin Ports. In August 1973, the Minneapolis-based company announced its intention to construct a new 33-million-dollar facility in Duluth. The news was a joint release issued by the Seaway Port Authority of Duluth and Rep. John A. Blatnik (D-Minn). A spokesperson for the Port Authority in its house organ *Minnesota's World Port* wrote:

> The three-phase project is an amplification of a two-year campaign to construct a $4.2 million meal handling facility in Duluth, which has now become the first phase of a program to retain grain meal cargo traffic in the port by improving handling facilities and to expand that element of the port's international trade.

The facility would be constructed on Cargill's property by the Port Authority, with Cargill operating the facility under a thirty-year lease. The Port Authority issued 13.5 million dollars in revenue bonds. Additional funding came from a 1.5-million-dollar grant by the Economic Development Administration, with some smaller funding from the Iron Range Resources and Rehabilitation Commission. C. Thomas Burke, executive director for the Seaway Port Authority of Duluth, said in an interview for the Duluth Chamber of Commerce publication *Duluthian*, "Duluth's meal handling facility will be the most modern in the United States."

There was an upward trend for grain by-products, pellets and meal because of their ability to retain high protein when pelletized. High demand for human consumption as a food ingredient as well as livestock feed was driving a strong international market. Duluth-Superior was behind in its ability to handle and ship this type of commodity. In the previous year, 1972, the port had shipped a "record 517,000 tons" of grain by-product.

The initial drive for a new meal plant in the port began in 1970, led by Port Authority Commissioner Conrad Fredin.[364] A preliminary

---

364 "Duluth Port Gains $15 Million Elevator Complex," *Minnesota's World Port* 9, no. 2 (Summer 1973).

study conducted in 1972 by George Lloyd Levin, Inc. consulting engineers in St. Paul, reported that without the facility, the Port of Duluth "would lose not only the meal capacity being handled but any hope of expanding trade in that area in the future."[365]

"We look forward to building and operating a highly modern and efficient export elevator in Duluth," stated H. Robert Diercks, chairman of the board of Cargill, Inc. "It will have features that do not exist in the Port and that will make Duluth more competitive with other Great Lakes and seaboard ports." He went on to say the elevator in Duluth would be the only facility in the harbor to handle meal, like linseed meal and soybean meal in addition to grain.

> **For this reason, the new terminal promises opportunities for Duluth to participate to a much greater extent in the heavy volume of this country's protein meal and grain shipments to expanding world markets. Nearly all the meal business, for example, now goes to other U.S. ports with more competitive facilities.**[366]

Cargill's investment, along with the monies from the Seaway Port Authority, pushed the cost of the project close to 34 million dollars.

One of the first tasks in the Cargill expansion was the razing of Elevator *E*. The elevator had been abandoned due to structural defects, which made it unsafe for operation. The lost capacity was one of the reasons behind the decision to build a new elevator. Elevator *E* was originally part of the Union Improvement and Elevator Company system built in 1884. In 1899, the Consolidated Elevator Company made upgrades to the elevator that became a complete rebuild. In 1962, as part of its renovation, Cargill removed most of the machinery from the elevator, effectively relegating the building to a storage annex.

---

365 : "The Port of Duluth takes a giant step," Waterfront Notes, *Duluthian*, July 1973.

366 "Cargill: Faith in the Future of the Port," *Minnesota's World Port* 9, no. 2 (Summer 1973).

**Cargill *B* facility: A-frame storage (center), and ship loading berths *B1* (left), *B2* (right).**
Photo: Copyright Cargill, Incorporated. Used with permission.

Cargill's new ship-loading facility was constructed on the north side of the property. The 5.4-million-bushel terminal was a high-tech, computerized plant. On the south side of the facility, the dock located across from the Northland Pier became known as the Cargill Commodities Dock, at which inbound grains arriving by ship or rail were unloaded into a shore-side hopper. The dock is commonly referred to as *B2*.

Prior to the advent of self-unloading vessel technology, grain arriving at elevators from ships was unloaded with a "marine leg," a vertical conveyor system with buckets attached to a canvas or rubber belt. When the leg is lowered into the cargo hold of a vessel, it scoops the grain from the ship and raises it to the top of the elevator. The invention of the marine leg is largely credited to Joseph Dart, who first employed his device in Buffalo. Many but not all of the elevators in the port had at least one marine leg. Elevator *E*, for example, had two legs capable of unloading 20,000 bushels per hour,[367] but most were in the range of 10,000 to 15,000 bushels per hour. When the

---

367 Note: Data from Norris Grain Company, circa 1945.

Farmers Union elevator put its unloader into action in August 1943, it was said to be the fastest in the harbor, capable of unloading 25,000 bushels per hour.[368]

New, six-foot, four-inch-wide conveyor belts manufactured by Goodyear were installed to increase speed in grain handling. A computerized system remotely monitored all aspects of the grain handling, from input to sampling, weighing and inventory control. As reported in the *Duluth Herald*:[369]

> **Metal buckets attached to the surface of the belts will lift corn, soybeans, wheat and other grains more than 200 feet vertically to other belts that run horizontally atop the storage silos at the facility. The "mouth" of each bucket measures 12 by 7 3/4 inches with a depth of 7 inches. The buckets virtually cover the entire belt surface. Goodyear said the belts are made of eight-ply fabric and rubber construction with an electrically conductive cover designed to prevent buildup of static electricity.**

The main storage complex., Cargill *B*, consists of a series of concrete bins. The silos stretch for nearly a block reaching a height of 103 feet. The dockside ship loader at berth one (*B1*) can deliver a maximum of 140,000 bushels per hour. At the Cargill dock, there were no remote controls or spouts. Two loading rigs, each with its own operator perched in a cab above the hold, loaded the ships.

Prior to this, nearly all the elevators used "pull spouts" to load, recalled veteran stevedore Chuck Ilenda.

> **Back in the early 70s, this now this is before Cargill *B1*, virtually every elevator had pull spouts. They would have a rope on each side of the end of the spout and**

---

368 "40 Years Ago - Aug. 15, 1943," *Superior Evening Telegram*, August 15, 1983.

369 "Wide belts to speed up grain handling," *Duluth Herald*, March 22, 1976.

> you had to have a dock man that would pull the spout up and down, and the longshoremen would pull it right and left on the ship. The dock man worked for the elevator and was employed by the elevator, and he stayed on the dock. So, all he did was swing the spouts in and out and raise them up and down.

Dedication ceremonies for the new facility took place in September 1977.[370] Two months later, on November 16, 1977, the new headhouse caught fire in one of the lifting legs. Flames spread to a horizontal conveyor in a dust collection system causing two belts to fall. Fighting the fire was difficult for the Duluth Fire Department. Reaching the top of the 200-foot concrete tower clogged with smoke was a challenging obstacle. The fire burned out of control for over five hours before being subdued. The Upper Lakes Shipping vessel *St. Lawrence Prospector*, which was loading at the elevator, shifted over to *B2*.

Damage to the new elevator was estimated to be in excess of one million dollars. Fortunately, the fire occurred during the off-season for shipping, giving the company time to make repairs.[371] The new elevator was again dedicated, this time on December 20, 1977. In addition to the storage silos and new ship loader, the complex housed the new A-frame grain by-products building. The A-frame was built to store bulk commodities such as soybeans and sugar beet pellets. Its design is unique among elevator buildings in the Twin Ports.[372] "In terms of handling speed and efficiency, this is the most advanced facility on the Great Lakes," said Cargill vice president Clifford M. Roberts, Jr. at the dedication ceremony.[373]

---

370 "Cargill, New and Newest Twin Ports Facility Is Most Advanced on Great Lakes," *Superior Evening Telegram*, February 28, 1978.

371 "Elevator Fire Damage in Excess of $1 Million," *Duluth News Tribune*, November 16, 1977.

372 "New Construction on the Twin Ports Waterfront," *Minnesota's World Port* (Fall, 1978).

373 "Newest Twin Ports facility is most advanced on Great Lakes," *Superior Evening Telegram*, February 28, 1978.

Following the completion of the new Cargill elevator and the *B1* loading dock, Cargill announced the closing of Cargill *D*, the former Peavey headhouse located on the south end of Rice's Point. The firm cited the high cost of meeting state and federal air quality standards as the reason for the shutdown. Additionally, a downturn in the market resulting from the Soviet grain embargo was listed as part of the Cargill decision to close.[374] (The elevator was used to store government grain as late as the 1980s until the federal surplus program ended.)

\* \* \*

In May 1977, the Omaha-based commodities company ConAgra actively entered the grain handling business. The McMillan Company became its first acquisition. Included in the purchase were the McMillan Elevator *M* and the former Daisy Mill and annex located in Superior. ConAgra continued moving quickly, and, by December, had acquired the Burdick Grain Company. Burdick Grain managed the operation of *M* for ConAgra.[375] Jay Van Horn recalled:

> **McMillan was too successful. They went nuts! Things were going so good they started doing stupid things. They started playing the commodities market... futures... and they started spending money like crazy. Well, in 1976, they suddenly found themselves strapped for cash. They didn't have the money to go buy grain, so they would have grain to sell. That was how they made their money. All they were depending on then was their business with Dreyfus... and Dreyfus wasn't helping the situation in that I think Dreyfus wanted Elevator *M* for themselves. So, they finally got to the point where they had to sell. They couldn't operate; they just didn't have the money anymore.**[376]

---

374 "Cargill To Close Export Terminal," *Duluth News Tribune*, April 19, 1980.
375 Jay Van Horn, interview with author, Superior, WI, 1994.
376 Ibid.

Dreyfus was looking at Elevator *M*, explained Van Horn. Roy Leighton, executive vice president of Dreyfus, toured the elevator.

> They knew what it was and what it could do. And Peavey got in the act and they came and surveyed *M*. There was a traitor in the McMillan crowd and an outfit by the name of ConAgra became aware of Elevator *M* being for sale, and ConAgra was just thinking of breaking into the merchandising end of the grain industry; expanding.
>
> ConAgra went and looked into the McMillan Company and what they found was Howard McMillan had put up 80% of the money to form the company, but he'd taken in eight partners. The eight partners put up the balance, put up 20% of the money, but he gave each of the partners an equal vote on the board. ConAgra went and approached these people and they got five of them to give them their proxies to vote the stock.
>
> As I've been told, a fellow by the name of Bud Morrison from ConAgra came to Minneapolis and went in, made an appointment to see Howard McMillan and told him, "Mr. McMillan, we're going to call a board meeting at one o'clock today in the conference room downstairs in the grain exchange." McMillan supposedly told him what the hell are you talking about? I'm the head of this company. I'll decide when the board meetings are held." "No, I've got the proxy to vote five of your board members stock and we've decided to call a board meeting." They ended up stealing the McMillan Company from Howard. Instead of him getting the $7 million he was asking for he ended up keeping his house, which he stuck an IOU in the company till and put his house up as collateral.

ConAgra took over. In December 1977, it bought out Burdick Grain. Burdick had a long history with Elevator *M*, recalled former superintendent Van Horn. Osborne-McMillan produced malting barley for Burdick. The processed barley was shipped by boat and rail. Van Horn said they were handling about 8 million bushels per year.[377]

> When ConAgra bought Burdick, it was the perfect match-up. Burdick had Belco *1* and *2*[378] and Belco *5*, in Minneapolis, and all of the McMillan facilities [it was just Shoreham and Elevator *M* left] because Howard McMillan had sold Thief River Falls to Harvest States… so we were operated by Burdick Grain. Once ConAgra took over, we got really busy. We operated that way until 1983 when ConAgra bought Peavey Company, and then all of Burdick's facilities were put under Peavey's operation. That created a lot of hard feelings in Burdick Grain because Peavey was made the operator, and Burdick was supposed to go under.
>
> A fellow by the name of Brooks Fields, who was the executive vice-president of Burdick Grain, called Bud Morrison in Omaha and told him he could shove his you know what job… that he'd be damned if he'd work for a bunch of people who had lost money every year for the nine years when Burdick Grain had made nothing but profits. And he quit over the phone. Alan Burdick hung around for a while until he saw what kind of an operation Peavey was going to be, and he quit. At

---

377 Ibid.

378 Note: Two of the three Burdick elevators (Belco 1 and Belco 2) were destroyed by fire in St. Louis Park, Minnesota, on May 11, 1977. Burdick Grain Co. owned the elevators since 1950. The elevators were built for the Great Western Grain Elevator in 1893. In 1939, Hales Hunter purchased the elevators, changing the name to Belco.

> the time he quit, he was supposedly the biggest single stockholder in ConAgra. Because he had traded Burdick Grain strictly for ConAgra stock. Peavey had tried to solve all its problems by hiring people. So when Peavey was going broke and had to sell, they were like a big bureaucracy, and they just couldn't make money anymore.

\* \* \*

The fear expressed by grain millers about working in the older wood structures was borne out in January 1978. It was the Multifoods No. 4 house that would burn next. Cap 5 had been razed because of its age and structural deterioration. The fire at Capitol 4 became one of the most spectacular elevator blazes witnessed in the port.[379] Hollis Graves, part owner and local manager, recalled the night of the fire.

> It was terrible. It was on a Saturday night. I was going to church, and we were loading barley out of this elevator, where we had a good barley business. We were loading cars out, and they called me just as I was going to go to church and said there's smoke coming out of the ventilator. I asked them if the sprinkler system had gone off or any other devices and they said "No." I said, "Call the fire department. Get down there and see where the trouble is." When I drove down, I could see smoke coming, wisps off the top.

The fire was first reported around mid-afternoon on Saturday, January 21. Firefighters had brought the blaze under control by 3:30, but a dust explosion somewhere in the upper story of the elevator ended all hope of containing the fire. Graves said when he arrived, his crew told him where the fire was and that it was out.

---

[379] "Fire Consumes City Grain Elevator," *Duluth News Tribune*, January 22, 1978.

> I asked the millwrights to go upstairs with the firemen. I mean the "upstairs," take a look, make sure everything was alright up there. I wanted to call Minneapolis. I wanted to let them know there was a problem. If it did catch on fire, I didn't want them to hear it on the radio, so I went down there. First, I called them and told them everything was alright, and I stepped out of the door to go back and I could see black smoke starting to come. Then I knew there was a problem. I called and told them I was afraid it was going to burn up, which it did in a grand fire.

Moored next to the fully engulfed elevator was the ice-locked steamer *Harry L. Allen*. The vessel's fuel bunkers added the possibility of another explosion.

The remains of Capitol No. 4 smoldered through the night. Morning brought a grim scene of charred wood and twisted metal. The local papers covered the blaze with spectacular photographs showing the fire as it raged at its peak. International Multifoods listed the age of the elevator as being built in 1889 and declared an intent to quickly rebuild on the same site.

The ice-crusted hulk of the lake carrier *Harry L. Allen* displayed considerable topside damage from fallen debris. Tremendous heat generated by the fire caused sections of the deck housing to warp. The Steinbrenner fleet vessel was eventually declared a total loss and sent to the scrapyard.

Hollis Graves, Jr., elevator operations manager for Capitol at the time of the fire, felt that enough safeguards had been placed in Cap 4 to prevent a fire from destroying the elevator. "We had fixed the thing all up, with automatic bearings, all the safety devices you could think of," he said, adding, "I thought we were in pretty good shape… I thought the thing was actually fireproof. Once the wood caught on fire, well, that was all there was to it."[380]

Graves looked fondly upon Cap *4*.

---

380 Hollis Graves, Jr., interview with author, Duluth, MN, 1994.

> That was a fast little elevator. It really did a fast, good job in those days. It held about a million bushels, and the other elevator (Cap 5) held close to 500,000. It was a fast little place; they could really handle grain. In the early days, they cleaned a lot of flax, but times change so quickly in grain, you know. So, we used it then for a barley house, and Ralph McCarthy and my brother John were down, and they were running that, and they did a good business. Eventually we took it all up to 6 and put the barley cleaning machinery up there and made it all under one operation."

International Multifoods made good on their declaration to rebuild. In June, they announced a decision by its board of directors to issue bonds for construction of a new concrete annex to Elevator 6 at an estimated cost of 4 million dollars. A portion of the construction was financed through industrial development dock and wharf revenue bonds issued by the Seaway Port Authority of Duluth.

August 1978 saw the new concrete bins, considered part of Capitol 7, underway on the former Imperial Mill location. The Minneapolis firm of McKenzie-Hague-Giles was awarded the contract. They had recently been involved in Duluth in the construction of the new Cargill elevator. The Multifoods annex consisted of twenty-eight bins with a capacity of a million bushels.[381]

Capitol 4 was the last surviving remnant of Duluth's Imperial Mill. Multifoods razed the main mill building during the 1950s, and Cap 5 was demolished in 1977, nearly a year before the fire.

Hollis Graves, Jr. was the last of the Graves family to be associated with the Duluth elevator industry. His brother John was already working for Capitol when Hollis, Jr. started as a laborer out of college. "We were drying corn. In those days, they dried corn on the evening shift and did everything else around the place, and then I became a foreman. I was in charge of all incoming grain. It started

---

381 "Work Underway On New Grain Elevator," *Superior Evening Telegram*, August 8, 1978.

out to be train cars." As time went on, he became superintendent and later the manager of the company. He had big shoes to fill.

> My father was in there, and he was the superintendent of the elevators, and then he retired. He had a heart problem. That was when International owned it. When he retired, International retained me as a superintendent. My brother Johnny was down here at *4* house on the barley. Then Ralph (McCarthy) retired, and Johnny went up to run the barley business, and he was going to go to Minneapolis. They asked if I'd come up and manage the company, which I did for it must have been fifteen years or so.[382]

The destruction of Capitol No. *4* marked the end of the wooden grain elevator at Duluth. This left the Globe Elevator and Elevators *M* and *O* in Superior as the lone surviving wood frame elevators left in the Twin Ports. It was somehow fitting that it literally went out in a blaze of glory.

\* \* \*

Events at the end of the 1970s brought additional changes to Superior's East End elevators. Elevator *O* was sold to the city of Superior in 1979. The age of the wooden structure and its potential OSHA violations continued to keep the elevator closed and unusable. Elevator *O* was one of Superior's oldest grain elevators. The structure was built in 1893 as Elevator *K* for the Superior Terminal Elevator Company. When the Osborne-McMillan purchase took place in 1954, the elevator was renamed Elevator *O*.

The City of Superior now owned the elevator site and initially attempted to find a buyer to take over the operation of the elevator. Unsuccessful, the city voted to sell the property with the intent to demolish the structures.

---

[382] Hollis Graves, Jr., interview with author, Duluth, MN, February 12, 1994.

As plans progressed towards demolition, a group of Duluth developers came forward in 1979 with a proposal, albeit an unusual one, for the property. They proposed turning the elevator into luxury condominiums. A series of legal maneuvers by the consortium managed to delay even further the demolition of Elevator O. Petitions to the city council finally ended in September 1983 when the council voted to discontinue any further negotiations and proceed with the demolition.[383]

Before the legal proceedings, salvage work was already underway at the elevator. The timber harvested from the site was reportedly equivalent to 27,000 acres. A large amount of scrap metal was also salvaged.

While the city focused on its old elevator, talks were underway with the Louis Dreyfus Company for a proposed twenty-six-million-dollar elevator facility on Connors Point. Plans called for a 3.2-million-bushel elevator on a thirty-two-acre project site. The City of Superior agreed to apply for state and federal grants and considered issuing tax increment or industrial revenue bonds to assist with the costs. Pat Kluempke, regional manager for Dreyfus, anticipated that anywhere from sixty-five to seventy new jobs would be created. When questioned about a new elevator amidst the Russian grain embargo, Kluempke said Dreyfus would not commit capital unless it was warranted.[384]

In early July, it was announced that construction would begin in October. The City of Superior was awarded a thirty-nine-million-dollar urban development action grant to assist in building the estimated 27-million-dollar facility. As the mayor and civic leaders applauded the grant and the potential elevator, the reality of building on the Connors Point site was beginning to sink in… and along with it came two big pitfalls—dredging and rail access.

A feasibility study conducted by R. S. Fling & Partners of Columbus, Ohio, stated that:

---

383 "Superior Oks Razing of Elevator," *Duluth News Tribune*, September 7, 1983.

384 "Connors Point to be Site of Dreyfus Grain Elevator," *Superior Evening Telegram*, February 28, 1978.

> The land contours of Superior Bay and the location of the shiploaders dictate the need for extensive dredging. The site will require approximately 125,000 cubic yards of dredging, which will allow a ship to berth under its own power. "Rail access is a major constraint," added James McCarville, Superior port director. "The site is served by the Chicago & North Western, Soo Line and Burlington Northern railways, but the C & NW tracks on Connors Point—which have the most direct access to the proposed elevator site—are extremely congested."

As the talks and studies continued into the next year, it was obvious that progress toward an elevator was stalling. In October 1981, Louis Dreyfus canceled plans for the elevator, citing the rising project costs as the major factor. "The construction price rose from $25 million to $32 million." Another factor was the deregulation of the railroads, allowing lines like Burlington Northern to offer cheaper rates for moving grain to ports on the West Coast, the Gulf and even arch-rivals Milwaukee and Chicago.[385]

The nearly eight million dollars in state and federal grants secured by the City of Superior put the mayor and civic leaders in the difficult position of trying to find a new developer for the Connors Point site or lose the funding. A potential second dock for low-sulfur western coal shipments was among the ideas being discussed, but in the end, nothing was developed. For Mayor Hagen, who worked very hard to get the elevator project, it was a lost opportunity.

Years later, the story unfolded through off-the-record comments gleaned from informal conversations that went something along the lines of the Connecticut office of Louis Dreyfus felt that there wasn't enough capacity for grain on the Great Lakes and proposed the idea of building at Superior. After developing the plan, the final step in the process was to present a proposal to one of the appropriate division presidents of Dreyfus in Paris. After listening to the proposal, that

---

385 "Grain elevator project dropped," *Duluth News Tribune*, October 16, 1981.

president reportedly asked only one question in a tone that spoke volumes: "Why are we planning to do this?"

Nobody raised their hand to answer.[386]

\* \* \*

The adaptation of grain-loading spouts to accommodate oceangoing vessels did not end with the opening of the St. Lawrence Seaway System in 1959. Changes evolving with automated technology resulted in modifications well into the late 1970s when General Mills added a large 26-inch spout dubbed "Big Thunder" to Elevator *A* in Duluth. In several instances, these modifications caused friction between elevator operators and the International Longshoreman's Association because of the direct impact on labor contracts. Such was the case in 1977 when ADM Grain Company installed three large towers with electrified spouts along the wharf at Elevator *S* six feet from the water's edge. The ILA Local Union No. 1037 filed suit against ADM on April 18, 1978, for violation of its contract.[387]

The suit gives insight into the relationship between the elevators, the longshoremen and the grain millers.

> Prior to the opening of the St. Lawrence Seaway in 1959, grain was loaded through three spouts attached to the Employer's elevator, each of which was manned by a grain miller who performed the vertical and telescopic functions by means of manually turned cranks on winches located on the elevator wall some 30 feet from the nearest side of the ship. Longshoremen aboard ship controlled the lateral movements of the spouts by ropes attached thereto and, through hand

---

386 Ron Johnson, interview with author, January 5, 2024.

387 Chairman Fanning and Members Jenkins and Penfello, "Decision and Determination of Dispute," August 25, 1978. Local Union No. 1037, I International Longshoremen's Association, AFL-CIO *and* ADM Grain Company, a subsidiary of Archer-Daniels-Midland Company *and* Local Union No. 118, American Federation of Grain Millers, AFL-CIO. Case 18-CD-223-1.

signals and/or shouting, directed the grain millers, who were unable to see the holds, to start, slow, or stop the grain flow, and to raise, or lower, or telescope the spout.

The opening of the Seaway and a corresponding influx of ships caused the Employer to enlarge the flow capacity of two of the spouts, on which it also electrified the grain flow, vertical and telescopic mechanisms. Each of these spouts was operated by a grain miller by means of controls positioned beneath each spout. These two employees also were responsible for operating the remaining mechanical spout, and the Employer thus reduced its dock force by one.

In 1969, the Employer centralized the electrified controls by moving them to a dockhouse located on the dock where one grain miller only was required to operate all spouts. That grain miller, however, still had no view of the ships' deck or holds and, consequently, longshoremen continued to perform the lateral spout work.

In 1977, the Employer sought to accommodate increasingly larger sized ships by constructing three towers which it situated 6 feet from the water's edge of the dock and on which larger sized electrified spouts were installed. The electrified controls for these spouts, however, now included a control for lateral movements of the spout. The Employer also constructed in the middle tower a "cab" positioned about 30 feet above dock level which was to house the electrical control panel for all spouts and a grain miller operator, contractually classified as a dockman, automated.

> By late 1977, all construction and electrical work had been completed save for a voice communication system linking the longshoremen aboard ship with the cab. The Employer surmounted his deficiency by transferring the electrified spout control panel from grain millers operators on the dock to longshoremen on the deck, thereby incurring Grain Millers displeasure expressed through oral and written grievances alleging contractual violations which the Employer admitted to Grain Millers had occurred.
>
> On November 28, 1977, the Employer agreed to return the control panel to grain millers after completion of the voice communication system, which occurred prior to the beginning of the 1978 shipping season. Longshoremen, therefore, continued to operate all spout movements until the close of the shipping season in December 1977.
>
> Beginning on April 15, 1978, the first day of the 1978 shipping season, and continuing to date, grain millers have operated all of the electrified spout controls from the cab. The loss of the electrified controls caused ILA to engage in a strike from April 17 through 20.

The arbitrators of the dispute ruled in favor of ADM and its use of the Grain Millers, with which the company had a collective bargaining agreement. ADM did not have any labor agreement with the ILA. In the arbitrators' conclusion, the following text outlines the thinking of the judges.

> Upon the record as a whole, and after full consideration of all relevant factors involved. Particularly the collective-bargaining agreement between the Employer and Grain Millers; the realized and potential economies

**and efficiencies flowing from the Employer's managerial control over the disputed work and the employees performing same: the efficiency and economy of operation realized by combining in one operator control of both grain flow and spout movements: the Employer's assignment and preference: and the absence of any probative evidence that performance of the disputed work from the elevated cab poses a safety hazard to longshoremen on deck, we conclude that employees of the Employer who are represented by Grain Millers are entitled to perform the work in dispute. and we shall determine the dispute in their favor.**

**Accordingly, we shall award the disputed work to the Employer's employees represented by Grain Millers, but not to that Union or its members. We also find that ILA is not entitled by means proscribed by Section 8(b)(4)(D) of the Act to force or require the Employer to assign the disputed work to employees represented by it. Our present determination is limited to the particular controversy giving rise to this proceeding.**

There was one bright spot to end the decade. At the end of January 1979, General Mills began constructing an addition to their Elevator *A*. The 900,000-bushel annex would be a series of three steel tanks on the west end of the concrete storage silos adjoining the workhouse. Initial estimates placed the project cost at 1.4 million dollars to be financed with revenue bonds from the Seaway Port Authority. The tanks increased the elevator's capacity by approximately 45 percent.

# 16
# The 1980s: Old Faces, New Names

The decade of the 1980s opened with Cargill's April announcement of its intent to close Cargill C (formerly Occident) in Duluth. The firm stated that decreased grain activity in the port, along with the high costs associated with compliance to federal air quality standards, were the reasons for the shutdown.[388] This raised controversy in the port. A committee was sent to Chicago to meet with officials of the federally operated Environmental Protection Agency, who contended that Cargill and several other Twin Ports elevator companies were in violation of the federal standards.

The *Duluth News Tribune* reported that officials in the Chicago division of the EPA did not think the costs to bring Cargill C into compliance were unusually high. David Ullrich of the EPA forcefully stated that the closing was related more to the poor grain economy than air quality issues. "Based on all the information we have, [the closing] isn't due to environmental requirements, but supply and demand for grain, and the effect of the Soviet embargo."[389]

Delmar Kloewer, assistant vice president for commodity marketing at Cargill, countered this way, "With limited amount of additional business available to it, we cannot economically justify

---

388 "Cargill Blames Clean Air Rules for Shutdown," *Duluth News-Tribune*, May 17, 1980.
389 Ibid.

spending money necessary for Elevator C to meet all Minnesota Pollution Control Agency and federal Environmental Protection Agency emission standards."[390]

On Friday, May 16, 1980, at five o'clock in the afternoon, operations at Elevator C came to an end.[391] The closing resulted in the loss of jobs for sixteen grain millers at Elevator C and an additional thirteen at Elevator B. Cargill officials were considering using the elevator to store government surplus grain. As the verbal sparring continued, Cargill softened its position in a statement issued to the press by a company spokesman. "The volume of grain for export has been significantly reduced because of the new (partial Soviet) embargo, primarily with corn and wheat."[392]

Fairbanks Scale on the scale floor of the empty Peavey Duluth Terminal.
Photo: author.

---

[390] Wayne Nelson, "Cargill to close export terminal," *Duluth News-Tribune*, April 19, 1980.

[391] "Cargill Inc. reduces local operations," *Duluth News-Tribune*, May 16, 1980.

[392] Ibid.

Port officials at Duluth were concerned that Cargill would abandon the structures with no intent to vacate the 28-acre property. A similar situation occurred in Buffalo with Cargill regarding some of their former elevators in that city. In July 1980, Cargill announced its intent to place the property on the market. A proposed buyer, Italgrani U.S.A., Inc., a subsidiary of Italgrani Di Francesco Ambrosio of Naples, Italy, expressed interest in purchasing the property, seeking twenty million dollars in industrial bonds from the Seaway Port Authority.

Italgrani U.S.A., an international grain trading firm, filed an application with the Securities Division of the Minnesota Department of Commerce to secure funding for the proposed purchase. The Italian firm expected to pay 7.7 million dollars to purchase the two elevators with an additional 4.5 million for the purchase and installation of equipment, 4.5 million for construction on the site and 3 million for "architectural and legal fees, interest and contingencies."[393]

The Italian firm was a privately held company operating four durum mills in Italy, "accounting for about 80 percent of all durum milling in that country," reported the *Duluth Herald*, "and three import terminals on the Mediterranean and Adriatic Seas. The company has offices in Canada, France, Switzerland and Argentina, and its subsidiary has recently purchased a minority interest in a fleet of barges on the Mississippi River, a four-million-bushel river terminal in St. Louis and several country elevators in Missouri."[394]

Six months later, Italgrani U.S.A. backed away from the purchase, citing difficulty finding banks willing to back the industrial revenue bonds. Sources at the Port Authority stated that the firm was waiting for interest rates on the bonds to drop below the thirteen percent market rate. At the time, Italgrani was the fourth largest exporter of grain from the port, shipping durum wheat from North Dakota to its pasta mills in Italy.[395]

---

393 Bill Beck, "Italian group may buy idle elevators," *Duluth Herald*, January 1, 1981.
394 Ibid.
395 "Firm postpones plans to buy elevator," *Duluth News-Tribune*, July 15,

Cargill was unable to find a developer for the site or another grain company interested in the elevators. The property has since passed into the hands of the Seaway Port Authority of Duluth and is used for the open storage for off-loaded cargo. The property underwent some significant upgrades to its dock infrastructure and storage for its break bulk cargo business. One of the last known vessels to load at Cargill C was the Yugoslavian vessel *Solta*, taking a partial cargo of government surplus wheat on September 26, 1985.[396]

\* \* \*

The softening of the market alluded to by Cargill was felt across the board by all the elevators. The decline couldn't be attributed to any one factor or assigned to any specific grain company. It was a frustrating situation for everyone involved.

The hard-won grain deals with the Soviet Union that propelled the early 1970s grain rush had been polarized by trade embargoes. The restrictions placed a tangible hardship on the Duluth-Superior elevators. The movement of grain destined for more traditional European markets was also on the decline. The 1970s saw a marked increase in agricultural production in Europe, Russia and Ukraine, which led to a decreased dependence upon Western grain imports. Here, again, was another factor in the decreased flow of grain from the Twin Ports. It was easy to point fingers at the Soviet Union and Europe.

On the home front, a trend that began as early as the 1960s profoundly affected the Twin Ports market. The growth of grain shipments south along the Mississippi River was diverting a tremendous amount of grain away from the Great Lakes basin. Many of the major players at Duluth-Superior were already involved in this trade as well. Cargill and Continental, among others, operate large shipment facilities along the river.

Critics felt the St. Lawrence Seaway was antiquated before it was even completed. Twenty years later, that aspect became more

---

1981.
    396 "Waterfront Business," *Duluth Herald*, September 26, 1985.

apparent to shippers using the Great Lakes grain distribution channel. The technology involving vessel construction continued evolving during the sixties and seventies, unrestricted by the size of the Seaway. The Seaway remained static and further out of date.

To stay competitive with the rising costs of crew labor, newer and more automated vessels were designed with larger capacity and fewer crew. As a result, these deep-draft vessels were not capable of coming into the Seaway system, further restricting the flow of trade in the Twin Ports. The Great Lakes shipping industry also began expanding the size of vessels to more effectively compete for commodities such as iron ore and coal. They, too, are restricted by the Seaway in the opposite manner of international vessels by not being able to get out.

The Lake Superior ports of Duluth-Superior and Thunder Bay have increasingly reverted back to being a transfer point, this time for the movement of grain to ports like Montreal, Quebec City and Baie Comeau along the upper St. Lawrence River. The large amount of grain shipped from the Twin Ports during the 1980s was hauled on Canadian bottoms. The use of American flag vessels in the Great Lakes grain trade is virtually non-existent.

\* \* \*

By the start of 1980, International Multifoods had been working with Buhler-Miag of Minneapolis to install a large Buhler ship loader mounted on a 95-foot boom along the north wall of Capitol 6. The drawings indicated numerous conflicts with the support structure and location of the existing 16-inch spouts.[397] Spout No. 1, a high spout located 64.7 feet above the dock, was one of the few not impacted by the new loader. Spouts No. 2 and 3, indicated as low spouts, were no longer used. High shipping Spout No. 2, at 70 feet, and intermediate Spout No. 4, at 60 feet, were both in conflict with the new boom. The spout support for High Spout No. 3 was also in

---

397 Drawing WS-22, Buhler-Miag, Inc., International Multifoods, exterior elevation. Collection of Lake Superior Marine Museum Association, Capitol Elevator collection.

conflict with the new boom. Low Spout No. 5, on the western side of the north wall, was no longer in operation.

The new Cargill B facility in Duluth made the news again as a second fire in its short history caused an estimated $250,000 in damages.[398] This fire started at the bottom of one of the lifting legs that carries grain to the top of the 200-foot-tall headhouse. The fire then spread to one of the 40-foot horizontal belts and into the dust collection system, much like the 1977 fire, which started at the top of the structure in that instance. That fire caused close to a million dollars in damages. "The bottom of the lifting leg and the horizontal conveyor belt are located about ten feet underground where trucks dump the grain," said DFD assistant fire chief Robert Smith.[399]

In Superior, the Farmers Union Grain Terminal Association underwent a name change. The St. Paul cooperative merged with the Washington State Northwest Growers Association in 1983. The newly merged entity adopted the agricultural-sounding name of Harvest States Cooperatives.[400]

In a similar move the previous year, the Omaha commodity giant ConAgra Foods, Inc. purchased the Peavey Company. The Peavey Grain Company was retained as the elevator division for ConAgra, and Elevator M was placed under the supervision of Peavey Grain. This marked the second time Peavey operated the elevator.[401] The Burdick Grain Company, who originally operated M for ConAgra, became a part of the Peavey elevator division. While under Burdick's control, ConAgra invested nearly a million dollars into Elevator M beginning in 1980. A new truck dump was added to handle the increased demand for sunflower seeds. The new addition was equipped with a camera surveillance system to monitor the

---

[398] Carla Wheeler, "Cargill fire causes $250,000 damage," *Duluth News-Tribune*, October 29, 1982.

[399] Ibid.

[400] "Harvest States Cooperatives: Only the Name is Changed," *Superior Evening Telegram*, February 25, 1984.

[401] Clifford E. Clark Jr., *Minnesota In a Century of Change* (St. Paul: MHS Press, 1989), 269.

truck operation. A computer was installed to "allow all scaling and inspection to be done away from the truck dump area," a first for Twin Port elevators.[402]

The demolition of the former neighbor Elevator O (original Elevator K) proved slow and laborious. Elevator O shut down in 1972 and was undergoing a long-term demolition by Tri-State Salvage of Superior. The elevator's exterior walls, built with two-inch by ten-inch white pine, were expected to be salvaged and sold, as well as the ten-gauge galvanized iron sheeting covering the exterior with a "fire-proof" coating. The *Superior Evening Telegram* pointed out that "The condition of the white pine is amazing. Considering that it was installed in 1893. A sample of the wood is being sent to the forest lab in Madison to determine the age of the trees the mill material was cut from. The age of the trees may vary from 100 to 200 years in age."[403]

Attempts to level the elevator and salvage the timber were not totally successful, so the next step was to dynamite the structure, which was also largely unsuccessful. Dust billowing from the building gave the dramatic appearance of an explosion. "Key supports inside the elevator were cut and removed and cables were strung to pull in just the right places. The plan called for the structure to fall like an elaborate house of cards… When all the pushing and shoving was done, she remained standing, albeit somewhat disheveled looking."[404]

The end finally came on August 25, 1984. To dismantle the elevator and salvage the timber, cutting torches severed the steel support rods in the structure. The torches generated numerous sparks, continually causing small fires in the scrap piles around the demolition site.[405] The Saturday afternoon blaze originated in the same part of the building where a fire had been put out the previous day.

---

402 "Modernization underway at Elevator M," *Superior Evening Telegram*, July 29, 1980.

403 "Elevator O wood said to be in great shape," *Superior Evening Telegram*, December 21, 1979.

404 "Port Logbook," *Minnesota's World Port* (Duluth Seaway Port Authority, Spring 1980), 20.

405 The *Duluth News Tribune* erroneously reported the date of this fire as July 1984 in its coverage of two other elevator fires in the years following this fire.

Workers leaving for the weekend thought they had fully extinguished the fire, but it slowly rekindled itself into a full-fledged blaze. The alarm call came in at 2:48 in the afternoon. The Superior Fire Department responded with five trucks and twenty men. At the peak of the fire, the flames reached upwards of several hundred feet into the sky. With the elevator under demolition, fire-fighting efforts were focused on saving the nearby Elevator M.

Fire department officials said, "The fire started in the lower level on the north side of the elevator. Hot flames destroyed the north side and with the help of the prevailing southwest winds, the structure gave way around 4:30 p.m. Burning wreckage was blown over into Superior Bay."[406] The result of the fire was a total loss of the structure, the oldest of the east end elevators.

\* \* \*

The early years of the decade were characterized by a major economic downturn dubbed the Reagan Recession, the deepest since World War II. "The unemployment rate hovered between 7 percent and 8 percent from the summer of 1980 to the fall of 1981 when it began to rise quickly. By March 1982, it had reached 9 percent, and in December of that year the unemployment rate stood at its recession peak of 10.8 percent. The jobless rate slowly receded over the next few years, falling to 8.3 percent by the end of 1983 and to 7.2 percent by the 1984 presidential election."[407]

In the Twin Ports, the most visible signs of the recession were the idling of many of the large Great Lakes iron ore freighters and the loss of grain cargoes following President Carter's embargo on the Soviet grain trade. It would take a couple of years for the elevators to feel the pinch, but the impact was just as dramatic. The Farmers Union elevator went from over 150 employees between the two houses to just a handful.

---

[406] "Torches Blamed for Elevator Fire," *Superior Evening Telegram*, August 27, 1984.

[407] Richard C. Auxier, "Reagan's Recession," Pew Research Center, December 14, 2010, https://bit.ly/48WBne6.

## The Grain Terminal Elevators of Duluth-Superior

After about seven years as a laborer in the union (American Federation of Grain Millers Local 118), Dick Carlson had moved into the position of car puller at No. *1* house at the Farmer's Union. "I ran the hydraulic cables that pulled in each car individually to dump the cars." During the busy fall grain rush, literally hundreds of trucks would be lined up to dump grain at either the No. *1* or No. *2* house at Farmers Union, recalled Carlson. "We were probably doing about 200 trucks a day. We were going twenty-four hours a day on trucks."

As a laborer, Carlson was frequently called upon to help out in other roles if someone called in sick. "You had to know quite a few of the positions. Back then the young guys never got the chance to be one of the operators, like the car dump operator or a truck dump operator. You were always outside." On any given day, he could be out in the lot lining up trucks or probing box cars or trucks for grain samples. Carlson recalled:

> **Sometimes I was out probing, which is getting on top of the rail cars or crawling into boxcars and getting samples out of them. I probed quite a bit. There were all different kinds of things; you'd help on the inspection part of it of the grain by running it through the machines, recording the dockage and recording sunken and broken in it and the test weights.**

At the time, circa 1985, the labor force was divided between the No. *1* house (Tower slip side) and the No. *2* house (Hughitt slip side), with no crossover of employees. "I started at number 65, and there was 15 to 20 underneath me," Carlson recalled.

> **When you started, you were a laborer, and either you worked at No. *1* house or No. *2*, either you worked one or the other, that was it. When business slowed down and when they laid off, either they were going to do most of the business at *1* house or they were going to**

> do most business at 2 house.[408] So, I remember guys that were hired before me were getting laid off at 2 house, and I was still working.

Carlson recalls that each house employed about 80 people. Included among this number were non-elevator personnel such as state (approximately 25) and four federal grain inspectors. In 1983, the recession caught up with Carlson.

> I got laid off from 1983 to 1985. I was one week shy of two years being laid off from the elevator. If I would have been off one more week, I would have lost my seniority, and they didn't have to call me back. I was the last one to save seniority on that big layoff.

When he finally returned to work at the elevator, the Farmers Union was now Harvest States Cooperative, and more changes were in the offing. Carlson moved up the union ranks from car puller to the job of floorman, responsible for opening the gates at the bottom of the bins.

> I was given a list of how much to open the bins down in the basement for the blends, and that's what I did. I started the bins and gave the blend as needed. It was a pretty simple process with big implications if it wasn't done right.
>
> We had phones in the basement—they would call and tell you back off the grain a little bit or take a couple of notches off this bin, say bin 356 and add it over to 546 and stuff like that. You had what we called the ticket, and you made sure you kept a pencil on you because you're

---

408 Note: The Farmers Union/Harvest States House No. 2 was used primarily for storing and shipping malting and feed barley.

> always making changes. You always wanted to keep track of the changes that you made, because if something went wrong, you didn't want someone to tell you, 'Hey, what were you doing? You could say, "Here's what I did."

The grain was treated with pesticides such as carbon tetrachloride to prevent an infestation of insects. While lethal on insects, it caused health issues among elevator employees as well as deck crews on vessels sweeping out cargo holds. "It happened when I was there too, but I wasn't around it at the time," recalled Carlson. "Guys working in basements opening the bins didn't have N-95 dust masks back in the day, so the guys wore a handkerchief over their nose and mouth. Guys opening their bins down there and come up and they're bleeding from the nose from the stuff."

The Farmers Union headhouse, annexes and ship loading gallery on the Tower Avenue slip. Photo: author.

The mid-1980s brought more significant changes to Harvest States' Superior operation. Under superintendent Jim Veltum, the elevator began finding ways to eliminate jobs to create efficiencies in operations. The introduction of locomotives at the elevator meant a move away from using cables to pull the rail cars in, and the dependance upon the Lake Superior Terminal and Transfer (LST&T) and Burlington Northern to switch cars in and out of the elevator. The changes were difficult but necessary.

Carlson eventually became a house superintendent or foreman until he was hired directly by Harvest States, leaving the union to, in essence, become a "company man." He remained with the elevator, rising to terminal manager years before his retirement in September 2020.

\* \* \*

The expansion of ConAgra into the Duluth-Superior marketplace took on dramatic proportions in 1986 with the announced deal to purchase the Continental Grain Elevator. The Connors Point site had been operated by Continental since 1965 under a lease agreement with the Chicago and North Western Railroad.[409]

Negotiations between Continental and the Chicago and North Western had reached an impasse. The railroad wanted to sell while Continental wanted a new lease. The grain market had been depressed for several years. Continental believed the worth of the elevator was decreased as a result of the lower operating revenues and felt the lease or sale price should reflect this change. All the Twin Ports elevators showed decreased volume in the early eighties. It was speculated that Continental did not foresee a return to the volume it had previously seen and, therefore, did not think it prudent to outright purchase the elevator.[410]

ConAgra was interested in strengthening its handling of commodities in the port. To accomplish this would mean getting out of the Globe Elevator. The facility was a great one when it was built in 1887, but after nearly a hundred years, it was showing its age. The Globe was no longer the efficient, cost-effective plant it once had been. Its days were numbered.

---

[409] "ConAgra Acquires Continental Elevator," *Superior Evening Telegram*, June 4, 1986.

[410] John Parrington, interview with author, Minneapolis, MN, 1993.

ConAgra/Peavey believed that the acquisition of the Continental elevator would give them the facility they needed in their distribution network. They entered into negotiations with the Chicago and North Western and reached an agreement over the elevator in early 1986. Continental Grain had thirty days to vacate the elevator.

The Peavey Grain Company, a division of ConAgra, took control of the Continental Elevator in July of 1986. The facility was renamed the Peavey Connors Point Elevator. Peavey continued operating the Globe Elevator facility until 1988, when it was permanently shut down. The Connors Point Elevator remained one of the more active elevators in the Twin Ports harbor.[411] Mick Sertich, who had worked at Globe prior to its closing, was named superintendent, recruited by ConAgra to return to the Twin Ports to run the operation.

"ConAgra went in there and bought it from the railroad, kind of right out from under Continental, from what I heard," said Sertich. "Anyway, my old boss called me and asked me if I'd be interested in moving back and being a superintendent at the place, and it just all worked out."

Continental Grain continued active operations in Superior for two more years. During this time, it shipped grain through the Harvest States elevators. It finally closed its doors for good in the Twin Ports after the close of the 1988 season. [See the Appendix.]

When ConAgra/Peavey Grain took over in 1988, the elevator was in excellent condition. "It was a solid facility for one thing, meaning it worked. It was probably 50 percent faster in operating, for loading out and unloading," recalled Sertich. "We had three shipping legs there to load a vessel and they were 25,000 bushel each, so you could easily get 70,000 bushel an hour load-out speed. That's pretty fast."

On average, a Seaway-sized saltwater vessel loads around 700,000 to 750,000 bushels of grain, or 20,411 metric tons, equivalent to 45 million pounds in United States measurements.[412] Peavey Connors Point supervisor Sertich found the salties difficult to load

---

411 Jay Van Horn, interview with author, 1994.

412 Note: Tonnage in pounds is based on 750,000 bushels of spring wheat. Saltwater vessels use the metric system for measurement.

for a variety of reasons. "They'd have to check their marks constantly and take a little bit, like 1,000 bushel of grain at a time, because they kept figuring out all their fuel and water they we're going to use before to get out of the Seaway. They wanted every pound of grain on anything going overseas, and I don't blame them."

They often had to stop loading when the vessel couldn't take the grain quickly because it still had ballast. Until they pumped the ballast out, you couldn't load. "Sometimes you'd just load eight hours, and then they'd have to pump ballast all night long," said Sertich. "The lakers were easier to load. It was quicker, and they could move faster. These guys knew, almost to the pound, how many bushels you were gonna put on their vessel."

Peavey's move into the Continental site proved to be a timely one for the company. On October 27, 1986, the company suffered a severe setback with a fire at Elevator *M* that destroyed the workhouse in an early morning blaze. "A Superior police squad patrolling nearby reported the fire about 1 a.m. By the time firefighters arrived, the elevator's 200-foot-tall wooden workhouse near 21st Avenue East on Superior Bay was engulfed in flames."[413] A small grain dust explosion a half hour into the fire toppled the building.

Two days later, as small fires continued burning, ConAgra officials assessed the damage. The fire was believed to have begun in the upper part of the workhouse, but because of the extensive damage, finding the exact source was difficult. About 140,000 bushels of grain stored in the headhouse were destroyed in the fire. Industry experts within the port believed that with the weakened grain economy, ConAgra would not readily rebuild on the site.[414]

After the fire, Peavey idled the facility for several years. In 1990, after three years, ConAgra reopened Elevator *M*, using it to store imported Canadian oats and some spring wheat for several seasons until ConAgra leased the elevator to Hansen-Mueller of Omaha.

---

413 M. L. Levandowski, "Fire guts Superior grain elevator," *Superior Evening Telegram*, October 28, 1986.

414 Al Miller, "Officials probe smoldering rubble for cause of Peavey elevator blaze," *Duluth News-Tribune & Herald*, October 29, 1986.

Because of a lack of track space to accommodate large unit trains, a hopper was installed at Elevator *M* so that oats and possibly other grains could be brought in by self-unloading vessels.

\* \* \*

General Mills announced plans to construct a bagging plant adjacent to its Duluth elevator on the opposite side of the harbor. Like the Cargill plant, this was a joint effort between General Mills and the Duluth Seaway Port Authority. The house publication of the Port Authority, *Minnesota's World Port*, reported, "The plant is being built with Port Authority tax levy proceeds. Estimated cost of the project is $550,000. General Mills will manage the new facility under an agreement with the Port Authority."[415] The plant was expected to bag spring wheat, durum wheat, barley, corn, sunflower seeds, beet pulp pellets and various specialty grains. The facility had a bagging capacity of 1,200 tons daily.

The bagging facility was an idea generated by the Seaway Port Authority of Duluth to obtain federal and state money for construction of an infrastructure that would also utilize the port's freight terminal for shipment of the bagged products. The movement of containerized goods through the port was never going to be economical because of the size restrictions of the St. Lawrence Seaway System. The Port Authority's attempt to use pre-bagged food was an attempt to offset the loss of revenue by not being competitive in the container market. The Food for Peace program was its biggest customer.

"The bagging plant was a very unique situation," recalled former Seaway Port Authority of Duluth Trade Development Director Ron Johnson. "That never would have happened except for the guy that was running Elevator *A*. He took on the challenge. If he'd have been a so-so leader, headquarters would never have let him do it. The port went to the grain companies and asked, 'Would you consider doing this?' and General Mills was the only one that took the challenge."

---

415 "New Bagging Plant in Duluth," *Minnesota's World Port* 20, no. 1 (1985): 4.

For the Port Authority, the main impetus for the bagging plant was to enable participation in the Food for Peace program. Food for Peace had its origins in the Eisenhower administration as a formal program to provide food relief to countries experiencing natural disasters or the impacts of war. The Agricultural Trade Development and Assistance Act was signed into law in 1954 and became known as Public Law 480.

"The port knew they were losing general cargo because of containerization, and they tried containerization, but it just didn't work," Johnson recalled. "They were trying to do anything that could provide jobs and cargo through the port terminal, and if you could bag grain and work with USDA and PL-480, then it was kind of value added by providing jobs for the warehouse and ships coming in."[416]

The first cargo was grain destined for famine relief, so the first bags were ceremoniously filled by dignitaries, including Minnesota Lt. Governor Marlene Johnson,[417] before they were loaded onto pallets and delivered to the Port Authority dock for loading onto ships. The African Famine Relief program captured big headlines in Duluth, with photos of ships loading in sub-zero weather—very dramatic moments for the Port. A General Mills spokesman said the bagging plant represented the ideal blend of private and public cooperation designed to enhance the Port's competitive position. Port officials were actively pursuing additional business for the plant.

* * *

In April 1989, Dick Pomeroy, a veteran reporter for the *Superior Evening Telegram*, broke the story that ADM would not be renewing its lease on the Great Northern elevators in Superior. His source within the company said employees were notified that "they will be terminated unless conditions in the grain industry produce

---

416 Ron Johnson, interview with author, January 5, 2024.
417 "African Relief Cargo First Through Bagging Plant," *Minnesota's World Port* 20, no. 1 (1985).

some changes that make it advantageous to continue with its leased operation of the big elevator complex in Superior." ADM had leased the 13-million-bushel elevator complex since 1937.

Grain shipments out of the Twin Ports during the late 1980s had dropped to one-third the volume of the 1970s. Pomeroy noted that ADM and Globe in Superior, and Capitol 6 and General Mills in Duluth had shipped very little grain in recent years, while most of the grain went through Harvest States, Peavey ConAgra, and Cargill in Duluth.[418]

Jim Revell, ADM vice president for operation in Minneapolis, was quoted the following day saying, "We just don't want to be in Duluth-Superior. We just don't think its profitable," The lease was due to expire at the end of December. A spokesman for Burlington Northern, owner of the elevator, expressed doubt in finding a new tenant. On April 28, 1989, the order was given to close the elevator, according to Harold Hackleman, manager of ADM's Minneapolis office. "It just wasn't cost-effective to continue operating the elevator."[419]

Fortuitously for the BN, the American public was in the midst of the craze over oat bran, "the magic bullet for cholesterol," driving demand for the cereal through the roof. General Mills needed more storage space, and Elevator *S* had plenty available, so in July, General Mills entered into a one-year lease agreement with an option for a second year.

The primary benefit for General Mills in acquiring control of the elevator was an increase in its grain storage capacity. At its Duluth location, General Mills installed a hopper on Elevator *A* to receive Canadian oats imported on self-unloading vessels. The lack of track space to accommodate the larger unit trains was likely a driving factor in having the oats brought in by ship. The Canada Steamship Lines vessel *Tadoussac* arrived on April 14 with the first import of oats, with many more shipments brought into Duluth that season.

---

418 Dick Pomeroy, "ADM ending its elevator lease," *Superior Evening Telegram*, April 19, 1988.
419 "ADM elevator closed Friday," *Superior Evening Telegram*, May 1, 1989.

"Ships probably also will bring oats into the Great Northern elevator," commented a spokesman for General Mills.[420] After the July announcement, General Mills installed an unloading hopper at Elevator S to receive imported grains. Just like at General Mills' Duluth elevator, the Canadian vessel *Tadoussac* was the first to unload into the new hopper at S. It was nearly a year later, in 1990, that the American steamer *Kinsman Enterprise* took the first load of grain out of Elevator S for General Mills.[421] Of note, on December 8, 1989, the *Kapetan Andreas G* took the final load of grain for ADM from Elevator S, closing its fifty-two-year chapter in the elevator's timeline.

Critics of Elevator S said it was an expensive elevator to run, citing the large number of receiving legs, the small bin sizes and the elaborate spouting system that required more maintenance and manpower than the profits could justify. Doug Christensen was appointed manager of the General Mills plant in 1992. Christensen started out sweeping grain for ADM as a young man. Working out of his office at General Mills Elevator A in Duluth, Christensen had a crew of twenty-five men working between the Duluth and Superior elevators.

In an interview, Christensen explained how most of their imported grain used to arrive by rail, but now 90 percent arrived by ship. Conversely, nearly all the grain exported used to go by ship, whereas, in 1994, 60 percent went by rail. "Ninety percent of General Mills' grain is sold domestically. Some is shipped by rail to General Mills plants and made into cereals. Barley is shipped to malting plants."[422]

The decade closed with Cargill "donating" Cargill C and D to the Duluth Seaway Port Authority. After the initial interest by Italgrani U.S.A. waned, no company showed any interest in the aged facilities. An appraisal of the property conducted for the Port Authority placed its value around 4 million dollars. Cargill reportedly pledged to pay

---

420 "General Mills to lease ADM elevator for year," *Duluth News-Tribune*, July 15, 1989.
421 General Mills Elevator S: elevator loading logbook.
422 "Growing With Grain," *North Star Port* 26, no. 4 (Winter 1994–95).

nearly forty thousand dollars in 1990 property taxes and the first seventy-five thousand for razing the structures.[423] The cost to remove asbestos from pipes throughout the elevator and from the boilers was estimated at six thousand dollars. It subsequently cost the port of Duluth three million dollars to demolish the elevators plus conduct ground contamination clean-up to make the acreage shovel-ready. Under the Seaway Port of Duluth, the former Occident Terminal became Garfield *C*, and the Peavey side became Garfield *D*.

---

423 Wayne Nelson, "Cargill offers land to port," *Duluth News-Tribune*, December 14, 1989.

# 17
# 1990–2000: Stability

Since its foundational years as a grain port, Duluth prospered. Slightly over a hundred years afterward, wheat was still the money maker, but other grains had made inroads into the market. Rumors of its death were exaggerated. The high protein wheat is sought after by millers around the world.

Don Lilleboe, in his *Prairie Perspective* column for the Duluth Seaway Port Authority, wrote, "So, more than 120 years after the prairies of western Minnesota and the eastern Dakotas first felt the bite of the farmer's plow, and more than a century after the first notable quantities of Northern Plains wheat rode the rails to Duluth, the region's wheat industry remains vital and vibrant—and mighty important to the Twin Ports of Duluth-Superior."

A study funded by the Minnesota Association of Wheat Growers and the Minnesota Wheat Research and Promotion Council, conducted by North Dakota State University, concluded that "Minnesota's wheat industry generated a total of 1.3 billion dollars in economic activity in the state alone during 1992."[424]

Don Lilleboe wrote, "The relationship between wheat and the Port of Duluth-Superior provides a prime example of this national and international influence." He noted that in 1992, nearly 26.1

---

[424] Don Lilleboe, "Wheat Yields Grains of Economic Truth," Prairie Perspective, *Minnesota's World Port* (Summer 1994): 10.

million bushels of Minnesota-grown wheat entered the Twin Ports. Nearly 70.5 percent left the harbor on ships. "Add in all the wheat flowing into the Twin Ports during 1992 from states such as North Dakota, South Dakota, and Montana, and it's clear that wheat and Duluth-Superior are impressive and important partners."

Statistics show that in 1979 and 1989, grain shipments through the Twin Ports peaked at 7.89 and 8.15 million metric tons, respectively. Since that time, the port has seen a steady decline. On average, with the two peak years, grain shipped between 1979 and 1992 totaled 69.14 million metric tons. The deregulation of rail and truck rates in the 1970s made shipments to the West Coast and Gulf more attractive.

The Red River Valley of Minnesota and North Dakota continues to be the largest tributary of grain into the port. Cargill, which averaged 75 million bushels annually, was down to 40 to 50 million in recent years. The Russian grain embargo is thought to have caused some of the drop in volume. According to Lilleboe, "In December 1979, the Soviet Union invaded Afghanistan. President Jimmy Carter slapped a grain embargo against the Russians, and nervous grain traders around the world became hesitant about contracting for American grain."[425]

In the early 1990s, U. S. Wheat Associates, the national market development association for wheat growers, was test marketing a combination of American spring wheat and native West African grains as a wheat-based food product for the Ivory Coast and other sub-Saharan African countries.[426] Spring wheat and durum wheat, used to make pasta, are two of the largest grain commodities exported from the port. As grain science developed, wheat promotion organizations conducted research, continually looking for new markets.

\* \* \*

At the start of the decade of the 1990s, International Multifoods was the oldest continuous tenant in the Board of Trade building,

---

425 "Going With the Grain," *Minnesota's World Port* (Spring 1993).
426 "New Wheat Tested in West Africa," *Minnesota's World Port* (Fall 1991).

occupying the same corner office above First Street and Third Avenue West since the early 1900s. Tom Miller, who was appointed superintendent for Multifoods in 1989, said that most of the grains it handled were spring wheat with some barley and durum wheat. "Our marketing people have done a great job finding specialty markets for our wheat," said Miller in an interview for *North Star Port*. "We ship wheat grown in western Minnesota and the Dakotas—some of the finest in the US. It tests out low in damage, high in protein and has a very high-test weight."

Two years later, Multifoods was looking to sell its Duluth elevator. By the end of October 1991, a deal was pending to sell the business to Omaha-based AgProcessing Limited Partnership (AGP LP).[427] "Multifoods is selling its agribusiness assets so it can focus on other food-related businesses," reported the *Duluth News-Tribune*.[428] Multifoods' grain division had operated Elevator 6 and Annex 7 since 1947 with the acquisition of the Capitol Elevator Company. (Elevator 5 had been razed and 4 destroyed by fire.) The sale was for a reported 146 million dollars in cash. AGP LP was a joint venture, owned 80 percent by AgProcessing and 20 percent by Archer Daniels Midland of Decatur, Illinois. AgProcessing itself was owned by 392 cooperatives, including Harvest States and Land O' Lakes, at that time.[429] Miller stayed on as elevator superintendent with AGP after the sale.

Across the bay, ConAgra sold its aging Globe Elevator to J. R. Jensen Construction for demolition, consolidating its operations to the Peavey Connors Point elevator. Mick Sertich, elevator manager/superintendent of the Peavey Connors Point elevator, managed the final days of the Globe, basically cleaning out the remaining grain so the elevator could be sold.

While growing up, Mick was exposed to the grain industry through his father, Mark Sertich. The elder Sertich worked for

---

[427] "Sale of Grain Elevator Pending," *Duluth News Tribune*, October 30, 1991.

[428] David Algeo, "Sale of grain elevator pending," *Duluth News-Tribune*, October 30, 1991.

[429] "Maritime and Development," *Minnesota's World Port* (Spring 1992).

Peavey Producer Service out of an office in the Duluth Board of Trade, handling accounts in western Minnesota, the Dakotas and Montana before retiring from the Peavey office at the Globe elevator in 1983.

After high school, Mick moved to Grand Forks, working with his brother as a helper for a refrigeration company. While living in Grand Forks, Mick heard that the Globe Elevator in Superior was hiring, so he applied for the job and was brought on board. "I think it was like seventy-five cents an hour more. That was a lot of money back in '72. So, I accepted the job and moved back from Grand Forks to Duluth and started working just as a bobcat operator unloading boxcars and sweeping and cleaning—just a laborer, you know. I worked my way up to superintendent at the Globe." Sertich talked candidly about how the Globe operated from the time he came on board in 1972 until the final years. Sertich said:

> It had a lot of conveyor systems in it. It was labor intensive. There were probably 50 to 60 guys working there at one time. You could run two 12-hour shifts or three 8-hour shifts, and I mean it ran around the clock pretty much because there was so much grain going out of the port at the time.

Sertich said it was hard just keeping up. They would dump 130 trucks a day and rail cars around the clock. In the 70s, most of the rail cars were box cars. "They had to be unloaded with an electric bobcat. It probably took forty-five minutes to an hour depending how good you were as an operator."

Sertich recalled that some of the wooden bins in the Globe leaked where the timbers had eventually bowed with age.

> You always had to put the same kind of grain, meaning spring wheat or drum or sunflower seeds or soybean, you always had to put that next to the bin that you put it in because everything was intertwined there. It's all

> 2 x 12 white pine linked together, so if you ran one bin down and you had a different commodity in the next bin over it would start leaking into the bin that you were pulling out of, to say load a ship or whatever and that's a no-no. That's an unload. Nobody wanted that.

By the 1970s, the No. *3* house was used for unloading box cars but was no longer connected to the No. *2*. The houses were linked on the bottom so you could pull grain from *3* House into *2* House and *1* House for a ship or rail cars, but there was nothing connecting them on top, so it became a separate entity. Unloaded boxcars went into *3* House, and then if they needed grain, they'd pull it out of the bottom.

**The Peavey Globe Elevator House *1* in the summer of 1976.**
Photo: author.

Number *3* house had its own conveying system, its own pits to put the grain in, and unloading legs. They could dump two cars at a time, and each boxcar had its own elevating legs. Upstairs in No. *3* were two conveyor belts with a tripper on each belt that would trip

## The Grain Terminal Elevators of Duluth-Superior

the grain into the right bin.[430] That had to be operated manually. On cold winter days, it was hard for workers to stay warm, especially up in the top of the annexes, where the equipment had to be coaxed into working.

The Globe handled 75 percent spring wheat, 20 percent durum wheat and 5 percent feed barley. The bulk of the grain was shipped overseas to places like North Africa, South Africa, Algiers and Italy. Roughly 30 percent of the wheat went domestically to Buffalo, where ConAgra had a flour mill. The grains were sourced from western Minnesota, North Dakota and Montana. Sertich explained, "If our market needed some different quality spring wheat, and say North Dakota had some wheat that went bad from the growing season, and Montana had a lot better, we would buy from Montana. At that time, I think there were 26-car trains and 52-car trains, but if we needed it, we had elevators in Montana."

Sertich stayed at the Globe until ConAgra closed the elevator in 1985, leaving them with Elevator *M* and the Daisy Mill at the East End of Superior. "They cut way back," Sertich said. "We had seven management people, superintendents and foremen and stuff like that, and they let seven of us go, and I was number seven… there was no market. All they had was the government storage. They laid everybody off and just tried to keep the storage there to make revenue."

The consolidation of Peavey's elevator operations to Connors Point meant the end of the Globe Elevator. The demolition didn't occur, partly because the cost of environmental clean-up of the property was prohibitive. Rather than be saddled with the vacant elevators for years, Jensen, after scrapping out most of the equipment

---

430 Note: The introduction of the conveyor belt tripper to the grain industry increased the efficiency of the elevators and decreased labor costs. A tripper is a structure that removes grain from a conveyor belt. It can be moved along the belt to remove grain at different positions. The tripper was developed in the early 1900s in the coal industry as a means of removing debris from active mining areas. From its introduction to today, all elevators use trippers to transfer grain to storage bins. The belt and tripper are usually located on the bin floor.

like the garners and scale hoppers, found a willing buyer in Gordon Oftedahl, who purchased the property in 2004.

Oftedahl wanted to turn the parcel into an RV park and marina, which would require razing the buildings. Tangentially, David Hozza, the former Twin Cities investment banker, saw the potential for recycling the wood. He partnered with Judy Peres to found and start Wisconsin Woodchuck LLC in 2006, contracting with Oftedahl to remove the wood one plank at a time.[431]

In 1998, Harvest States Cooperatives merged with Cenex to become Cenex Harvest States. The firm adopted "CHS" as its brand name before officially becoming CHS Inc. in 2003. The Superior complex can hold eighteen million bushels. Cenex-Harvest States ships 80 percent of its outbound grain by ship. About 70 percent of inbound grain arrives by rail. Durum wheat accounts for the largest volume, most destined for Morocco and Tunisia, where it is made into "couscous." Barley is shipped to North Africa, Israel and Saudi Arabia.

In May 1998, ConAgra, Inc. and Farmland Industries, Inc. agreed to form a grain-basis alliance to "improve both companies' services to farmers and grain marketing and export activities." The new company was split into two branches—Concourse Grain, LLC, and Farmland-Atwood, LLC. The Superior elevator on Connors Point was leased to and operated by Concourse Grain.

In a ConAgra press release, Fred Page, president of ConAgra Grain Companies, stated, "ConAgra will benefit from access to the Galveston port, greater utilization of its Great Lakes and Mississippi River export facilities and better access to hard red winter wheat."[432] The partnership didn't work out, and after a year, Concourse Grain, LLC went away when the agreement expired on May 22, 1999. In

---

431 In 2013, the project was halted when Wisconsin Woodchuck defaulted on their loan.

432 "ConAgra and Farmland Form Grain Marketing, Service Alliance," ConAgra News Room, May 18, 1998, https://www.conagrabrands.com/news-room/news-conagra-and-farmland-form-grain-marketing-service-alliance-778574

little less than a decade, Farmland filed for bankruptcy. Farmland, the nation's largest farmer-owned cooperative, "got into a cash crunch caused in part by high costs and weak sales in its fertilizer business," according to the *Minneapolis Star Tribune*.[433]

From a commodity perspective, 1998 was the first year that sugar beet pulp was exported from the port. Sugar beets are grown primarily in Minnesota and North Dakota, but the export product is a compressed pellet. "Beet pulp is the vegetable matter that remains after sugar is extracted from the beet. This vegetable matter is then mechanically pressed, dried to reduce moisture content and then turned into a five-sixteenths-inch pellet to capture its nutritional matter and improve its handling characteristics."[434] That season, 34,000 metric tons of beet pulp pellets were loaded out of the port.

From the start of 1901 to the end of December 1999, a hundred shipping seasons had come and gone as the century came quietly to a close.

---

433 "Smithfield, Not Cargill, to Buy Pork Business," *Minneapolis Star Tribune*, October 14, 2003.

434 "Say this 10 times real fast: Beet Pulp Pellets!" *North Star Port* (Fall 2007).

# 18
# 2000–2023: Changing Players

The turn of the century introduced the first ownership of local elevators by foreign interests and a shift toward ownership by hedge fund companies rather than traditional agricultural commodity firms. The overall volume of grain moving through the port was down from the numbers posted a century earlier, but it still accounted for a steady yearly total. The first two decades of the twenty-first century reflect the changing global view and the interdependency of nations around the globe.

One big change was the elimination of grain inspection from the Minnesota side of the harbor. Inspection would continue in Superior, as explained in a paper to the Joint Committee on Finance in Madison.[435] The paper also examined the factors behind the decreased level of grain exports from the harbor. For example, in Superior, the shipping volume of grain had decreased from approximately 256 million bushels in 1999 to approximately 142 million bushels in 2003 (a decrease of nearly 45%). In calendar year 2004, grain volume increased slightly to approximately 146 million bushels.

Superior officials stated that grain volume levels reached their lowest level in twenty-seven years in 2003. They believe that the

---

435 "Grain Inspection Program (Agriculture, Trade and Consumer Protection) Joint Committee on Finance, Paper #141, May 5, 2005, pp. 5–6. Legislative Fiscal Bureau, Madison, Wisconsin.

combination of increased prices, reduced number of employees and expected increasing grain volume yielded a modest surplus in 2004–05, with improving financial conditions because of increased grain volumes. However, DATCP and DOA officials projected the state's combined grain inspection program to continue to be in deficit through the 2005–07 biennium.

Superior officials argued that one of the reasons for a decrease in grain volume at the port over the previous few years was tariffs on foreign steel, making it more expensive than domestic steel. Superior officials stated that when foreign steel was shipped to the US, it was typically back-loaded with grain to Europe. However, with the increase in the price of foreign steel relative to domestic steel, fewer shiploads of steel had been delivered to the US, which had also decreased the amount of grain that back-loaded to Europe. With the end of these tariffs in December 2003, Superior officials expected the grain volume to increase.

In August 2005, the Federal Register reported that the Minnesota Department of Agriculture announced a voluntary cancellation of their services as grain inspectors in the port. The Minnesota Railroad and Warehouse Commission had served the port's elevator industry well, standing steadfast in times of controversy. Grain Inspection Office continued operating in Superior as a part of the Department of Agriculture, Trade and Consumer Protection: Under an agreement with the United States Department of Agriculture's (USDA) Federal Grain Inspection Service, the Wisconsin Department of Agriculture, Trade and Consumer Protection (DATCP) administers the state's grain inspection program. Inspection services are funded from program revenues derived from fees charged for inspection services.

* * *

The excitement at the opening of the Peavey Duluth Terminal in 1901 and its innovative use of concrete as a construction material lasted exactly one hundred years before efforts began to remove the concrete silos to make room for new development. The Port Authority Board of Commissioners awarded a 1.05 million dollar contract for the demolition of the former Peavey/Cargill elevator to Isle Engineering of Finland, Minnesota, in 1988.[436]

The contractual completion for the demolition was the following June. Work began on August 30 with the removal of the top stories of the Peavey headhouse, but from that point, it became a struggle to meet deadlines, which led to the cancellation of the contract after attempts to collapse the concrete silos by dynamite failed.

Billington Contracting Inc. was hired to finish the demolition. In a pre-project visual survey of the elevator property, employees of Billington unearthed about a dozen sticks of dynamite as well as an equal number of blasting caps before eventually finding a suspicious-looking storage box. According to a local newspaper, "It was a strong box which had two padlocks on it," Davis Helberg, executive director of the Seaway Port Authority, said, "…and was found in a cavity on the sea side. It almost looked like a bunker from World War II with a box nestled inside of it. It was found to contain 2 1/2 cases of dynamite."[437] The hidden explosives were believed to have been there for many years, and the mystery of how they were left there remains unsolved.

\* \* \*

In the spring of 2006, ConAgra announced the sale of its grain operations to Ospraie Management, LLC, a New York hedge firm "that invests in commodities and basic industries worldwide across public and private markets. The company, through its venture arm, makes agriculture-focused investments that seek to reduce environmental impact."[438]

In 2006, Ospraie launched the Ospraie Special Opportunities Fund, which holds private equity stakes in commodities and basic

---

436 Letter from Lisa Marciniak, Port Promotion Manager, to Richard Langlee, Vista Fleet, providing schedule of demolition, August 26, 1997. Collection of Lake Superior Marine Museum Association, folder on Duluth-Superior-Elevators-Garfield "C."

437 "Explosives found at demolition site," *Duluth Budgeteer*, August 23, 2002, https://bit.ly/4afkqfV.

438 "Ospraie Management, LLC," Wikipedia, https://bit.ly/3Po0a3V.

## The Grain Terminal Elevators of Duluth-Superior

industry companies. The fund was the lead investor as the company completed its 2.8-billion-dollar deal with ConAgra Foods, Inc. Included in the purchase was the Peavey Company elevator on Connors Point in Superior, Elevator *M*, and the former Daisy flour mill, all part of a 2.8-billion-dollar deal with ConAgra Foods. Ospraie created a subsidiary called Gavilon, LLC to operate the Superior elevator, which was renamed Connors Point Terminal.

While the elevator was operated by ConAgra Peavey Grain, it doubled its rail capacity in 1990. Gavilon's newly acquired Superior elevator could unload 11,000 rail cars a year and 27,000 trucks. On the ship loading side, the elevator can load up to 75,000 bushels an hour. Grain from twenty-five bins can be blended to meet customer specifications. About 70 percent of the volume of the Connors Point elevator is spring wheat, followed by barley, oats, sunflower seeds and feed grains. "We ship out 60 million bushels a year to Italy, West Africa, Cyprus, Israel and Saudi Arabia," said then superintendent Len Kucza in an interview shortly after the acquisition. "There will always be a need for grain coming from the Twin Ports. Some ports around the world can't handle bigger ships that load on the west coast or in New Orleans."[439]

During the 1990s, ConAgra purchased the adjacent dock property to its west, the former Meehan Seaway Services dock, also known as the municipal dock, used for overflow storage. "It was a good buy when they bought it because there was grain in it," recalled Sertich. "We unloaded some cars, one an hour, but you could only do ten rail cars at a time before the railroad had to switch them out, so you've got four guys over there standing by watching it come out of the cars, pretty slow, but in the market, when the price of grain was right, it worked. It probably still does. They were looking for storage, that's what they bought it for. They didn't buy it to do any blending."

\* \* \*

---

[439] "Growing With Grain: Peavey," *North Star Port* 26, no. 4 (Winter 1994–95).

The conclusion of the 2007 shipping season saw a late surge in the movement of grain, up 42 percent for a total of 3,178,848 metric tons. Overall, totals were down. In January 2008, Cargill sold its entire Duluth export terminal to Riverland Ag, a spin-off of Whitebox Commodities Holding Corporation, "a grain handling, storage and trading business" a subsidiary of Whitebox Advisors, LLC, a Minneapolis-based hedge fund group founded in 1999.

The sale of Cargill's Duluth facility came as a shock to many in the industry but was part of a larger strategy developed by John Stich, president of Riverland Ag. Stich was initially contacted by Nick Swenson, portfolio manager and partner at Whitebox Advisors, to work as a consultant.[440] Prior to his involvement with Whitebox, Stich had a long history and knowledge of the grain industry. His father, Duane Stich, was the vice president of Bunge Corporation in Minneapolis and president of the Minneapolis Grain Exchange in the late 1970s when the Soviet Union brokered a five-year deal with the United States for the purchase of six to eight million metric tons of grain.[441]

Following along the lines of his father, John started grading grain while in high school and loaded barges on the Minnesota River in Savage, Minnesota, while attending college. After graduating from the University of Minnesota, Stich started his career in 1990 as a trader with the Peavey Grain Company in Davenport, Iowa, before becoming a grain merchandiser with the DeBruce Grain Company of Kansas City.

In 1995, after leaving DeBruce, Stich went to Great Falls, Montana, where he worked for General Mills as a merchandiser of feed barley, malting barley and oats for country elevators in Montana and Idaho. In 1997, he transferred to Minneapolis as senior commodity merchandiser manager, overseeing the movement of wheat to a General Mills flour mill in Buffalo, the procurement of wheat to all five General Mills cereal plants producing Wheaties and

---

440 John Stich, interview with author, January 24, 2024.
441 "Surprise Soviet Wheat Sales to Affect Prices," *Valley Morning Star*, Harlington, Texas, November 12, 1977.

managing ship logistics with George Steinbrenner's Kinsman fleet to supply wheat to Buffalo while merchandising the wheat program at Elevators S and X in Superior.

"I started working for Swenson as a consultant," Stich explained. This was in June of 2006 when ethanol production was beginning a rapid stage of growth. "Swenson wanted me to look around and see if there were any opportunities in grain. I knew of all these assets in town. ConAgra had these assets, and there were other assets that were woefully under-traded and under-utilized, and storage rates were quite cheap. They were paying less than three cents a month per bushel, tops, and were leasing facilities basically for malt barley moving to Anheuser Busch."

Stich decided to contact Matt Gibson, a colleague working for the ConAgra Trade Group, to ask if they'd be interested in selling a couple of their facilities in Minneapolis. They were. "He was very excited about it," said Stich, who negotiated the purchase of three ConAgra facilities in Minneapolis and Shakopee (Electric Steel and Malt One, Shakopee). Stich perceived the value of these facilities as exceedingly cheap compared with the cost of new construction, plus they were an established mechanism for shipping oats and spring wheat. "If I bought grain and put it in there, I could deliver against my hedges and get my money back," said Stich, "and I can also force carry, wider carry in the marketplace. So, I bought those facilities."

That fall, in 2006, Whitebox hired Stich full-time at its office across from Lake Calhoun in Minneapolis.[442] At the same time, Whitebox Holding Corporation was spun out as Riverland Ag, its own C Corp, with Stich at the helm. "I built out the space on the same floor as Whitebox, just across the hall, and started building my trading team." With a large amount of capital to work with, Stich sought more opportunities, with Cargill's Duluth elevator squarely in his vision.

"That property was owned lock stock and barrel by Cargill, and it's about sixty-five acres. They built it in late 70s to ship soy beans,

---

442 Note: Lake Calhoun has since been renamed Lake Bde-Maka-Ska in honor of the indigenous populations that lived here.

soy bean meal and wheat to Russia. That all ended when Jimmy Carter screwed the farmers over with the grain embargo after Russia invaded Afghanistan and also politicized the Olympics," opined Stich about the facility they referred to as the crown jewel.

"My thought was, we have a saying in the grain business… everything is for sale. All you've got to do is pick up the phone and call somebody. I ended up paying 20 million dollars for a 14-million-dollar space with a hundred-car unloader. You can unload a vessel and load a vessel simultaneously. There was also a million-bushel elevator up there, the older one on that property, that wasn't being utilized because they hadn't repaired the roof. I spent $115,000 to redo the roof, so for eleven-and-a-half cents per bushel, I had an additional million-bushels of storage space."

In these contracts, and certainly in the Cargill one, there was a right of refusal to buy back the facility in case we went bankrupt, said Stich. "I don't recall if that was in the ConAgra ones, but that was in a couple of the contracts, certainly in the Cargill one. I was like, no problem," explained Stich, "because I knew this was going to work."

In June 2008, Riverland Ag acquired the former Lake & Rail Elevator on the Buffalo River, garnering another flurry of media reports. Reporter Sharon Linstedt, covering the sale for the *Buffalo News*, wrote:

> Whitebox and other investment groups are going beyond the buying and selling of financial derivatives linked to commodities, like corn, soy beans and wheat, and putting serious dollars directly into agricultural crops and infrastructure. Grain elevators are of particular interest because they can store inventory for future sales at higher yields.[443]

Well over a hundred years after A. J. Sawyer and Charles Pillsbury went head-to-head over futures trading in 1892, the practice remains

---

443 Sharon Linstedt, "'Lake & Rail' grain elevator purchased by Minnesota firm," *Buffalo News*, June 13, 2008.

at the heart of the grain industry, as does hedging. To the layman, futures hedging establishes a price either before or after harvest. By establishing a price, the producer protects against price declines, but also generally eliminates any potential gain if prices rise. It is a way to manage risk and help reduce a potentially large loss. Stitch explained:

> What you do when you hedge is you buy cash grain, and then you sell futures. And then, when you sell a cash grain back out, you buy the futures back. You end up living in what we call a "basis" world, meaning once you know that concept, the value, the futures and the price of the grain products really don't matter anymore. It's all about the basis value. What price did you pay? And the basis means is what the price is relative to the futures. So, you're trading above and below the futures value.

That same year, back in Duluth, the former Cap 6 elevator, owned at the time by AGP Grain Ltd., sold its subsidiary Ag Processing, Inc. to Columbia Grain of Portland, Oregon.[444] According to Mike Maranell, senior vice president of corporate and member relations for AGP Inc., "This [sale] happens to be a small portion of our grain group, which includes the North Dakota locations along with Duluth, Minnesota."

In a public statement, Maranell said, "We will actually reposition now our efforts and assets within our grain group and concentrate on our Nebraska, Kansas, Iowa, Minnesota and South Dakota marketing agreements and assets we also operate in Texas. We will also continue to operate the Antwerp, Belgium, and the Barcelona, Spain, offices as well."[445]

Columbia Grain wasn't interested in the Duluth elevator, and as a result, John Stich found himself again in the right place at the

---

444 "AGP sells AGP Grain Ltd.," *All About Feed*, April 8, 2008, https://bit.ly/3PtqODt.

445 Byron Sims, "Ag Processing sells grain Subsidiary Assets," *Ethanol Producer Magazine*, August 7, 2008, https://shorturl.at/txy27.

right time when Mike Wong at Columbia Grain reached out to him about the Duluth elevator. Stich said:

> I knew Mike Wong from my days with General Mills out in Montana. He was now the number two guy at Columbia. They were going to buy all these assets. They wanted the origination in North Dakota, and Wong asked if I'd like to buy the Duluth facility. I said yes.

Stich recalled offering 2 million dollars, which Columbia accepted but added additional money as part of the closing, eventually paying 2.5 million dollars for the elevator.

"It was like one of those 'I buy, I sell, Peter-Paul' things," said Stich, adding:

> I think it might have happened the same day, like they closed the morning, and then I closed with them in the afternoon, or maybe it was still the next morning. But that was sort of how that worked out. They already had size-ups. When you buy these facilities, say there's grain in them, the federal warehouse guys go in and do a measure up on everything. That was already taken care of, all that due diligence.

Concurrent with the purchase of the Duluth elevators, the names of the facilities changed as well. The AGP elevator became Riverland Ag *Duluth Lake Port Storage* and Cargill became Riverland Ag *Duluth Storage*. The new names, as well as Riverland Ag, came from Nick Swenson.

At Riverland Ag, the whole concept was buying space and expanding position. Coincidently, during the summer of 2007, Canadian farms yielded a massive harvest of high-quality oats. Stich explained his perspective this way:

> It's better to be lucky than good, you might say, or timing is everything. I bought five thousand rail cars of oats out of Canada; that's twenty-five million bushels of oats. General Mills grinds around twenty-two or twenty-three million bushels a year, so it was more than what General Mills grinds to make Cheerios. I bought those oats at under delivery value and stuffed Duluth and Minneapolis. I was also starting expansions at Shakopee and at Malt One. It was like 25, 30, 35 percent of the open interest on the oat contract on the Chicago Board of Trade. I mean, it was just huge, the size of the positions.

> I got all the facilities in my clutch deliverable for oats, some of them were not regular for delivery for spring wheat, and expanded that footprint. My job was to provide carry to the market. That's how you make money.

The concept of Riverland Ag was to buy commodities that turned into a food ingredient for multi-billion-dollar branded equities, oats for cereals, for flour, for Cheerios, and by continuing contracts with Anheuser Busch while upping the rent. "I really jacked up the rent on these guys. They were paying next to nothing for storage space for malting barley for their Budweiser beer."

Cargill had a long-term contract with Anheuser Busch to store malting barley at a very cheap rate. Shortly after Riverland Ag closed on the Duluth elevator, Anheuser Busch was purchased in 2008 by InBev, a company founded in 2004 with the merger of the Brazilian Companhia de Bebidas das Américas (AmBev) and the Belgian Interbrew SA.[446]

"They started canceling all the contracts as soon as the leases were up on my storage with Anheuser Busch," recalled Stich. InBev

---

[446] "Anheuser-Busch InBev," Britannica, March 10, 2024, www.britannica.com/topic/Anheuser-Busch-InBev.

began drawing out all the malt barley stored in Duluth. "That storage… it was worth millions and millions of dollars for a three-year type of a deal. So that never happened."

In addition to the malt barley, at the time of the purchase by Riverland Ag the Cargill facility in Duluth had a little bit of wheat, some oats and fertilizer in the A-frame. "It would store anything—you want to talk about beautiful facility. When I bought it, it was still state of the art. I mean, the leg speeds and the dust collection. It was absolutely Rolls Royce, Rockstar, amazing facility," said Stich admiringly.

Two years into the ownership, the collapse of the stock market brought an abrupt end to everything Stich and Riverland Ag had built up. Riverland Ag was very successful, recalls Stich:

> I didn't sell, but you have to remember the economy was on fire. The stock market went down to like 6,000 points or something, and my boss had lost a lot of money. I didn't want to sell the company. It was my baby. I just birthed it, and we were making excellent returns, north of 25 percent, but hedge fund guys really aren't that bright. They also eat their young, so my boss went the way of the dodo, and they wanted to get rid of Riverland Ag so they could get the cash back out of it. I was sitting on $100 million—$50 million in equity in the assets, $50 million in retained earnings—so they could go buy cheap stocks.

Following the market collapse, Whitebox Advisers sold its grain assets and the Riverland Ag name to Toronto-based hedge fund Ceres Global Ag. Stich was replaced as president by his vice president shortly after the transaction.[447] In a press release issued on June 11 in Toronto, Ceres Global Ag Corp. issued the following statement:[448]

---

447 Note: Ceres Ag is not associated with Ceres Terminals, founded in Chicago in 1958. Ceres began stevedoring in Duluth-Superior in 1959 with the opening of the St. Lawrence Seaway System.

448 "Ceres Global Ag Corp announces closing of acquisition of Riverland

> ("Ceres" or the "Corporation") is pleased today to announce the closing of the Corporation's previously announced acquisition of 100% of the outstanding shares of Whitebox Commodities Holdings Corp. (the "Acquisition"). On April 27, 2010, the Corporation announced that it had entered into a definitive share purchase agreement to acquire 100% of the outstanding shares of Whitebox Commodities Holdings Corp. from various funds advised by Whitebox Advisors LLC, based in Minneapolis (the "Whitebox Funds"). Founded in 2006 by the Whitebox Funds, Whitebox Commodities Holdings Corp. operates under the trade name "Riverland Ag."

The former AGP Elevator 6 operated as the Riverland Ag Duluth Lake Port until 2016, when Ceres Global Riverland Ag closed the elevator. An estimated million dollars in repairs were needed to shore up a crumbling sea wall on the main elevator, an amount Ceres Global Ag was unwilling to spend. As a result, the elevator was purchased in 2017 by Ted Smith and Nick Patterson. Smith was the owner of the local marine contracting firm Marine Tech, and for many years, it staged a fleet of small tugs and barges at the head of the Northland Pier. As Marine Tech grew, adding vessels created an even greater need for space. When news of the elevator's potential sale came up, Smith and Patterson formed TN, LLC to purchase the site.[449]

In summary, throughout 2007, three elevators (Cargill, ConAgra and AGP) were acquired by hedge fund companies. The port was benefiting from a good harvest in 2007. Ag writer Tracy Saylor in the *North Star Port* noted,

> Consider too that many farmers already sold a good share of their anticipated new crop wheat last spring, in the $4 to $5 range. And while the wheat price has

---

Ag," *Cision*, June 11, 2010, https://shorturl.at/oyXZ1.
  449 "Look Who bought a grain elevator!" *North Star Port* (Fall 2017): 9.

never been higher, expenses for farm inputs such as diesel and fertilizer are at their highest too. All in all, though, it's still been a storybook year for wheat.

Worldwide, grain stocks were down due to a drought in Australia, lower acreage and production in Canada, and drought in Eastern Europe, Ukraine, and northern Africa. Saylor noted the shifting times throughout his article, but for the moment, everyone was enjoying the surge.

> The more wheat that's moved out of Duluth-Superior, the better the price of wheat in the Northern Plains. Spurred by increasingly volatile weather and more grain grown for biofuels, today's grain prices may signal a new paradigm in the grain markets. Expecting $9 wheat to persist would be a stretch, but the odds are good we won't have to wait another 11 years to see stable high-priced wheat again.[450]

\* \* \*

The following year, 2008, a small grain outfit in Omaha called Hansen-Mueller emerged with the purchase of Elevator *M* and the Daisy Mill and annex from ConAgra. The firm had been leasing the elevators for their specialty grains for several years. Elevator *M* was listed on the Minneapolis Grain Exchange as having a capacity of 2.5 million bushels, while the former flour/durum mill and annex could store 1.5 million bushels. The Dairy Mill and annex were being used exclusively by Hansen-Mueller for storing oats, which were shipped by rail to customers out of state.[451]

Across the harbor, modifications were made at CHS to allow the loading of a new export product, distilled dried grains with

---

450 Tracy Saylor, "Duluth-Superior's High-Quality Port," *North Star Port* (Fall 2007).

451 "A Guide to the Twin Ports," *Grain Journal* (Nov/Dec 2009): 85.

solubles (DDGS), a by-product of ethanol production that was being marketed as a high-protein feed for livestock. CHS loaded the DDGS product on the Hughitt Avenue slip side of their Superior facility. DDGS accounted for the largest share of export containerized grain commodities. The feed came in a high-quality, highly digestible form or a low-quality, less-digestible pellet.

Information from the USDA's Economic Research Service department provided a summation of the value of dried distiller grains and their modification for long-distance overseas shipping:[452]

> Dried distillers grains are a major coproduct from the production of ethanol from grain. DDGs are typically used as a protein-rich animal feed. While distillers' grains are sold locally in wet form, weight precludes shipping long distances. For longer distances, DDGs are dried to about 10 percent moisture to reduce weight. Value-additive innovation continues in the ethanol coproducts space, including the growing use of pelletized DDGs. Pellets provide a storable, easily handled form of DDGs that are compressed into small nuggets that can be bagged or shipped in bulk. DDGs substitute roughly 1-to-1 for corn grain in feed rations. When blended into the animal feed, DDGs provide a high-protein meal that is readily available to the animals. DDGs are most commonly used in feeding cattle, dairy cows, swine, and some poultry.

"We decided that 2 House would handle all the DDG's, traveling from all the way from down in Iowa or out in South Dakota from these different plants that were mashing the corn to get the ethanol

---

452 David W. Olson and Thomas Capehart, "Dried Distillers Grains (DDGs) Have Emerged as a Key Ethanol Coproduct," *Amber Waves*, US Department of Agriculture, October 1, 2019, https://shorturl.at/qILRY.

out," recalled CHS terminal manager Dick Carlson. "Before it comes in, it's dried, and put in the cars, but if they didn't dry it enough, it was almost like concrete in these cars."

CHS installed a hydraulic machine they called "the spike" that sat above the rail cars when they came on the car dump. One worker would open the tops of the hopper car, "and you had one guy that ran the stick, as we called it," Carlson said. "As we had the bottoms open, he'd try to poke it through to help the grain out of there. These DDGs never touched the silos. When you unloaded it, it went up, was weighed, and went right to the ship. You didn't want to get into a silo because if it does the same thing that it did in the rail car, how are you going to get it out?"

Transferring the DDG from the rail car to the ship loader was inherently an arduous process. Carlson recalled his anxiety as the first cargo of DDG was loaded onto a saltwater ship.

> It was a little bit more than a week. I think it was 60, almost 60 hours. You only had one spout because you're coming single out of a car, so the Longshoremen had seven guys on that ship, one spout, and you're paying for that. And I can't remember what it ended up to, the bill for the Longshoremen. It was over $200,000 dollars for the longshoreman alone.

The time and expenditure for outside labor made CHS take a closer look at their own numbers to determine if this was going to be affordable going forward. "From the elevator, we had so many guys running the car dumps, one guy up on the scale floor, and one guy that was the dock guy, so if the longshoremen needed a different spout, he'd hand them the spout, and it came close to $450,000 to load the ship."

In total, CHS loaded only four small, river-sized ships with a capacity of 350,000 bushels, roughly half what a regular saltwater vessel could carry. Even after renegotiating their contract with the ILA to reduce the manpower needed for the single spout loading of DDG, the long-term prospect for the cargo still didn't make sense economically, and CHS dropped the product as an export commodity at Superior.

\* \* \*

After more than a century of operations, the first introduction of foreign ownership interests in the Twin Ports elevators occurred in 2012 with the acquisition of Gavilon Grain by the Japanese trading house Marubeni Corp., as reported by World Grain.com on May 29, 2012, from Tokyo:

> Marubeni Corp., a Japanese trading company, announced on May 29 that it has entered into an agreement to acquire Omaha, Nebraska, US-based Gavilon Holdings, LLC, a grain, fertilizer and energy commodities company, for $3.6 billion.

As part of the deal, Marubeni agreed to take on Gavilon's $2 billion of debt and used cash and loans to fund the deal. It was reported that Glencore International PLC, Bunge Ltd, Mitsui & Co. and Mitsubishi Corp. had also shown interest in Gavilon.[453]

Privately held Gavilon LLC, one of the largest grain, processing and merchandising companies in the US, was established in 2008 with the sale by ConAgra Foods' trading and merchandising business to Ospraie Management LLC Special Opportunities Fund in a $2.1 billion transaction. With the sale, the business was renamed Gavilon LLC. Ospraie remains the principal owner of the business.

Since it became a privately held company, Gavilon has grown rapidly with a number of significant actions, including acquisitions and capital expenditures. Gavilon operates 300 facilities and regional offices worldwide. The company estimated its business mix, measured as share of earnings, at 62 percent grain and ingredients (mostly origination, storage and distribution), 20 percent energy (storage, transportation and logistics) and 18 percent fertilizer (distribution).

---

453 "Marubeni to acquire Gavilon for $3.6 billion," World-Grain.com, May 29, 2012, https://shorturl.at/hpGV5.

According to the 2012 Grain & Milling Annual, Gavilon was the third largest grain storage company in the US.

There were no reported changes in the operations of the elevator on Connors Point, which continued operations under the Gavilon brand name.

\* \* \*

The span of the past two decades has seen the undertaking of extensive rehabilitation projects designed to repair and rebuild crumbling dock infrastructures at the elevators and other commodities docks within the harbor. CHS brought in the local engineering firm of AMI Consulting, Inc. to assess its dock infrastructure, beginning a long-term rehabilitation program to ensure another fifty years of operation. The work recommended by AMI commenced in 2003 with the first phase of rebuilding along the Tower Avenue slip. A second repair phase occurred in 2006, completing that side of the elevator complex. To offset the costs, Superior city officials applied for funding through the Wisconsin's harbor assistance program, part of the Wisconsin Highway Department.

In 2009, Gavilon Grain received 2 million dollars in harbor assistance for their $2.7 million dock refurbishment to install 795 feet of coated sheet piling, a concrete dock cap and a new water system at the Peavey Connors Point elevator.[454]

In 2012, the City of Superior applied for another grant (4.7 million dollars) from the Wisconsin Harbor Assistance Program to help General Mills install new sheet piling and tiebacks along the loading slip at Elevator S. The aging timber crib bulkhead had deteriorated to the point that it had the potential to fall into the slip.[455] The timber wharf at Elevator S was the only one of its kind left within the harbor. Its warped and distorted planking was a hazard to sailors when mooring a vessel. It was reported that General Mills employed

---

[454] "Wisconsin grant will stimulate harbor construction," *Business North*, December 9, 2009.

[455] "Superior gets state grant to repair dock," *Duluth News Tribune*, June 12, 2012.

thirty-one workers at the Superior facility and annually handled about 8 million bushels. For the City of Superior, the investment in the dock wall was essentially an investment in retaining an important business in the city.

The engineering firm of Krech-Ojard was awarded the project, which was funded by a grant from the Wisconsin Harbor Assistance Program/Wisconsin Department of Transportation. The scope of the project included replacing the 1,200-foot dock comprised of a retaining wall of wood cribbing and piling and sheet pile with a timber deck. New mooring dolphins were installed the length of the approach to the ship loading dock and the elevator's wooden wharf was replaced by a concrete surface. The following year, a major change was made to the eastern side of the main workhouse cupola with the removal of four of the elevator's nine receiving legs, its steel girder support towers and some structural maintenance to the remaining metal towers.

The repairs came on the heels of General Mills' outright purchase of the 20-acre facility from the Burlington Northern Railroad in the summer of 2012, ending over a century of ownership by the railroad and its predecessor, the Great Northern. Prior to the purchase, John Stich at Riverland Ag had spent roughly eighteen months negotiating with the BN to purchase the elevator, eventually arriving at an agreement that came on the heels of the market crash and the sale of Riverland Ag.

After leaving Riverland, Stich independently attempted to convince Lansing Grain and the Andersons from Ohio to buy the elevators around 2011, but after touring the facility, those firms determined that the facility was too old. Exactly how General Mills became aware of the proposed sale is unclear, but it had invested a lot of money in the elevator for dust collection, quality control and efficiency and purchased the elevator to protect their interests.[456]

In 2018, Superior worked again on behalf of CHS to obtain a 1.7-million-dollar grant from the Wisconsin Harbor Assistance Program (HAP) to complete the final phase of the project designed

---

[456] John Stich, interview with author, January 24, 2024.

by AMI. The scope of this portion repaired 590 feet of the old dock wall on the Hughitt Avenue slip with new sheet piling and a concrete dock cap.

> AMI Consulting Engineers has been tracking degradation of the east wall for 14 years, which requires immediate remediation to prevent soil failure through one of the oldest areas of the dock wall affected by severe corrosion found in the harbor. About 50 percent of the steel has been lost, according to 2016–17 inspections of the facility.[457]

At the time of the repairs, CHS employed over fifty full-time employees and was the largest shipper of grain in the harbor by volume. The Hughitt Avenue house stores and ships about 20 million bushels of grain annually.

Roen Salvage was contracted to rebuild the wall and laydown area for vessels, a job completed in 2017. The total cost of the project was estimated to be as high as $3.26 million dollars. "The investment shows that CHS considers its Superior grain terminal a valuable asset and one that it will be holding onto for many years to come," said Jason Serck, Superior's economic development, planning and port director, in an article for *North Star Port*.[458]

\* \* \*

The annual volume of grain leaving the port in the past decade (2010–2020) became somewhat of a roller coaster ride—one good year followed by a disappointing one. 2016 was a good year. In July, the *Algoma Harvester* loaded a record 30,000,045 metric tons of grain. "On September 7, we loaded her with 30,007,542 metric tons (1,102,639 bushels) of spring wheat bound for Canada," said Duluth

---

[457] "Superior grain facility receives state money," *Duluth News Tribune*, January 13, 2018.

[458] "$1.7 million Grant to Shore up CHS Dock Walls," *North Star Port* (Spring 2018): 15.

Storage elevator superintendent for Ceres Terminals Ben Herstad.[459] The record breaker was its ninth vessel for the season. The following season, grain exports at the port were a meager 1 million metric tons, down 40 percent from the previous year.

History went up in flames on December 17, 2018, when the former Globe Elevator in Superior caught fire. The elevator headhouse was in the process of demolition by two firms, Wisconsin Woodchuck and the Old Globe Wood Company, to salvage the wood for resale. The fire was believed to have started when a worker cut through a nail or spike, causing a spark. The property owner, Gordy Oftedahl, was on site and called in the fire. Damage was estimated at 2.5 million dollars, including the buildings, a bobcat and $450,000 in previously salvaged wood that had already been sold. The lone remnant of the former Duluth Elevator Company/Globe Elevator is the No. 3 house, which was in a state of disassembly as of 2023.

The final shuffle of ownership on Rice's Point occurred in late 2020 when the Duluth Seaway Port Authority announced its purchase of the Riverland Ag Duluth Lake Port Elevator 6. The site encompasses 7.5 acres, including a 3.5-acre slip. The price of the transaction between the Duluth Seaway Port Authority and TN LLC was $950,000.

> The site's more immediate future could involve demolition of the grain elevator structures, or the Port Authority could seek to accommodate the storage and trade of a non-agricultural bulk commodity with the existing elevators. Regardless, rehabilitation of the pier's dock walls will be a priority to secure the site and open possibilities for future freight-related use, stated a Port Authority media representative.[460]

---

459 "Loads of Grain for 2016," *North Star Port* (Fall 2016): 11.
460 "Port Authority to Purchase Duluth Lake Port Dock," *North Star Port* (Fall 2020): 22.

The dock wall, repaired in part by Krech-Ojard, is believed to be beyond repair to the point that loading grain into the elevator could cause it to collapse into the dock. As of 2023, the Port Authority planned to raze the elevator.

The former General Mills Elevator *A*, idled in 2015, was purchased by Hansen-Mueller in the spring of 2022. The Omaha company has been shipping grain by rail car out of the old Daisy Flour Mill and Elevator *M* in Superior since 2008 and was looking to expand its operations to include shipping overseas via the Great Lakes. Hansen-Mueller is interested in importing and exporting small grains grown in the US and Canada to domestic and foreign destinations. The first rail car of grain arrived on September 20, 2022, and the first ship to load at the elevator in ten years arrived in June 2023 when the Dutch vessel *Maxima* loaded around 12,000 short tons of beet pulp pellets destined for the Netherlands.

**Spout floor in General Mills Elevator *A*. This elevator is built primarily of ceramic tile.** Photo: author.

Hansen-Mueller was founded in 1979 in Omaha, Nebraska, by Jack Hansen and his cousin Randy Mueller. At the time, they were merchandising grain in the lower half of South Dakota, Nebraska and western Iowa. Since then, Hansen-Mueller has expanded with key acquisitions and, as of 2020, operates twenty-four facilities in eleven states. The Duluth elevator is managed by Josh Hansen, the founder's son.

On October 3, 2022, Netherlands-based Viterra announced the purchase of Gavilon Grain via Viterra USA Investment LLC of Minneapolis, a wholly owned subsidiary of Maurbeni America Corporation. The Gavilon name remained active until the end of February 2023, when the company became Viterra.[461] The facility is now called Viterra Connors Point Terminal. "The purchase price for the acquisition is US $1.125 billion plus working capital and is subject to certain price adjustments," stated a spokesperson for Viterra in a press release.[462]

David Mattiske, chief executive officer of Viterra Limited, stated,

> Gavilon's business has all the key attributes that support our long-term strategic plan and allows us to provide additional value to our customers at origination and destination. This acquisition further strengthens our global network by providing us with a material presence in every major exporting region and makes us one of the largest origination businesses in our industry.[463]

Viterra is a global supplier of...

> ...essential food and feed products to the world. Viterra handles over 100 million metric tons of agricultural products annually, including grains, oilseeds, pulses, rice, sugar, and vegetable oil, as well as a wide

---

461 "Gavilon Rebrands to Viterra," Viterra, February 27, 2023, https://rb.gy/9nqugn.

462 "Viterra completes its acquisition of Gavilon," Viterra, October 3, 2022, https://rb.gy/hn4nfe.

463 Ibid.

variety of animal feed products. We purchase agricultural products directly from producers and suppliers in over 65 countries and deliver them to customers in over 125 countries.[464]

Viterra, a privately held company headquartered in Rotterdam, operates a network of grain elevators, special crops facilities, processing plants and port terminals across Canada and parts of the United States. Viterra was acquired by the Swiss company Glencore for $6.1 billion in 2012 and operates as part of Glencore's global agricultural division. "We are one of the largest global diversified natural resource companies in the world," states Glencore on their webpage.

In July 2022, Columbia Grain International purchased eight Gavilon Grain facilities in Montana and North Dakota, except for two facilities in Montana and the elevator on Connors Point. Gavilon has since been rebranded as Viterra, effective February 2023. The Viterra Connors Point Terminal in Superior is used by Viterra as its Great Lakes shipping elevator for domestic spring wheat.

* * *

In 2023, Twin Ports grain exports hit the lowest level in 133 years. It was a shocking headline to many casual followers of the port's grain activities. "The amount of grain leaving the Duluth-Superior port this shipping season hit its lowest level since 1890, in a year that also ended with a decrease in coal and total tonnage," wrote reporter Jana Hollingsworth for the Minneapolis *Star Tribune*.

Each successive year seems to add another chapter to the decline. Severe drought in Montana, the Dakotas and northwest Minnesota, which began before planting season and lasted through harvest, was the cause of decreased levels of production for spring wheat and durum wheat according to the USDA's Small Grains Report issued in September 2021.

On January 22, 2022 *Grainnet* reported that,

---

464 "What We Do," Viterra, https://rb.gy/d092kf.

> The Port of Duluth-Superior recovered last year from the pandemic-induced lows of 2020 but without help from grain, previously its No. 1 export. Grain suffered a steep drop to 808,498 short tons for the 2021 season, amounting to the second-lowest seasonal grain total for the port since 1890.

When questioned about the decrease, Deb DeLuca, executive director of the Duluth Seaway Port Authority, said,

> Grain is a dynamic commodity, and the port faced a number of headwinds in 2022, including two years of tightening grain supplies worldwide, further exacerbated by the war in Ukraine, a very strong dollar, extremely elevated transportation costs and competition from other countries' less expensive wheat.

Since the opening of the St. Lawrence Seaway, the export of grain from Duluth-Superior has transitioned from a vibrant domestic trade to an international trade that is markedly different than it was 150 years ago, not so much in point of origin but in destination.[465]

The majority of grain exported from Duluth/Superior originates in Ulen, Minnesota, and in Bisbee and Parshall, North Dakota. There are three alternative coastal ports that compete with the grain exported via Duluth/Superior. These are the ports of Portland, Oregon; Quebec City and New Orleans. The grain could be railed to Portland or neighboring ports of Kalama, Longview and Vancouver, could move to Quebec City from the inland origins directly by rail to Quebec export elevators, or first to Duluth/Superior, where it would be loaded onto a laker (not requiring pilots) for a shipment to an

---

465 John C. Martin Associates, LLC DBA Martin Associates, "Analysis of Great Lakes Pilotage Costs on Great Lakes Shipping and the Potential Impact of Increases in U.S. Pilotage Charges" (Lancaster, PA: June 28, 2017), 43–44. Prepared for: United States Coast Guard.

export elevator, and then reloaded onto a deep draft vessel calling Quebec for transit to the overseas destination.

To move the grain from the origins serving Duluth/Superior to New Orleans (or other Lower Mississippi River ports), the grain would be railed to St. Louis and then put on a barge for transport to a Lower Mississippi River export grain elevator. With respect to export destinations, grain is exported from Duluth/Superior primarily to Africa (the Port of Algiers), the United Kingdom (the Port of Felixstowe), Northern Europe (the Port of Hamburg), the Mediterranean (the Port of Livorno) and Central and South America (the Port of Cartagena). Currently, the Middle East and Asia are not major markets for grain exported from Duluth/Superior.

In today's market, there is virtually no domestic shipment of grain from the port on American or Canadian lakers. The largest volume of grain leaving the harbor is on foreign vessels, many calling here after unloading an import elsewhere on the lakes. Imagine what it must be like for a young foreign national to be on board a ship arriving in a city like Chicago, then sailing up the great Lake Michigan and Superior to the Twin Ports. The grain trade has brought the world to our doorstep and has changed the way we view our world.

In 2024, the remaining active Duluth export grain elevators are Hansen-Mueller Elevator *A* and Ceres Global Ag's Duluth Storage. In Superior, they are Cenex-Harvest States, the largest exporter of grain by volume in the port; General Mills, which operates Elevators *S* and *X*; and annexes Viterra Connors Point Terminal and Hansen-Mueller's Elevator *M* and Daisy Mill.[466] Elevator *S*, built in 1900, is the oldest terminal elevator in the port, the lone example of a steel elevator. Hansen-Mueller's Elevator *A* is the oldest on the Duluth side of the harbor and the lone example of a ceramic tile elevator in the harbor. On occasion, a ship will unload into the hopper at the end

---

466 Note: The former Daisy Mill (1893) in Superior is not considered a terminal elevator but could be considered the oldest grain facility in the harbor. The former Meehan Seaway Services dock, owned by Viterra, is an overflow storage facility and not equipped to load vessels.

of the headhouse at Elevator *M*. The former Capitol/International Multifoods Elevator *6* is structurally unsound and will never be used again for grain storage or export. The Duluth Seaway Port Authority owns the elevator.

# Conclusion

For the moment, putting smaller quantities of "specialty" grains into containers for shipment overseas has gained traction in the port but is not expected to become a high-volume staple. Grain has found other ways to move, other places to go—down to the Gulf, out to the West Coast, by rail, by barge. The post-Civil War men who came to Duluth to merge their ambition with Duluth's potential lived to see the growth of a great industry, participated in it through good and bad, and when it came time to move on, became another piece of the story of the grain elevators of Duluth-Superior.

    The wheat yields from the Red River valley were the best in the world. The railroads built an intricate network of tracks, and alongside them, country line elevators sprang up to feed the system. Like water, grain finds a way to flow. And flow it did through the great grain elevators in the port of Duluth-Superior. The volume of grain that these elevators once supported is not likely to return. A hundred years ago, when Duluth-Superior replaced Milwaukee and Chicago as the major trans-shipment points for Upper Midwest grains moving east to Buffalo, Duluth-Superior was the premier grain shipping port on the Great Lakes.

    Like the wind on the prairie, there is always a ripple of change that we can't see while in its midst. If we seek to define the state of the terminal elevators at Duluth-Superior today, there are several areas to examine to obtain an overall definition. From an economic standpoint, they provide a large monetary tax base plus full and part-time employment, which can be measured yearly with the traffic of grain. The first quarter of the century showed an overall decline in volume in each decade. Stability seems to be the keyword in the harbor. A century prior to this, the grain elevators were struggling to keep up with the rapidly increasing volume. It is easy to see that the Twin Ports grain industry has reached peaks that will never again be attained.

If we look at the elevators from an operational point of view, there are also noticeable differences. There are very few small operations at the Twin Ports. The control of grain flowing in and out of the harbor is done on trading floors hundreds and thousands of miles away. You no longer see ships pulling beneath the loading spouts at Duluth from the office windows of the grain commission houses in the Board of Trade. That view has been replaced by large commodity scoreboards.

Grain is moved around the world electronically—transferred to remote locations via smaller terminal screens in an age where buyers and traders seldom see an elevator, let alone the bottom of a cargo hold. The action is controlled by major corporations and hedge fund companies and handled in multinational offices. The world of ag processing and merchandising lives in a culture of a quarter percent profit per bushel of grain. The room for error and loss is too slim for small organizations to competitively survive. This is not unique to the Twin Ports but is prevalent in other major markets as well.

Considered as an architectural group, the terminal elevators at Duluth-Superior provide us with a diversity unequaled anywhere. It has been over a hundred years since the present-day Globe Elevator system was constructed. Today, the remains of the complex represent the last example of a wood-cribbed terminal elevator in the Twin Ports. The same comparison can be applied to the Great Northern Elevator *S* with its steel construction or to the *A* workhouse at Hansen-Mueller shaped with circular tile bins.

Industrial archeologists have noted the significance of steel in elevators in recent years. At Superior, the General Mills Elevator *S* stands as a prime example of a working steel house. The massive cupola rises above the concrete annexes that surround it. Engineer and designer Max Toltz is considered a genius among his peers, and Elevator *S* strongly supports this credit. The spired towers that enclose the receiving legs on the elevator's eastern wall stand castle-like, ready to defend any claim that this is not a supremely designed and executed elevator. It is believed to be one of the oldest working terminal grain elevators in the United States.

In Duluth, there were two examples of a tile elevator, another method that evolved from turn-of-the-century experimentation. On the Peavey site, in the end, gaping holes dotted the upper stories where the wall was opened to remove machinery. Tile shards littered the base of the elevator walls, broken and cracked like discarded China until it was removed. On the opposite end of Rice's Point, Hansen-Mueller's Elevator *A* is the only active baked ceramic tile-constructed elevator in the harbor. It is also the lone surviving elevator constructed by Barnett & Record.

The Peavey-Duluth Terminal became the site where reinforced concrete was given its first large-scale attempt to succeed. A century ago, concrete was considered experimental yet was simultaneously proclaimed and heralded as the forerunner of the future. Concrete was the revolutionary material the builders were seeking. The silo, no longer burdened by the need to be encased in a fireproof sheeting of corrugated metal, stood alone. The exterior profile of the modern elevator is a direct result of the combined use of the workhouse and unenclosed silo.

The use of reinforced concrete in elevator construction quickly became dominant after 1910. The erection of the Farmers Union grain terminal and subsequent annexes during the 1940s stands today as a classic example of this form of elevator. Towering silos stretch longitudinally from the headhouse, presenting an overwhelming visual panorama. The cylindrical form freed the builder from the constraints of space, allowing for virtually unlimited upward expansion. The Farmers Union elevator was the tallest in the world when completed. Fifty years later, it stands as a fully functional monument to the classic usage of the reinforced concrete elevator technique.

These elevators have stood over the growth and decline of an industry. They have weathered a century of conflicts and multiple generations. They have seen the shifts in economics, the subtle changes in operation and ownership. If we are to believe that history itself is a living entity, then the sweat of a hot summer's day of work rolling down the faces of young men unloading a grain car by shovel has itself been passed down over the years, too. It has been absorbed in the ground, into the grain of the wood, permeating that path which men to follow will tread upon. The power lines have swayed, ice-sheathed through bitter winters. Corrugated iron siding has burned hot through blistering summers. The air has the smell and feel of grain dust, transforming it into a tangible substance. It is what we call tradition—a tradition of utilization. It is a viewpoint that moves elevators out of the workforce when economics make them non-viable yet retain a presence of grandeur.

There were no plans drawn up for the ultimate survival of these elevators, nothing to leave for their preservation, no contingencies outlined during incorporation. Elevator historian Bob Frame recommends "preservation through documentation, particularly through the Historic American Engineering Record (HAER) of the National Park Service. Today, some documentation can be done with laser scanning, in addition to photography and measured drawings.

The blueprints show no notes for historical detail. The structures at Duluth-Superior have become significant only through the passing of time, not through the labor of their industry. The grain elevators here have found their place in a regional or national historical context, yet despite such generosity bestowed upon them, they continue daily to work and function as has every elevator built in the Twin Ports as a clearinghouse for grains to the world.

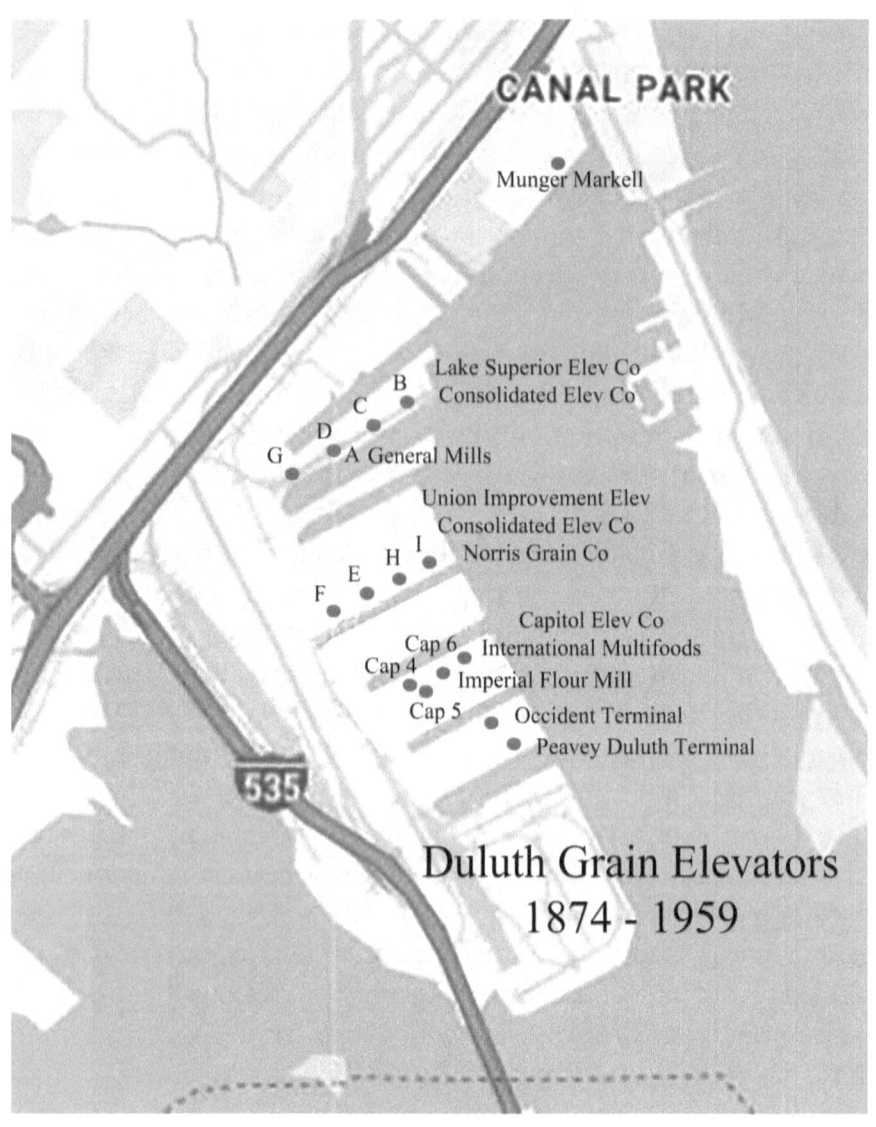

Duluth 1874-1959

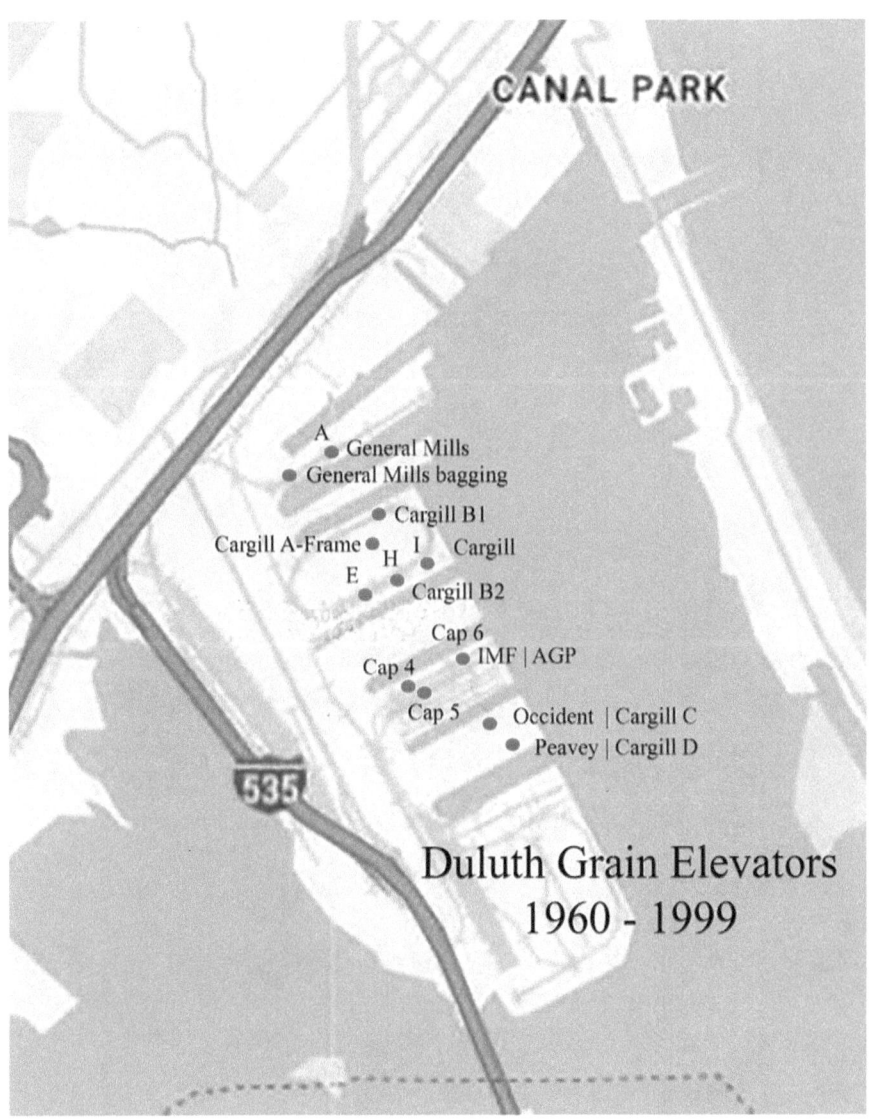

Duluth 1960-1997

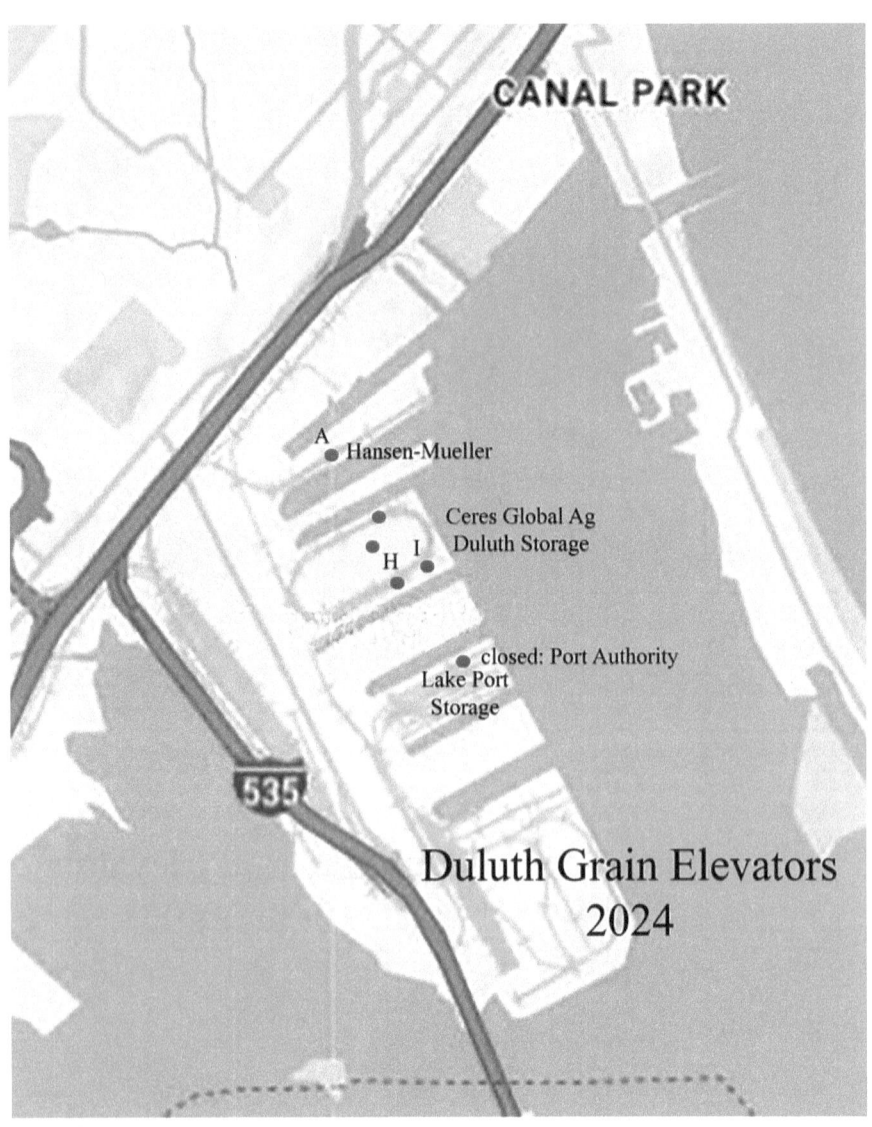

## The Grain Terminal Elevators of Duluth-Superior

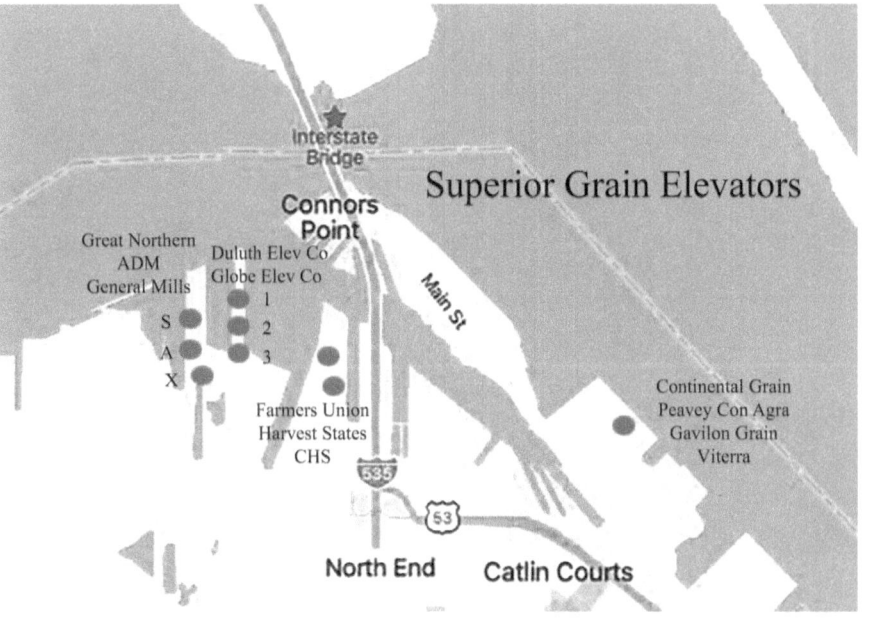

**Superior**

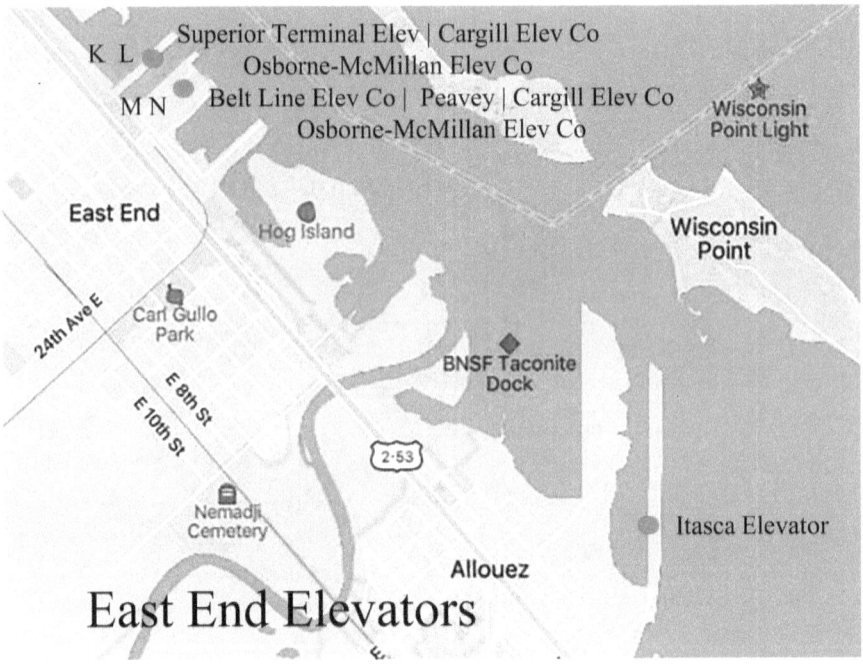

**East End**

# Appendix

**Page 20:**

As detailed by *The Duluth Minnesotian*, this portion of the tour describes the complexity of the structure's interior.

> Upon these "Cross-walls" at proper points or intervals, heavy dimension stones were cemented as "Cap-stones" to serve as points of rest for the 14 by 14 inch Post Timbers, 14 feet long, three of which posts rest on each Cap-stone and either as direct uprights or lateral braces support both the exterior and interior "Bin" walls, and in fact the entire superstructure: assisted by the heavy stringers of Norway pine, consisting of two timbers 7x14 inches, bolted together and tied to each other by bolts, and these again bolted upon and supported by the posts and post-braces.

### The Storage Part of the House

> Upon these posts and stringers, the Storage Part of the house is built, exclusively of two-inch plank laid flatwise and strongly spiked together, up to the eaves of the main structure, a distance of 40 feet. Above this again is

the Cupola, a strong-frame or network of timbers, principally 10 by 10 inches, well braced: admitted by all to be one of the handsomest pieces of framing ever put up in the Northwest. The Grain Bins are 90 in number, each 10 by 11, and of the depth of 45 feet, and each capable of containing 4,000 bushels of wheat, making the total capacity of the present elevator house 306,000 bushels... There are 5 Receiving Elevators, and 3 Shipping Elevators - which elevators are endless belts of leather 22 inches wide and all of them are fastened 1,800 six-quart buckets or cups of the best xxx tin, bound with hoop iron, which revolve around iron pulleys 5 feet in diameter at the top and 2 feet at the bottom - and are capable of hoisting about 4,000 bushels per hour. When the buckets of an elevator belt are filled, it is loaded with a little over 20 bushels of wheat. Five cars can be unloaded simultaneously: and allowing 15 minutes for moving, unloading and switching out each train of five cars, the capacity of the Elevator is to unload 480 cars in 24 hours, containing in every three cars, on the average, 1,000 bushels. Is not a uninteresting computation, that to produce the leather required in all these elevator belts, required the hides of over 500 cattle!

All the receiving and shipping elevators are set in large cast-iron boots, in which the bottom pulley revolves: and these boots again rest in capacious water-tight tanks, rendering elevator "foot" both fire-proof and water-proof, the journal of each pulley being besides furnished with Moulton's improved oil cups or floating cork lubricators... All the Receiving Elevator Belts are driven at the top of the building, in the Cupola, by a line 4½ inch iron shafting with universal joint couplings and oscillating boxes, and extending the whole length of the house - not driven directly by the Elevator pulleys being placed upon the line shaft, but by a novel and most capital arrangement of friction pulleys made of wood, 15 inches in diameter, which pulleys are placed upon the line shaft and there work directly under and in frictional contact with the 5-foot iron pulley on which the belt revolves, giving it motion when lowered into contact with it, or otherwise, as the case may be. Each Elevator belt first discharges into a Weighing Hopper, and thence the grain is spouted into receiving "bins."

# Page 21:

The Shipping Elevators, of which there are three, are driven in the same manner, by the same friction pulley arrangement, on a counter-shaft, put in motion by a cross-belt from the main line shaft - these Elevators and their accompanying Shipping "Bins" are located on the front or water side of the building.

We have alluded in the above to the Weighing Hoppers and Weigh Scales. These are located in the Cupola, on what is called the Scale Floor, which is next below the top or Shaft Floor, and there is one Scale for each Elevator Belt - that is, there are 5 Receiving Scales of the capacity of 500 bushels at a draft, and 3 Shipping Scales of the capacity of 300 bushels each. A revolving spout with cut off slide, is attached to each Weighing Hopper, and capable of being connected with 24 "Bins." On the water front, there are 5 shipping spouts: of which two would be generally used in loading vessels; and the weighing and loading could go on at the rate of about 30,000 bushels per hour.

## Page 52:

The amended articles of incorporation, hand-written in pencil on ledger paper detail the origins of the Great Northern Elevator Company of Minnesota, and its Superior elevator, sometimes referred to as the "Hill" elevator. Unusual for incorporation papers is a two-page "Introduction" to preface the document.[467]

> The Great Northern Elevator Company was incorporated under the laws of the State of Minnesota in November 1886 and had for its general object to –
>
> "build, construct, lease or purchase, and to maintain and operate grain elevators and Warehouses in such numbers and at such points and places in the State of Minnesota, Wisconsin and elsewhere, or said corporations may determine"
>
> However, its primary object appears to have been the business of taking on, under lease, the operations of an elevator of 1,800,000 bushel capacity in Superior, Wisconsin, erected by the Lake Superior & Southwestern Railway Company with funds advanced by the St. Paul, Minneapolis & Manitoba Railway Company.
>
> The Lake Superior & Southwestern Railway Company was a creation of the Manitoba Company, the latter causing the organization of the Eastern Railway Company of Minnesota and thereupon merged the properties and interests of the Lake Superior Company with that company on January 10, 1888.

---

467 "Great Northern Elevator Company, Introduction" Great Northern Railway Company Records. Box 132.D.17.4 (F), Folder F1 Great Northern Elevator Company (Minnesota) Histories, undated. Minnesota Historical Society.

Article two of Articles of Incorporation of the Great Northern Elevator Company provides that –

> the time of the commencement of this corporation shall be the 10th day of November 1886 and the same shall continue for thirty years thereafter"

> Therefore the charter not having been amended or extended in this respect the corporate existence of the company terminated November 10, 1916.

There are no records of the company in possession of the Great Northern Railway Company other than the stock certificate books in which the issued stock certificates were never pasted back to the stubs, thus indicating that they were not turned in by the holders and are still outstanding, although of no value.

There is also on file a copy of the contract dated November 17, 1886 between the Elevator Company and the Lake Superior & Southwestern Railway Company covering the leasing of the elevator at Superior constructed by the latter company from November 19, 1886 to August 1, 1890. The Great Northern Law Department has no record of this lease.

The Articles of Incorporation and amendment thereto of the Great Northern Elevator Company as presented herein, were copied from the record books in the office of the Secretary of State Minnesota.

The Great Northern Elevator Company here under review had no connection with a company of a similar name incorporated under the laws of the State of New York by the Great Northern Railway Company which constructed and operated an elevator at Buffalo, New York, nor with a company of the same name which contemplated the building of an elevator on or near Smith's Cove in Seattle, Washington.

In an amendment to the Articles of Incorporation, dated January 10, 1888, noted R. C. Burdick's appointment as president of the

Great Northern Elevator Company, and W. C. Farrington replacing Adolphus Bode as secretary.

> As stated under the caption "Introduction", the only records of this company in possession of the Great Northern Railway Company are the stock certificate book to which the issued stock certificates have not been returned and a hand written copy of a lease dated November 17, 1886, between the Lake Superior & Southwestern Railway Company and the Great Northern Elevator Company covering the leasing by the latter of a grain elevator constructed by the Lake Superior Company for a period from November 17, 1896 to August 1, 1890 for a consideration of 46,000 per annum. On January 10, 1888 the properties of the Lake Superior & Southwestern Railway Company were merged with those of Eastern Railway of Minnesota.
>
> Both the Lake Superior Company and the Eastern Company were owned and controlled by the St. Paul Minneapolis & Manitoba Railway Company and its book records and those of the Eastern Company reflect rental payments under the lease of November 17, 1886, at the rate of $3000 per month to and including September 1888. The records do not indicate the reason for the termination of the lease which had for its expiration date August 1, 1890, but effective October 1, 1888 the Eastern Railway Company of Minnesota commenced formal operations between Hinckley, Minnesota, and Superior, Wisconsin and the same date, according to the books, also took over the operation of the grain elevator at the latter point.

## Page 155:

By the end of the decade, the Duluth grain trade had changed considerably since its early years. The Federal Trade Commission published Volume III of its report on the grain trade in December, 1921, providing a good summary of the trade at Duluth since its inception until 1897 "or thereabouts..."[468]

> At Duluth, up until 1897 or thereabouts the main function of the terminal elevators was to store grain for account of others. Their only source of income were the established charges for storing, handling, and cleaning, and these operations were subject to the supervision of the railroad and warehouse commission of Minnesota. About 1897 the competition at the mills at Minneapolis for cash grain began to influence prices so largely that dealers and shippers could see no profit for themselves in buying the cash grain under such competitive conditions unless purchasers from them were in sight. They had formerly been able to hedge and send the grain to store while waiting for such purchasers, but the mill buying so narrowed the spread between cash and future prices, even at the season of heaviest receipts, that the holding of grain by a merchant with no elevator and the paying of storage charges for any considerable period involved a loss on the hedge not compensated by any opportunity to find meanwhile a better market for the cash grain. This caused a decline in the volume of grain placed in storage by dealers unable to make a profit from storage charges on grain handled for the account of others. The elevator companies therefore went into the market themselves as buyers of grain, contenting themselves with earning on a larger quantity of grain a

---

468 U. S. Government. *Report of the Federal Trade Commission on The Grain Trade, Vol. III Terminal Grain Marketing.* December 21, 1921. Minneapolis Public Library FT1.2: G762² Vol 3.

"carrying charge" smaller per unit than the public rate supplemented by opportunities for profit from mixing, conditioning, and spreading.

There have been no public elevators in Duluth since 1916. The elevator companies are the predominant buyers on the market and there is very little grain placed in store for other concerns.

## Page 253:

Looking back on Continental's twenty years of operation at Superior, John Parrington remembered the rivalry between the elevators during the boom years in the early 1970s. It was a busy time that took a lot of hard work, often combined with a little ingenuity to get the grain out.

> I was accused one time of stopping a ship that was going down to Elevator *M*, and bringing it alongside to load it because we were full. The ship was leaving the terminal... we were dealing – trying to get it and replace it with a ship later on. At any rate, they let it go. It was going to Elevator *M*, no question about it, but we were still negotiating as she was underway. Just prior to – probably she had her nose at the head of Great Lakes Storage – when we finally filled it in. I went out there (on the dock), Jack Lyons was on the ship's bridge, and I shouted, "Jack, bring it over." It all came through and it was always said Parrington can do anything. He can even stop a ship from going to another elevator.[469]

---

[469] Parrington, John. Interview with author, Minneapolis, 1993.

# Chronology

| 1869 | Union Improvement & Elevator Company | Founded at Duluth |
|---|---|---|
| 1870 | Union Improvement & Elevator Company **Elevator A** | Constructed |
| 1872 | Munger, Markell & Company | Founded at Duluth |
| 1873-74 | Munger, Markell & Company **Elevator No. 1** | Constructed |
| 1878 | Union Improvement & Elevator Company **Elevator A** | Capacity expanded |
| 1880 | Lake Superior Elevator Company | Founded at Duluth |
| 1880 | Munger, Markell & Company **Elevator No. 1** | Destroyed by fire |
| 1880 | Lake Superior Elevator Company **Elevator B** | Constructed |
| 1881 | Duluth Board of Trade | Founded at Duluth |
| 1882 | Lake Superior Elevator Company **Elevator Annex C** | Constructed |
| 1883 | Lake Superior Elevator Company **Store House 1** | Constructed |
| 1884 | Duluth & Western Elevator Company | Founded at Duluth |
| 1884 | Duluth & Western Elevator Company **Elevator D** | Constructed |
| 1884 | Duluth & Western Elevator Company **Elevator E (Q)** | Constructed |

| | | |
|---|---|---|
| 1884 | Union Improvement & Elevator Company **Elevator E** | Constructed |
| 1884 | Union Improvement **Store House 2** | Constructed |
| 1884 | Lake Superior Elevator Company **Elevator D** | Constructed |
| 1885 | Duluth and Western Elevator Company | Sold to George H. Christian |
| 1885 | Union Improvement & Elevator Company **Annex F** | Constructed |
| 1885 | Lake Superior Elevator Company **Elevator Annex G** | Constructed |
| 1886 | Duluth & Western Elevator Company **Elevator E** | Capacity expanded |
| 1886 | Great Northern Elevator Company of Minnesota | Founded in Minnesota |
| 1886 | Duluth & Western Elevator Company **Elevator D and E** | Destroyed by fire, Nov 27, 1886 |
| 1886 | Union Improvement & Elevator Company **Elevator A** | Destroyed by fire, Nov 27, 1886 |
| 1886 | Union Improvement **Store House 3** | Constructed |
| 1886 | Great Northern Elevator Company **Elevator A** | Constructed |
| 1887 | Duluth Elevator Company | Founded at Duluth |
| 1887 | Duluth Elevator Company **House No. 1, No. 2, No. 3** | Constructed |
| 1887 | Union Improvement & Elevator Company **Elevator H** | Constructed |
| 1888 | Imperial Mill | Founded at Duluth |
| 1888 | Great Northern Elevator Company **Elevator X** | Constructed |
| 1889 | Imperial Mill (became Capitol) **Elevator 4** | Constructed |
| 1892 | Cargill Commission Company | Founded |
| 1893 | Superior Terminal Elevator Company | Founded |
| 1893 | Superior Terminal Elevator Company **Elevator K and L** | Constructed |

## The Grain Terminal Elevators of Duluth-Superior

| 1893 | Belt Line Elevator Company | Founded |
|---|---|---|
| 1893 | Belt Line Elevator Company **Elevator M and N** | Constructed |
| 1894 | Consolidated Elevator Company Merger of Union Improvement and Elevator Company and the Lake Superior Elevator Company | Founded |
| 1894 | Globe Elevator Company | Founded at Duluth |
| 1896 | Belt Line Elevator Company **Elevator M and N** | Purchased by F. H. Peavey Co. |
| 1896 | Belt Line Elevator Company | Reincorporated |
| 1898 | Peavey Grain Company | Founded in Chicago |
| 1899 | United States Flour Milling (became Capitol) **Elevator 5** | Wood frame, constructed |
| 1899 | Consolidated Elevator Company **Elevator E** | Rebuilt, added onto |
| 1900 | Itasca Elevator Company | Founded at Superior |
| 1900 | Itasca Elevator Company **Itasca Elevator** | Constructed |
| 1900 | F. H. Peavey Company **Duluth Terminal** and **Annex 1** | Constructed: Work house and Part 1 of annex |
| 1900 | Great Northern Elevator Company **Elevator S** | Constructed |
| 1901 | F. H. Peavey Company Duluth **Annex 2** | Constructed: Part 2 of annex |
| 1905 | Capitol Elevator Company | Founded at Duluth |
| 1906 | F. H. Peavey Company **Duluth Terminal** | Destroyed By Fire February 17, 1906 |
| 1906 | F. H. Peavey Company **Duluth Terminal** | Temporary wood headhouse |
| 1907 | F. H. Peavey Company **Duluth Terminal** | Tile Replacement Constructed |
| 1907 | Great Northern **Elevator A** | Destroyed By Fire November 9, 1907 |

| 1908 | Consolidated Elevator Company **Elevator D** | Destroyed By Fire June 25, 1908 |
|---|---|---|
| 1908 | Consolidated Elevator Company **Elevator D** | Tile replacement constructed |
| 1908 | Consolidated Elevator Company **Elevator D Annex** | Constructed - concrete |
| 1909 | Great Northern **Annex No. 1** | Constructed - concrete |
| 1912 | American Milling Company Elevator | Constructed – wood frame |
| 1913 | Consolidated Elevator Company **Elevator D Annex** | Constructed - concrete |
| 1914 | Belt Line Elevator Company and **Elevators M and N** | Sold by Peavey to Cargill |
| 1914 | Belt Line Elevator Company **Elevator M** | Destroyed By Fire April 26, 1914 |
| 1914 | Cargill Elevator Company **Elevator M** | Wood replacement constructed |
| 1915 | F. H. Peavey Company is now Globe Elevator Company | Name Change |
| 1917 | Spencer Kellogg and Sons | Purchases American Milling Company and elevator |
| 1917 | Capitol Elevator Company **Elevator 6 and 7, Annex A-2** | Constructed - concrete |
| 1917 | Itasca Elevator Company **Itasca Elevator** | Purchased by Julius Barnes |
| 1919 | Consolidated Elevator Company **Elevator I** | Constructed - concrete |
| 1923 | Occident Elevator Company **Occident Terminal** | Constructed - concrete |
| 1926 | Cargill Elevator Company **Elevator M** | Expanded - concrete |
| 1926 | Spencer Kellogg and Sons | Expanded - concrete |
| 1926 | Itasca Elevator Company **Itasca Elevator** | Expanded |

## The Grain Terminal Elevators of Duluth-Superior

| | | |
|---|---|---|
| 1928 | Capitol Elevator Company **Elevator 7, Annex A-3** | Expanded |
| 1928 | Great Northern **Annex No. 2** | Constructed |
| 1929 | Itasca Elevator Company **Itasca Elevator** | Expanded |
| 1930 | Itasca Elevator Company **Itasca Elevator** | Purchased by Cargill |
| 1929 | Occident Terminal Elevator | Expanded |
| 1930 | F. H. Peavey Company **Duluth Terminal** | Expanded |
| 1930 | Great Northern **Annex No. 3** | Constructed |
| 1934 | Spencer Kellogg and Sons | Expanded |
| 1937 | Consolidated Elevator Company **Elevator B and C** | Demolished |
| 1937 | Cargill, Inc. **Elevator N** | Demolished |
| 1937 | Great Northern Elevator | ADM takes over management From A. D. Thomson & Co. |
| 1938 | Farmers Union Grain Terminal Association | Founded in St. Paul |
| 1941 | Globe Elevator Company | Dissolved. Property distributed to F. H. Peavey Co. |
| 1941-42 | Farmers Union Grain Terminal Association | No. 1 house constructed Sections A, B, and C |
| 1942 | Great Northern **Elevator X** | Destroyed by Fire January 10, 1942 |
| 1943 | Consolidated Elevator Company | Purchased by General Mills, Inc. |
| 1944 | General Mills **Elevator A and B** | Renamed: Elevator D is now A Renamed: Annex G is now B |

| | | |
|---|---|---|
| 1944 | General Mills **Elevators F, E, H, and I** | Purchased by Norris Grain Co. |
| 1947 | Capitol Elevator Company | Purchased by International Milling Company |
| 1947 | Great Northern **Elevator X** | Replacement Constructed |
| 1949 | Spencer Kellogg and Sons Linseed Oil mill, Superior | Purchased by Farmers Union Grain Terminal Association |
| 1950 | FUGTA **Workhouse No. 3** (old Spencer Kellogg) | Expanded |
| 1950-51 | Farmers Union Grain Terminal Association **House No. 1** | Expanded, Sections D and E, (Tower Ave) |
| 1950-51 | FUGTA **Headhouse No. 2** and **Annexes F1, F2, and G** | Constructed (Hughitt Ave) |
| 1952 | Cargill, Inc. **Elevator M** | Purchased by Osborne-McMillan |
| 1954 | Cargill, Inc. **Elevator K and L** | Purchased by Osborne-McMillan |
| 1954 | Osborne and McMillan Elevator Company **Elevator O** | Renamed: Elevator K is now O |
| 1954 | Farmers Union Grain Terminal Association | Expanded, Tower Ave |
| 1958 | Osborne and McMillan Elevator Company **Elevator M** | Expanded, steel tanks |
| 1958-59 | Farmers Union Grain Terminal Association | Expanded, steel tanks |
| 1959 | St. Lawrence Seaway System opens | First ocean vessel, May 3, 1959 |
| 1960 | Norris Grain Company **Elevators E, F, H, and I** | Purchased by Cargill |
| 1960 | Occident Elevator Company **Occident Terminal** | Managed by Peavey Co. (Peavey purchased Russell-Miller in 1954) |

| | | |
|---|---|---|
| 1960 | Peavey Duluth Terminal | Loading gallery added |
| 1961 | Cargill, Inc. **Elevator F and H** | Demolished |
| 1962 | Farmers Union Grain Terminal Association **House No. 1** | Loading gallery added |
| 1962 | Cargill, Inc. **Elevator H** | Replacement Constructed (steel tanks) |
| 1962 | Cargill, Inc. **Elevator E** | Renovated |
| 1962 | Cargill, Inc. **Elevator B2** | Renamed: H and I now B2 |
| 1962 | Osborne and McMillan Elevator Company **Tank A** | Destroyed by explosion January 18, 1962 |
| 1962 | Osborne and McMillan Elevator Company **Elevator M** | Replaced tank with 4 concrete silos |
| 1965 | Continental Grain Company **Continental Elevator** | Constructed |
| 1969 | Cargill, Inc. **Itasca Elevator** | Demolished |
| 1969 | Osborne-McMillan Elevator Company | Purchased by McMillan Elevator Company |
| 1070 | McMillan Elevator Company | Operating as O&M Elevators |
| 1970 | International Milling becomes International Multifoods | Renamed |
| 1970 | Peavey Company **Occident Terminal** | Purchased by Cargill, Inc. |
| 1970 | Cargill, Inc. **Elevator C** | Renamed: Occident Terminal becomes Elevator C |
| 1970 | Cargill, Inc. **Elevator D** | Renamed: Peavey Duluth Terminal becomes Elevator D |
| 1971 | Duluth Board of Trade | Closed |

| 1972 | McMillan Elevator Company **Elevator O** | Closed |
|---|---|---|
| 1977 | FUGTA **Spencer Kellogg headhouse** | Demolished 1912 era headhouse |
| 1977 | International Multifoods, Inc. **Capitol 5** | Demolished |
| 1977 | General Mills, Inc. **Elevator A** | Expanded Steel tanks |
| 1977 | Cargill, Inc. **Elevator B and berth B1** | Constructed, concrete silos |
| 1977 | Cargill, Inc. **Elevator E** | Demolished |
| 1977 | McMillan Elevator Company **Elevator M** | Purchased by ConAgra |
| 1977 | ConAgra **Elevator M** | Managed by Burdick Grain Co. |
| 1978 | International Multifoods, Inc. **Capitol 4** | Destroyed by fire January 21, 1978 |
| 1978 | International Multifoods, Inc. **Capitol 7** | Expanded concrete silos |
| 1979 | McMillan Elevator Company **Elevator O** | Purchased by City of Superior |
| 1979 | General Mills, **Annex B** | Expanded: Steel tanks |
| 1980 | Cargill, Inc. **Elevator C** | Closed |
| 1980 | Cargill, Inc. **Elevator D** | Closed |
| 1982 | ConAgra **Elevator M** | Managed by Peavey Elevator Division of ConAgra |
| 1983 | Farmers Union Grain Terminal Association re-named as Harvest States Cooperative after merger | Renamed from FUGTA |
| 1984 | City of Superior **Elevator O** | Destroyed by fire August 25, 1984 |
| 1985 | ConAgra Peavey **Globe Elevator** | Closed |
| 1986 | Continental Grain Company **Continental Elevator** | Purchased by ConAgra, Peavey Elevator Division |

| 1986 | ConAgra **Peavey Connors Point Elevator** | Renamed: Peavey Connors Point |
|---|---|---|
| 1986 | General Mills Bagging plant | Constructed |
| 1986 | ConAgra Peavey **Elevator M** | Workhouse destroyed by fire October 27, 1986 |
| 1989 | Cargill, Inc. **Elevator C and D** | Purchased by Duluth Seaway Port Authority |
| 1989 | Duluth Seaway Port Authority **Garfield C and D** | Renamed |
| 1989 | General Mills **Elevator S and X** | Purchased from ADM |
| 1991 | AgProcessing Limited Partnership (AGP LP). **Capitol 6, and Annex 7** | Purchased from International Multifoods, Inc. |
| 1994 | ConAgra Peavey **Globe Elevator** | Sold for scrap to Jensen Construction Company |
| 1998 | **CHS** Harvest States Cooperative merges with Cenex | Merger |
| 1998 | **Concourse Grain LLC** ConAgra and Farmland merger | Founded |
| 1999 | **Garfield C and D** Former Occident Terminal and Peavey Duluth Terminal | Demolition |
| 1999 | **Concourse Grain LLC** | Dissolved |
| 2006 | ConAgra sells grain operations to Ospraie Management LLC. Operating as: **Gavilon Connors Point Terminal** | New ownership, Renamed |
| 2007 | Cargill sells Duluth facility Whitebox Commodities Holding Corporation. Operating as: **Riverland Ag Duluth Storage** | New ownership, Renamed |
| 2008 | Gavilon LLC formed: **Gavilon Connors Point Terminal, Elevator M, Daisy Mill** | New ownership |

| | | |
|---|---|---|
| 2008 | AGP Grain Ltd. sells Duluth elevator (former **Cap 6**) to Columbia Grain | New ownership |
| 2008 | Riverland Ag purchases Duluth Cap 6 from Columbia Grain, operating as **Riverland Ag Duluth Lake Port Storage** | New ownership, Renamed |
| 2008 | ConAgra sells **Elevator M** to Hansen-Mueller | Elevator sold |
| 2010 | Ceres Global Ag Corp purchases Riverland Ag Corp. | New ownership |
| 2010 | Ceres Global Ag **Ceres Global - Riverland Ag Duluth Lake Port, and Duluth Storage** | Elevators renamed |
| 2012 | General Mills buys **Elevator**(s) **S** and **X** from BN Railroad | General Mills S, X |
| 2012 | Marubeni buys **Gavilon Grain Connors Point Terminal** | Marubeni Corp buys Gavilon |
| 2017 | Ceres Global sells to **Duluth Lake Port Storage** to TN, LLC | New ownership |
| 2018 | Globe Elevator **House No. 1** | Destroyed by Fire December 17, 2018 |
| 2020 | Duluth Seaway Port Authority **purchases Ceres Global Ag / Riverland Ag Duluth Lake Port Elevator** | New ownership |
| 2022 | General Mills sells **Elevator A, Annex B** to Hansen-Mueller | New ownership |
| 2022 | Viterra USA Investment, LLC buys Gavilon Grain | New ownership |
| 2022 | Gavilon Connors Point operating as **Viterra Connors Point Terminal** | Renamed |

# Acknowledgments

I owe a debt of gratitude to all the elevator personnel who gave me their time to answer questions or escort me through their facilities. Many have passed away since I began this project in the early 1990s. I am grateful for the opportunity to share the stories they passed on to me. I hope my writing has shed a favorable light on this largely inaccessible industry. I would like thank Bill Hoffer, Superintendent at Elevator S in Superior, for sharing his knowledge of the elevator and allowing me to photograph its interior; Hollis Graves, Jr., the third generation of the Graves family to work at Capitol in Duluth; John Parrington, the sharp-tongued manager of Continental Grain in Superior; Jay Van Horn, superintendent at Elevator M in Superior's East End; Joe Burbul, chief millwright. and Doug Christensen, superintendent at General Mills; Mick Sertich, superintendent Peavey Connors Point; Tom Grosser, AGP, Duluth; Chuck Ilenda, Ceres Terminals, Inc.; Chuck Hilleren, Guthrie-Hubner Vessel Agent, Davis Helberg, Director, Duluth Seaway Port Authority; Ron Johnson, Trade Development Director, Duluth Seaway Port Authority; John Stich, president, Riverland Ag.; and Dick Carlson, superintendent, Cenex-Harvest States. A special nod to Pat Maas, Northeast Minnesota Historical Collections, and Kris Aho, Duluth Public Library.

In the battle of providing too much detail or straying off course or making something unreadable, I'd like to acknowledge the feedback from Professor Thomas Leslie, FAIA, the Illinois School of Architecture, University of Illinois at Urbana-Champaign; C. Patrick Labadie, historian and former director for twenty-seven years of the Duluth Marine Museum and researcher and historian of the Thunder Bay National Marine Sanctuary; and Bob Frame, engineering historian and noted Minnesota grain elevator expert.

I would like to thank and acknowledge everyone who contributed to my project, including Carrie and Darren Krueger; Felicity and Galen Pearson; Kim and Jonathan Heinrichs; Michael and Judy Boyle; Ray Boyle; Mike Boyle; Beverley Anich; Paul Haltvick; and Laura Jacobs, Archivist, Lake Superior Maritime Collection, JDH Library, UW-Superior.

# Index

## A
AGP Grain, Ltd., 275, 320
AMI Consulting Engineers, 284, 286
Adams, John Q., 32
AgProcessing Limited Partnership (AGP LP), 262, 275-76, 279, 319, 320-21
African Famine Relief, 256
American Federation of Grain Millers Local 112, 191
American Federation of Grain Millers Local 118, 191
Anchor Mill, 94
Anderson, Gov. Elmer, 195
Anderson Grain, 285
Anderson, William, 83
Anheuser Busch, 273, 277
Arlo, Leopold, 80

## B
Baie Comeau, 195-96, 245
Banning, William, 6
Barnard and Leas Manufacturing Company, 28
Barnett & Record Company, 90, 93-94, 104, 107, 111-114, 126, 141-42, 144, 146, 151, 155, 159, 161-63, 165, 296
Barnett, Lewis, 113-114
Barnum, George, 64-65, 174
Barnum Grain Company, 174
Barnum, Minnesota, 174

Bayfield, Wisconsin, 31
Belt Line Elevator Company, 91-96, 98, 103, 114, 149-50, 167, 204, 313-14
Belt Line Elevator M, 92, 94, 150-151, 161
Belt Line Elevator N, 92, 94, 313
Blatnik, Rep. John A., 223
Bode, Augustus, 307
Boston, Massachusetts, 6, 11, 100-01, 127
Bradstreet Commercial Agency, 45, 47
Buckingham, Alvah, 15
Buckingham, C. P., 15
Buffalo, New York, 24-25, 36, 58, 70, 112, 119, 141, 153, 158, 162, 165-66, 172, 174, 179-80, 183, 197, 200, 225, 243, 265, 272-73, 294, 307
Buffalo River, 273
Buhler-Miag, 245
Bunge, 188, 218, 272, 283
Bunker, Frank R., 43, 47
Burdick, R. C., 53, 307
Burdick Grain Company, 228, 230-31, 246, 318
Burdick Grain Belco Elevator 1, 230
Burdick Grain Belco Elevator 2, 230
Burdick Grain Belco Elevator 5, 230
Burke, C. Thomas, 223
Burlington Northern Railroad, 236, 251, 257, 285
Burnham, Daniel, 41

## C

C. H. Graves and Company, 8, 26, 37
CHS, 153, 191, 221, 266, 280-86, 319
Capitol Elevator Annex A-2, 314
Capitol Elevator Annex A-3, 163, 315
Capitol Elevator Company, 76, 109, 133-35, 148, 153, 163, 178-79, 206, 222, 262, 312-16
Capitol Elevator 4, 109, 262
Capitol Elevator 5, 135, 262, 313
Capitol Elevator 6, 134-35, 154, 206, 262, 314
Capitol Elevator 7, 163, 262, 314-15
Carlson, Dick, 153, 191, 221, 249-52, 282
Cass, George, 31
Cargill Berth B1, 225-26, 228, 318
Cargill Berth B2, 194, 225, 317
Cargill Commission Company, 84, 312
Cargill Commodities Dock, 225
Cargill Elevator Company, 84, 89, 149, 166, 192, 314
Cargill Elevator B, 226, 242, 246
Cargill Elevator C, 204, 241, 244, 258, 318-19
Cargill Elevator D, 204, 258, 318-19
Cargill Elevator E, 194, 224, 317-18
Cargill Elevator H, 193-94, 317
Cargill Elevator I, 193-94
Cargill Elevator M, 161, 316
Cargill Elevator N, 167
Cargill Grain Company, 166
Cargill, Inc., 84, 89, 93, 167, 192, 194, 195, 200, 223-24, 315-318
Cargill, James F., 85
Cargill, Samuel, 84, 89-90, 93
Cargill, Sylvester, 84
Cargill, William S., 90
Cargill, William Wallace, 89, 90, 114, 181
Carl Bolander and Sons, St. Paul, 202
Casey, Theodore B., 76
Carter, President Jimmy, 212, 214, 248, 261, 274
Ceres Global Ag Corporation, Toronto, 278-79, 287, 292, 320,
Ceres Global Ag Duluth Lake Port, 279
Ceres Global Ag Duluth Storage, 292
Ceres Terminals, 188, 278
Chase Elevator Company, 28-29
Chicago and North Western Railroad, 199, 252,
Chicago Board of Trade, 22, 75, 175, 277
Chicago, Illinois, 3, 12-13, 15, 17-18, 22, 24-25, 28, 37, 41, 51-52, 55, 58-59, 63, 71, 75, 81, 110-112, 127, 147, 151, 174-76, 188, 192, 236, 241, 278, 292, 294
Chicago, Minneapolis, St. Paul and Omaha Railroad
Chicago River, 14
Christensen, Doug, 258
Christian, George H., 43-44, 49, 312
Church, Bradford Clifford, 73
Clark, C. H., 101
Clarke & Company, 11
Clarke, J. Hinckley, 11
Cleveland, President Grover, 83
Clow and Nicholson Transportation Co., 37
Cofield, Craig, 44, 47
Columbia Grain, 275-76, 290, 320
ConAgra, 228-31, 246, 252-54, 257, 261, 265, 266, 270-71, 273-74, 279-80, 283, 318-20
ConAgra Elevator M, 177, 185, 246, 248, 254, 265, 271, 318-20
ConAgra Foods, Inc., 246, 271, 283
ConAgra Trade Group, 273
Concourse Grain, LLC, 266, 319
Connors Point, 89, 139, 199-200, 235-36, 252, 265-66, 271, 284, 290
Conover, Iowa, 84
Consolidated Elevator Company,

99-102, 104, 106, 110, 135, 140-44, 148-49, 154-155, 165, 167, 173-174, 176, 192, 224, 313-14
Consolidated Elevator B, 167, 315
Consolidated Elevator C, 167, 315
Consolidated Elevator D, 140, 142-43, 149, 167, 173, 313-14
Consolidated Elevator E, 80, 82, 100, 104-06, 110, 148, 313
Consolidated Elevator F
Consolidated Elevator G
Consolidated Elevator H, 100, 106, 148, 155
Consolidated Elevator I, 100, 155, 167, 314
Consolidated Land Company, 90
Continental Grain Company. 199-200, 202, 204-05, 252-53, 317, 319
Converse, William Freeman, 157-58
Cooke, Jay, 4, 6, 10-11, 23, 30, 76
Cook Industries, 220
Cooley, Jerome E., 37
Cottage Grove, Minnesota, 31
Crosby, John, 53, 64
Cromwell, Minnesota, 18
Cross, Albert, 72
Culver, Joshua B., 4
Cutler, Dwight G., 43, 47
Cutler-Magner Company, 43

**D**

Daisy Mill, 97, 150, 228, 265, 280, 292, 320
Dakota Southern Railway, 102
Dakota Territory, 30-31
Dalrymple, Oliver, 31
Davis, Wilmer W., 40, 43, 210
DeBruce Grain Company, 272
Decatur, Illinois, 176, 262
DeLuca, Deb, 291
Detroit Red Wings, 176
Dickens, Charles, 44
Diercks, H. Robert, 224

Distiller dried grains with solubles (DDGS), 280-82,
Dock Street, Duluth, 27
Douglas County, 91, 204
Duluth and Western Elevator Company, 43-49
Duluth and Western Elevator D, 44
Duluth and Western Elevator E (Q), 44-45, 47-50, 312
Duluth and Winnipeg Railroad, 76
Duluth Bay, 5
Duluth Board of Trade, 40-41, 47, 58, 67, 69-70, 83, 86-87, 91, 95, 100, 126-27, 131, 133, 137, 151-52, 174, 209-210, 263, 311, 318
Duluth Boat Club, 101
Duluth Curling Club, 101
Duluth Elevator Company, 64, 102, 171, 287, 312
Duluth Elevator Company Elevator 1, 63
Duluth Elevator Company Elevator 2, 63
Duluth Elevator Company Elevator 3, 63
Duluth Lake Port Storage, 276, 279, 287, 320,
Duluth Seaway Port Authority, 212, 255, 258, 260, 287, 291, 293, 319, 320
Duluth Storage, 276, 286, 292, 320,
Duluth Symphony Orchestra, 176
Duluth, Minnesota, 2-12, 14, 17, 20, 22-35, 37-45, 47, 49, 51-55, 58-70, 73-77, 79-87, 91, 98-102, 104, 106-107, 110-111, 115-118, 120, 126, 128, 133-135, 140-42, 144, 147-149, 151-53, 155, 157-158, 163-68, 173-74, 176, 179, 183-89, 192-93, 195-97, 201, 204-06, 209-211, 215, 218, 222-24, 233-35, 237, 241, 243-46, 252, 255-63, 272-73, 275-78, 280, 289-92, 294-97, 309-310
Dunwoody, William H., 53, 62, 64

**E**
East Dubuque, Illinois, 16
Eastern Railway Company, 72-73, 306, 308
Economic Development Administration, 223
Edward P. Allis Company, 93-94
Eldridge, North Dakota, 61
Electric Steel Elevator, Minneapolis, 273
Elevator O Ltd., 205
Elevator Row, Duluth, 39, 69
Environmental Protection Agency (EPA), 241-42
Equity Cooperative Exchange, 168

**F**
F. H. Peavey Company, 102-03, 110-11, 114, 118, 136, 141-42, 151, 171, 189, 313-15
Fagin and Company, 54
Fairbanks Scales, 28, 56, 66
Fargo, North Dakota, 206
Fargussen, Owen, 110, 210
Farmers Union Grain Terminal Association, 169-171, 179, 184, 191, 246, 315-18
Farmers Union Section A, 170, 315
Farmers Union Section B, 170, 315
Farmers Union Section C, 170, 315
Farmers Union Section D, 180, 316
Farmers Union Section E, 180, 316
Farmers Union Section F1, 181
Farmers Union Section F2, 181
Farmers Union Section G, 181
Farmers Union – Spencer Kellogg Section H, 164
Farmers Union – Spencer Kellogg Section I, 162
Farmers Union Head House No. 1
Farmers Union Head House No. 2, 181
Farmers Union Head House No. 3, 180-81
Farmland-Atwood, LLC, 266-67, 319
Farmland Industries, Inc., 266
Farrington, W. C., 53, 308
Federal Trade Commission, 155, 169, 309
Fedo, Mayor John, 214
Fegles Construction Company, 162
Fitzpatrick, Francis, 41
Fond du Lac, MN, 7
Foley Brothers, Inc., St. Paul, 201
Fort William, Ontario, 148, 188
Fox River, Wisconsin, 114
Franklin, Vermont, 114
Fredin, Conrad, 223
Freeman, Almeron A., 89, 139
Freeman Mill, 139
Fribourg, Michel, 200

**G**
Garfield Avenue, Duluth, 135, 192
Garfield C, 259, 319
Garfield D, 259, 319
Galveston, Texas, 266
Gasport, New York, 60
Gavilon Agriculture Investment, Inc.
Gavilon Grain, 283-84, 289-290, 319-20
Gavilon Holdings, LLC, 271, 283
Gavilon, LLC, 271, 283
General Mills, Inc., 173-74, 176, 237, 240, 255-58, 272, 276-77, 284-85, 292, 315, 320
General Mills Elevator A, 174, 255-58, 318
General Mills Elevator B, 174, 316, 318
General Mills Elevator D, 316
General Mills Elevator D, 316
General Mills Elevator E, 316
General Mills Elevator G, 316
General Mills Elevator H, 316
General Mills Elevator I, 316
General Mills Elevator S, 257-258,

284, 288, 319-20, 292, 319-320
General Mills Elevator X, 319-20
Geneva, Ohio, 9
George Lloyd Levin, Inc., 223
George W. Spencer and Company, 100
Gibson, Matt, 273
Gilford, New Hampshire, 12
Glencore International, Plc, 283, 290
Glischinski, Steve, 147
Globe Elevator Company, 96, 103, 128, 132, 139, 142, 149, 165, 171, 185, 313-15
Globe Elevator 1, 16, 20-21, 60, 63, 264, 287, 320
Globe Elevator 2, 263
Globe Elevator 3, 263, 287
Globe Elevator Division, 171, 189, 220-221, 234, 252-53, 256, 262-65, 319
Goodyear, 226
Goose River, North Dakota, 30
Grain Committee on National Affairs, 176
Grand Republic Mill, 139, 153
Grant, President Ulysses S., 23
Graves, Hollis F. Jr., 134-35, 231-33
Graves, Hollis, Sr. 178-179
Graves, Charles Hinman, 21, 28, 32, 76, 87
Graves, James, 133-35
Graves, John, 233
Great Lakes Storage, 310
Great Northern Elevator Company of Minnesota, 52-53, 59, 70, 73, 306-08, 312-13
Great Northern Elevator A, 53-55, 57, 70, 72, 118, 137-140, 144
Great Northern Elevator X, 70-72, 74, 138, 172-73, 312, 315
Great Northern Elevator X (2), 176-177, 316
Great Northern Elevator S, 119-24, 138-39, 144, 146, 163-64, 173, 182, 190, 217, 221, 237, 295-96, 313, 319

Great Northern Annex No. 146, 163
Great Northern Annex No. 2, 163
Great Northern Annex No. 3, 164
Great Northern Iron Ore Properties, 121
Great Northern Law Department, 307
Great Northern Railway Company, 307-08
Green, Charles B., 190
Grenvall, Axel, 134

**H**
Hackleman, Harold, 257
Hagen, Mayor Bruce, 236
Haglin, Charles H., 115-16, 145, 163
Halifax, Nova Scotia, 201
Hall, R. J., 79
Hallet and Carey, 158
Hamburg, Germany, 196, 292
Hansen, Jack, 288
Hansen, Josh, 289
Hansen-Mueller, 254, 280, 288-89, 320
Hansen-Mueller Elevator A, 288, 292, 295-96, 320
Hansen-Mueller Elevator M, 280, 288, 292-93
Harris, Samuel Arthur, 103
Harris, Scotten and Company, Chicago, 175
Harvest States Cooperative, 250, 318-19
Hatch, Rep. William H., 85-86, 89
Hatch Anti-Option Bill, 86
Heffelfinger, Frank, 114-115, 118, 141
Helberg, Davis, 212, 270
Hepworth, A. F., 101
Herstad, Ben, 287
Hill, James J., 53, 97, 120-21, 148, 168, 306
Hilleren, Chuck, 215-17
Hinchman, Charles S., 11
Hinckley, Minnesota, 52, 72, 308
Hoffer, Bill, 163-64

Hogeland, Albert H., 144, 146
Hooker, William T., 40, 210
Hozza, David, 266
Hudson, WI, 4
Hughitt Avenue slip, Superior, 89, 139, 152, 162, 180-81, 184, 190, 222, 249, 281, 286, 316

**I**

Illinois Central Railroad, 14
Imperial Mill, 38, 73, 76, 107, 133, 135, 154, 222, 233, 312
Ingles, J. David, 147
Interior Elevator, 115
International Longshoremen's Association Local 1037 (ILA), 188, 191, 209, 237, 239-40, 282
International Milling Company, 135, 178, 187, 205, 222, 316
International Multifoods, Inc., 178-79, 187, 205, 222, 231-33, 245, 261-62, 293, 317-19
Iron Range Resources and Rehabilitation Commission, 223
Isle Engineering, 270
Italgrani Di Francesco Ambrosio, Naples, Italy, 243
Italgrani USA, Inc., 243, 258
Itasca Corporation, 166
Itasca Elevator, 126-27, 151, 156, 163, 166, 183-84, 191-92, 202, 313-15, 317
Itasca Elevator Company, 151, 162, 166, 313-15

**J**

J. R. Jensen Construction, 262, 265, 319
J. T. Moulton and Sons, 28, 33, 42, 55, 59, 63, 67
James Stewart and Company, 77, 177
Jamestown, North Dakota, 61

Janesville, Wisconsin, 84
Jay Cooke & Company, 6
Jefferson, Robert E., 4
Jenks, James Messer, 127, 151
Jenks, Martin Lane, 128
Johnson, Ernest V., 114
Johnson, Lt. Gov. Marlene, 256
Johnson, Ron, 255-56
Johnson, Russell, 189

**K**

Kellogg, F. B., 101
Kelm, Erwin E., 195
Kemper and Draham, 61
Ketchum, Milo, 68, 120, 122, 144-45
Kitchi Gammi Club, 101
Kloewer, Delmar, 241
Kluempke, Pat, 235
Koski, Jim, 206-08
Krech-Ojard, 285, 288
Kucza, Len, 271

**L**

La Crosse, Wisconsin, 3, 84, 89-90, 128, 181
Lake & Rail Elevator, 274
Lake City, Minnesota, 114
Lake Michigan, 3, 52, 75, 84, 292
Lake Superior, 2, 4-5, 8-9, 12, 19, 23, 51, 77, 183, 188, 197, 245
Lake Superior and Mississippi Railroad, 4-7, 11-12, 27, 30, 43
Lake Superior and Southwestern Railway Co., 53, 306-08
Lake Superior Elevator Company, 32-33, 38, 41, 59, 62, 66-67, 76, 79, 83, 98-99, 101, 142, 167, 311-13
Lake Superior Elevator B, 32-33, 38, 42, 167, 311
Lake Superior Elevator C, 33, 42, 167, 311
Lake Superior Elevator D, 42, 79, 105,

141, 167, 312
Lake Superior Elevator G, 42, 312
Lake Superior Elevator Store House
   No. 1, 42, 67, 311
Lake Superior Elevator Store House
   No. 2, 67
Lake Superior Mill, 94
Lake Superior Terminal and Transfer
   Railway, 251
Lakewood Cemetery, Minneapolis, 89
Lamborn, Robert Henry, 11
Land O' Lakes, 262
Lansing Grain, 285
Larson, Henrietta, 39-40
Leighton, Roy, 229
Leitch, Gordon, 175
Leslie, Dr. Thomas, 13
Lilliboe, Don, 205
Lime Springs, Iowa, 84
Lindahl, Fred, 84-85
Linstedt, Sharon, 274
Listman Mill, 94, 167
Little Rock, Arkansas, 151
Locke, Edward, 43, 46-47, 49
Loftus, John, 79
London, England, 6, 32, 92
Louis Dreyfus Company, 235-36
Luce, Sidney, 9

**M**
MacMillan, Howard, Sr., 193, 219, 229
MacMillan, Howard, Jr., 219, 230
MacMillan, John Jr., 85, 192, 195
MacMillan, W. Duncan, 85
Madison, Wisconsin, 131-32, 247, 268
Mair, C. A., 101
Malt One Elevator, Minneapolis, 273, 277
Manitoba Company, 53-54, 306, 308
Manitoba Railway, 48, 52, 62, 72
Maranell, Mike, 275
Marine Tech, Inc., 279
Markell, Clinton, 9, 21, 27-28, 32, 40, 210
Marquette, Michigan, 6
Martin, Charles, 53
Marubeni America Corporation, 289
Marubeni Corp., 283, 320
Marvin, Luke Arthur, 32, 80
Mattiske, David, 289
McCarthy Bros. and Company, 133
McCarthy Bros. Grain Company, 133
McCarthy, Charles H., 178
McCarthy, J. V., 178
McCarthy, John R, 133, 178
McCarthy, Louis A., 178
McCarthy, Ralph, 233-234
McCarthy, Thomas G., 133
McCarthy, Walter, 135
McCarville, James, 236
McGregor and Western Railroad, 84
McIntyre & Wardell, 109
McKenzie, Duncan, 97
McKenzie, Hague Company,
   Minneapolis, 180, 233
McLennan, John A., 55-56, 71
McMillan, Cavour Langdon, 219
McMillan, John D., 181
McMillan Elevator Company Elevator
   M, 219-220, 228, 230, 317-318
McMillan, Howard Jr., 219, 228
McMillan, Howard Sr., 219
Meehan Seaway Services, 271, 292
Michigan Southern Railroad, 15
Miller, Alexander, 13
Miller, Tom, 261
Milwaukee, Wisconsin, 3, 22, 24-25,
   52, 75, 84, 93, 127-128, 236, 294
Minkota Mill, 139
Minneapolis, 24, 39, 43, 46-47, 49,
   62-65, 75-76, 87-90, 92-93, 102-103,
   111-115, 126-127, 133-135, 140-141,
   146-48, 157-158, 162, 164, 166, 178,
   180, 209-10, 219-220, 223, 229-230,
   232-34, 245, 257, 272-73, 277, 279,
   289, 309
Minneapolis Chamber of Commerce, 87

Minneapolis Grain Exchange, 128, 169, 210, 272, 280
Minneapolis, St. Paul and Atlantic, 147
Minnesota Association of Wheat Growers, 260
Minnesota Mining and Manufacturing, 135
Minnesota Point, 5, 7, 22
Minnesota Pollution Control Agency (MPCA), 242
Minnesota Railroad and Warehouse Commission, 68, 96, 129-31, 269
Minnesota Wheat Research and Promotion Council, 260
Minot, Henry, 72
Mississippi River, 3-4, 10, 16, 23-24, 52, 215, 243-44, 266, 292
Mitsubishi Corp., 283
Mitsui & Co., 283
Monarch Elevator Company, 171
Mondale, Vice-President Walter, 214
Montreal Pier, Superior, 90
Montreal, Quebec, 115, 120, 168, 175, 190, 245
Mork, E. Clifford, 195
Morton Salt, 179
Moulton, Gen. Jonathan, 12
Moulton, George Mayhew, 13-14, 17, 42
Moulton, Joseph Tilton, 10, 12-17, 20-21
Mueller, Randy, 288
Mulaner, Hank, 187
Munger, Gilbert, 27, 32, 38
Munger, Markell and Company, 27, 30-33, 36-38, 311
Munger, Markell and Company Elevator 1, 27, 30, 33, 36-38, 73, 311
Munger, Roger S., 27, 32, 38, 40, 73, 76, 210
Munger, Russell, 38

**N**
Nakhodka, Russia, 211

National Bank of Commerce, Minneapolis, 103
National Cargo Bureau, 216-17
Nettleton, George, 4
Nettleton, William, 4-5
New York City, New York, 6, 22, 55, 127, 152, 199-200, 270
Newberry and Dole Elevator, 13
Newcombe, Charles B., 11-12, 17-18, 23
Newport, Reese M., 75
Norris and Company, 175
Norris Grain Company, 174-76, 192, 225, 316
Norris Grain Elevator E, 176, 225, 316
Norris Grain Elevator F, 316
Norris Grain Elevator H, 176, 316
Norris Grain Elevator I, 176, 316
Norris, Bruce, 176
Norris, James, 174-76
Norris, James Dougan, Jr., 175-76
North Dakota Elevator Company, 61-62, 65
North Dakota State University, 260
North Western Leasing Company, 200
Northern Pacific Elevator Company, 76, 98
Northern Pacific Freight Shed No. 1, 141
Northern Pacific Railroad, 2, 6-7, 11-12, 23-24, 28-31, 52-53, 59, 61, 67, 76, 80, 105, 132, 142, 147-48, 150, 167, 173, 220,
Northern Steamship Company, 53
Northland Country Club, 100
Northland Pier, Duluth, 225, 279
Northwest Growers Association, 246
Northwestern Fuel Company, 158
Northwestern Grain Dealers Association, 43, 46, 49
Northwestern Manufacturing Company, 18
Northwestern National Bank, Minneapolis, 103

Nye, Raymond, 127
Nye-Jenks and Company, 127-28

## O
O&M Elevator L, 181-82
O&M Elevator M, 181-82, 197-98, 219-20, 228-29, 316-17
O&M Elevator O
Oakes, North Dakota
Oberstar, Sen. James L.
Occident Elevator Company
Occident Terminal Elevator
Occupational Safety and Health Administration (OSHA)
Oftedahl, Gordon
Ohio Central Barge and Coal Dock Co.
Old Globe Wood Company, LLC
Olmsted, Timothy Allen
Olson, Warren
Omaha, Nebraska
Osborne, Edward, 181-82
Osborne-McMillan Elevator Company (O&M), 114, 181-83, 193, 199, 218, 230, 234, 316-17
Osdel, John M., 13
Ospraie Management, LLC, 270-71, 319
Ospraie Special Opportunities Fund, 270, 283
Otsego, Michigan, 62

## P
Page, Fred, 266
Panic of 1873, 29, 43
Parker, F. H., 101
Parrington, John, 202, 205, 208, 310
Paton, Morton S., 101
Patterson, Nick, 279
Pattison, Martin, 121
Peavey Connors Point Elevator, 253, 262, 284, 319

Peavey Duluth Terminal Elevator, 118, 135-37, 141-42, 148-49, 163-64, 185, 204, 228, 242, 259, 269-270, 296, 313, 315, 317-19
Peavey Duluth Annex, 117-18
Peavey Elevator M, 254, 310
Peavey Grain Company, 110-11, 118, 246, 253, 271-72, 313
Peavey Producer Service, 263
Peavey, Frank H., 52-53, 62, 64-65, 87, 92, 102, 111-12, 114-15, 117-18
Peavey, George, 102-03, 118, 141
Peet, Emerson W., 99, 101
Peoria, Illinois, 28, 152
Peres, Judy, 266
Perham, Minnesota, 61
Perry, William B., 91
Phelps, Edmund Joseph, 91-92, 94, 98
Phelps, Melvin, 103
Philadelphia, Pennsylvania, 4, 6-7, 11, 23, 26, 57, 101, 120
Pillsbury, Charles A., 53, 88-89, 168, 274
Pokegema River, 64
Pomeroy, Dick, 256
Pope, Ralph, 91
Port Arthur, Ontario, 153, 188
Port Huron, Michigan, 127
Portage La Prairie, Manitoba, 148
Post, John, 9

## R
R. S. Fling and Partners, 235
Railway Express Delivery Agency, 134
Ray, James, 9
Readsboro, Vermont, 17
Reagan Recession, 248
Record, James, 114
Red River Valley, 24-25, 30-30, 61, 158, 261, 294
Red River Valley Elevator Company, 76
Revell, Jim, 257
Rice, Orin W., 4

Rice's Point, 2, 5, 32-33, 69, 76, 110, 134-35, 142, 153, 158, 191-92, 227, 287, 296
Rich, John M., 33
Richardson and Company, 175
Rico, Tony, 212
Ripley, George, 101
Riverland Ag Duluth Lake Port Storage, 276-79, 320
Riverland Ag Duluth Storage, 276, 320
Riverland Ag, Corp., 272-74, 285, 320
Robbins, Dr. A. B., 9, 146
Roberts, Clifford M. Jr., 227
Roen Salvage, 286
Rosenbaum and Norris Elevator, 174
Rupley, George, 32, 76, 78, 80-81, 83
Russell-Miller Milling Company, 157-58, 189, 317

**S**
S. F. Hodge and Company, 106
Salyards Grain Company, 135
Sanborn Map Company, 44, 67, 107
Sanborn, Judge Walter, 98, 132
Sargent, Gen. George B., 11
Sault Ste. Marie, Michigan, 24-25, 147, 211
Savage, Minnesota, 272
Sawyer, Andrew J., 40, 59-65, 87-89, 102, 210, 274
Saylor, Tracy, 279-280
Sea of Japan, 211
Seaver, J. H., 11
Serck, Jason, 286
Sertich, Mark, 262
Sertich, Mick, 253-54, 262-63, 265, 271
Severance, C. A., 101
Shepard, David, 53
Shippee, Lester, 3-4
Shoreham Elevator, 219, 230
Sioux City, Iowa, 102
Sloan, Dist. Attn Henry, 95

Smith, Robert, 195
Smith, Ghent R., 91
Smith, Ted, 279
Soo Line Railroad, 147-48, 236
Southwark Foundry and Machine Co., 57
Soviet Union, 205, 212, 214, 244, 261, 272
Spencer Kellogg and Sons, Inc., 152-53, 162, 165, 169, 180, 222, 314-316, 318
Spencer Kellogg Section H, 165
Spencer Kellogg Section I, 162
Spencer Kellogg Section J, 162
Spencer, George, 23, 40, 100-01
St. Cloud, Minnesota, 4
St. Croix River, 4, 10, 23
St. Francis Hospital, Superior, 95
St. Lawrence River, 183, 245
St. Lawrence Seaway System, 183, 185-86, 189, 191-92, 195-96, 200, 213, 237, 244, 255, 278, 291, 316
St. Louis County Historical Society, 21
St. Louis Hotel, Duluth, 100
St. Louis Park, Minnesota, 115-16, 118, 163, 230
St. Louis River, 7
St. Louis, Missouri, 77, 243, 292
St. Marys Canal, 6, 24
St. Paul and Duluth Railroad, 30, 43
St. Paul and Sioux City Railroad, 30
St. Paul, Minnesota, 3-5, 9, 23-24, 27, 32, 45, 53, 60, 83, 98-101, 105, 121, 130, 168, 180, 201-02, 224, 246, 308
Standard Milling Company, 133
Star Elevator Company, 92
Sterling, Illinois, 73
Stich, John, 272-78, 285
Stillwater, Minnesota, 9, 22, 24
Sturges and Buckingham Elevator's A and B, 15
Sturges, Solomon, 14-16, 21
Superior Fire Department, 248

Superior Manufacturing Company, 169
Superior Street, Duluth, 22, 40, 60, 100-01, 210
Superior Terminal Elevator Company, 89-91, 93, 96, 114, 149-50, 166, 204, 234, 312-13
Superior Terminal Elevator K, 90-91, 93, 234
Superior Terminal Elevator L, 90-91, 93
Superior, Wisconsin, 2, 4, 9, 28, 52-55, 58-59, 61-62, 64-65, 69-72, 75, 85, 89-91, 95-98, 102-04, 110-12, 114, 119, 121-22, 126-32, 137, 140, 144, 147, 149, 152-53, 156, 162-69, 172-173, 178-81, 183-186, 191-92, 198-200, 202-04, 206, 208-09, 215, 218-23, 228, 234-36, 244-47, 251-54, 256-58, 260-61, 263, 265-266, 268-69, 271, 273, 278, 280-81, 283-88, 290-95, 297, 306, 308, 310, 313, 318
Swenson, Nick, 272

**T**
Terminal Storage Company, 97
Thatcher, Mark W., 179,
Thief River Falls, Minnesota, 148, 219, 230
Thomas, George C., 11
Thompson, William, 90
Thomson, A. D., 76, 167-68, 315
Thomson, Alexander Douglas, 168
Thomson's Junction, 7, 12
Thunder Bay, Ontario, 183, 188, 245
TN LLC, 279, 287, 320
Toledo Pier, Superior, 90, 94
Toledo, Ohio, 15, 55
Toltz, Max, 120-21, 146, 296
Tower Avenue slip, 139, 170-72, 180, 183-84, 190, 249, 251, 284, 316
Town of Portland, 9
Tradax, 196
Traphagen, Oliver, 41

Tri-State Wreckage and Salvage, 205
Tull, Emory J., 90

**U**
U.S. Gypsum, 180
U.S. Wheat Association, 261
Ullrich, David, 241
Union Improvement and Elevator Company, 7-12, 21-23, 25, 27, 30, 32, 38, 42, 59, 62, 66-67, 75-77, 79, 98-99, 101, 105, 224
Union Improvement Elevator A, Duluth, 8, 22-23, 25
Union Improvement Elevator B, Stillwater, Minnesota, 23
Union Improvement Elevator C, Hastings, Minnesota, 23
Union Improvement Elevator E, 35, 42-43, 67, 77, 105, 224, 312
Union Improvement Elevator F, 43, 67, 77, 194, 312
Union Improvement Elevator H, 42-43, 66, 69, 77, 79, 194, 312
Union Improvement Warehouse 2, 67
Union Improvement Warehouse 3, 67
United States Department of Agriculture – Economic Research Service, 269
United States Electric Light Co., 58
United States Flour Milling Co., 107
Upper Lakes Steamship Company, 175, 227
Upshaw, H. P., 53

**V**
Valley City, North Dakota, 61
Van Brunt, Walter Jr., 17, 26, 40, 210
Van Dusen, George, 53, 87, 92
Van Dusen-Harrington Company, 92-93
Van Horn, Jay, 149, 161, 185, 198, 219, 228-30

Vancouver, Washington, 168, 291
Veltum, Jim, 251
Viterra, 288, 290
Viterra Connors Point Terminal, 288, 290, 292, 320
Viterra Limited, 288-89,
Viterra USA Investment, LLC, 288, 320

**W**
Walker, B. E., 101
Waltham Bleachery, 13
Washburn-Crosby Elevator A
Washburn-Crosby Mill, 93-94
Washburn, Sen. William, D., 85-89
Weare, Portus B., 62-63
Welland Canal, 183, 218
Wells, Frank, 118
Wells, Fred B., 141, 171
Western Knapp Engineering Company, 184, 193
Whitebox Advisors, LLC, 272-74
Whitebox Commodities Holding Corporation, 272-73
Whyte, William, 148
Winnipeg, Manitoba, 148, 152
Wirth, George, 100
Wisconsin Central Railway, 147-48
Wisconsin Grain and Warehouse Commission, 128, 130, 132, 140
Wisconsin Harbor Assistance Program, 284-85
Wisconsin Woodchuck, LLC, 266, 287
Witherspoon-Englar Company, Chicago, 112
Woodbridge, Dwight, 136-37
Works Progress Administration, 167
Wong, Mike, 276

**Y**
Youghiogheny and Ohio (Y&O), 199
Young, Sen George, North Dakota, 131

**Z**
Zachau, Harry, 177
Zenith Dredge Company, 189

**VESSELS**
*Adams*, 35
*Algoma Harvester*, 286
*Alva*, 138
*Atlantic Baroness*, 190
*B. W. Blanchard*, 80-81
*Beltana*, 196
*Canadoc*, 195
*Chili*, 138
*Cuba*, 58
*David W. Rust*, 78
*Fred E. Taplin*, 181
*Frost*, 6
*George Manolakis*, 190
*Harry L. Allen*, 232
*Herald*, 185
*Hiawatha*, 35
*J. P. Wells*, 181
*James E. Davidson*, 181
*James Norris*, 175
*Joe S. Morrow*, 202
*John J. Boland (1)*, 181
*Kapetan Andreas G.*, 258
*Keyes*, 6
*Kinsman Enterprise*, 258
*Maxima*, 288
*Meteor*, 172
*Murray Bay*, 190
*Onoko*, 70
*Paget Trader*, 201
*Penobscot*, 181
*Ramon de Larrinaga*, 185
*Saint Remi*, 186-87
*S. A. Parent*, 137
*Solta*, 244
*South Park*, 172
*St. Lawrence Prospector*, 227
*St. Paul*, 6
*T. R. McLagan*, 190

*Tadoussac*, 257-58
*Utica*, 138
*W. A. Rogers*, 137
*Zakarpatye*, 211

## NEWSPAPERS – JOURNALS et al
*American Elevator and Grain Trade*
*Boston Weekly Advertiser*
*Buffalo News*
*Chicago Tribune*
*Duluth Daily News*
*Duluth Evening Herald*
*Duluthian*
*Duluth Minnesotian*
*Duluth News-Tribune*
*Duluth Seaway Port Authority:*
　*Minnesota's World Port*
*Duluth Seaway Port Authority: North Star*
　*Port*
*Grainnet*
*Jamestown Weekly Alert*
*Minneapolis Journal*
*Minneapolis Star Tribune*
*Montreal Gazette*
*Northwestern Miller*
*St. Paul Globe*
*Superior Leader*
*Superior Times*
*Wausau Pilot*
*Weekly Northwestern Miller*
*Western Rural and American Stockman*

# About the Author

Patrick Lapinski, a native of Superior, is a researcher, historian, writer and photographer concentrating on the Great Lakes maritime industry. His work can be read and or viewed at http://www.inlandmariners.com. The author's writing and photography have been featured for many years in Great Lakes maritime publications. Lapinski is the author of four books and currently lives in Saint Paul.

www.ingramcontent.com/pod-product-compliance
Lightning Source LLC
Chambersburg PA
CBHW030520230426
43665CB00010B/698